HAITI AND THE AMERICAS

CARIBBEAN STUDIES SERIES

Anton L. Allahar and Shona N. Jackson
Series Editors

HAITI
AND THE
AMERICAS

Edited by

Carla Calargé, Raphael Dalleo,
Luis Duno-Gottberg, and Clevis Headley

University Press of Mississippi / Jackson

www.upress.state.ms.us

The University Press of Mississippi is a member
of the Association of American University Presses.

Chapter 3 incorporates material previously published in Jeff Karem,
*The Purloined Islands: Caribbean-U.S. Crosscurrents in Literature
and Culture, 1880–1959* (copyright 2011 by the Rector and Visitors
of the University of Virginia). Thanks to the University of Virginia
Press for permission to reprint brief portions from that book.

Portions of chapter 4 previously appeared in David P. Kilroy, *For Race and
Country: The Life and Career of Colonel Charles Young* (Praeger, 2003).

A version of the discussion of Colonel Murray in chapter 7 appeared
in French in Nadève Ménard, "La représentation de l'officier américain dans les romans haïtiens écrits durant l'occupation américaine," *Cahier des Anneaux de la Mémoire* 7 (2004): 253–67.

Two brief passages from chapter 9 appeared in Myriam J. A. Chancy,
"Desecrated Bodies/Phantom Limbs: Post-traumatic Reconstructions
of Corporeality in Haiti/Rwanda," *Atlantic Studies* 8, no. 1 (March 2011):
109–23; and *From Sugar to Revolution: Women's Visions of Haiti, Cuba,
and the Dominican Republic* (Wilfrid Laurier University Press, 2012).

First printing 2013

∞

Library of Congress Cataloging-in-Publication Data

Haiti and the Americas Conference (2010 : Florida Atlantic University)
Haiti and the Americas / edited by Carla Calargé . . . [et al.].
    p. cm. — (Caribbean studies series)
"The essays collected in this volume were presented at the "Haiti
and the Americas: Histories, Cultures, Imaginations" Conference
held at Florida Atlantic University from October 21 to 23, 2010."
    Includes bibliographical references and index.
ISBN 978-1-61703-757-3 (cloth : alk. paper) — ISBN 978-1-61703-
758-0 (ebook) 1. Haiti—Congresses. I. Calargé, Carla. II. Title.
            F1912.6.H35 2010
972.94—dc23   2012038298

British Library Cataloging-in-Publication Data available

Contents

Acknowledgments

The essays collected in this volume were presented at the "Haiti and the Americas: Histories, Cultures, Imaginations" conference held at Florida Atlantic University from October 21 to 23, 2010. We were not able to include all the contributions from that conference, but the conversations sparked by the other presentations and the audience contributions were important in the rewriting and rethinking of the essays collected here. For that reason, we want to thank everyone who took part in the conference, especially Isabelle Airey, Leslie Alexander, Diane Allerdyce, Aimee Kanner Arias, Alessandra Benedicty, Major Joseph Bernadel, Kristen Block, Graciella Cruz-Taura, Sika Dagbovie, Susan D'Aloia, Sara Fanning, Gérard Férère, Meagan Foster, Kaiama Glover, Mary Ann Gosser Esquilín, Mark Harvey, Bertin Louis, Elena Machado Sáez, Michelange Quay, Mariana Past, Jerry Philogene, Yvette Piggush, Rose Réjouis, Adam Rockenbach, Heather Russell, Melissa Sande, Patricia Saunders, Andrea Shaw, Adam Silvia, Faith Smith, Lara Stein Pardo, Robert Taber, Walteria Tucker, Adriana Umaña-Hossman, and Chantalle Verna. The conference benefited especially from the participation of a number of local nonprofit leaders: Nicole Toussaint-Prince and Dieunet Demosthene, from Toussaint L'Ouverture High School for Arts and Social Justice in Boynton Beach; Marli Lalanne and Daby Sully, from the Miami-based Konbit for Haiti; Gayle Williams, codirector of Digital Library of the Caribbean; and Rebecca Reichert, director of development at the Florida Association for Volunteer Action in the Caribbean and the Americas (FAVACA). All these individuals contributed to the discussions and investigations that form the context for this volume.

The "Haiti and the Americas" conference received generous funding from a number of departments, programs, and offices at both Rice University and Florida Atlantic University. From Rice, we want to thank Nicolas Shumway, dean of humanities; and José Aranda, chair of Hispanic studies. From FAU, we want to thank Manjunath Pendakur, dean of the Dorothy F. Schmidt College of Arts and Letters; Michael Moriarty, interim vice president for research; Charles Brown, vice president for student affairs; Corey King, associate vice president and dean of students; Barry Rosson, dean of the graduate college; Edward Pratt, dean of undergraduate studies; Maria Santamarina, university diversity officer; Noemi Marin, director of the peace studies program; Farshad Araghi, chair of sociology; Mike Harris, chair of anthropology; Michael Horswell, chair of languages, linguistics, and comparative literature; Wenying Xu, chair of English; Nicole Jacobsen, visual communications coordinator; Jackie Simpson, event planning specialist; and Larry Faerman, associate director of event planning and union programs. We also received financial support and in-kind donations from the Florida Humanities Council, the Figge Art Museum in Davenport, Iowa, and Puma.Creative; thanks to Claire Breukel, Mark Coetzee, and Andrew Wallace for helping us with those donations. The details of the conference were efficiently coordinated by Jacqueline Nichols, FAU Department of Philosophy program assistant; and Valorie Ebert, master's candidate in English. A number of other English graduate students donated their time in working on the conference, including Johanna Ayala, Kelly DeStefano, Jacob Henson, Jason Kaplan, Michael Linder, Jessica Pitts, and Emilija Stanic; we would also like to thank FAU's Philosophy Club and their president, Yona Rabinowitz, for helping out with the conference.

Publishing with the University Press of Mississippi has been a pleasure, thanks especially to the work of Walter Biggins, Bill Henry, Katie Keene, Shane Gong Stewart, and Todd Lape. Johanna Ayala compiled the index for this book, with her usual care and attention to detail.

HAITI AND THE AMERICAS

Introduction

—Raphael Dalleo

Ever since Columbus established his first settlement in the New World in the area near present-day Cap Haitien in 1492, Haiti has been a crossroads of the Americas. A crossroads is not only a geographic location but a place where past, present, and future intersect. *Haiti and the Americas* opens up the colonial and postcolonial archive to explore the implications of Haiti's status as crossroads while advancing a new archive of the counterdiscourses that Haiti's positioning has enabled. Recent scholarship has begun to reconstruct the centrality of Haiti to the New World experience, showing how Haiti has existed and been mobilized as symbol and specter for groups ranging from white Creole elites in the eighteenth century, to Latin American patriots and African American transnationalists in the nineteenth, to Caribbean anticolonialists in the twentieth, to international disaster capitalists in the twenty-first. In addition to assessing the existing scholarship, *Haiti and the Americas* points the way to new avenues of exploration and new correspondences made possible by thinking about Haiti's place in the Americas.

This book seeks to explore Haiti's positioning by becoming a crossroads itself in terms of disciplines and methodologies, bringing together work in history and cultural studies to apply the methods of archival research, art history, film studies, literary analysis, and political theory. Fields like African diaspora studies, American studies, Caribbean studies, Francophone studies, Latin American studies, and postcolonial studies have recently begun to reassess their own relationships to Haiti, its history, and its culture. These conversations often take place in isolation and without awareness of each other. *Haiti and the Americas* creates a dialogue between different fields and shows the diversity of approaches that are reclaiming Haiti's presence as a crossroads.

Haiti has long occupied this crucial place in the imaginary of the hemisphere, but ideas about, and images of, Haiti can appear paradoxical. Is it a land of tyranny and oppression or a beacon of freedom as the site of the world's only successful slave revolution? Is it a land of devilish practices or of a devoutly religious people? Does its status as the second independent nation in the hemisphere give it special lessons to teach about postcolonialism, or is its main lesson one of failure? Thinking about Haiti requires breaking through a thick layer of stereotypes, in which Haiti can appear as the furthest extreme of poverty, of political dysfunction, and of savagery, to develop approaches that can account for the complexity of Haitian history and culture. Media coverage since the earthquake of January 2010 fits easily into the narrative of Haiti as a dependent nation, unable to govern or even fend for itself, a site of lawlessness in need of more powerful neighbors to take control. Examining representations of Haiti from throughout the hemisphere makes it possible to contextualize the ways that Haiti has been represented over time, and to look at Haiti's own cultural expressions to think about alternative ways of imagining its culture and history.

Part I of *Haiti and the Americas* details a newly independent Haiti offering inspiration and support for hemispheric independence movements, first in South America and later in Cuba. From these exchanges with Latin America, part II looks at how Haitian thinkers at the turn of the twentieth century were creating the foundations of hemispheric Pan-Africanism, both intellectually and institutionally. Alongside this story of Haiti as an inspirational source, though, part II also shows the rise of international instruments of containment as Haiti shifted from a French to a U.S. imperial frame. The U.S. military presence in Haiti, beginning in the nineteenth century and culminating in occupation from 1915 to 1934, created a new set of affiliations and interactions between Haiti and the rest of the Americas that are the topic of part III. Finally, part IV turns to the ways in which the dominance of the United States regionally and globally continues to produce complicated racial and cultural relationships in a current moment characterized by complex global and postnational forms of imperialism. The book therefore explores the history of these hemispheric relationships, tracing a route from Simón Bolívar's sojourn in the young Haitian republic, to intellectual exchanges between Anténor Firmin, Benito Sylvain, Henry Sylvester Williams, and W. E. B. Du Bois at the turn of the twentieth century, to historical fiction written by Charles Chesnutt during the U.S. occupation, to the transnational hip-hop culture and NGO humanitarianism of today.

The Haitian Revolution in Transnational Context

The existing scholarship on Haiti's place in the Americas has focused primarily on the importance of the Haitian Revolution. *Haiti and the*

Americas takes its inspiration from this rich body of research rethinking one of the major revolutions in modern history, even as we expand from that focus to also examine other ways that Haiti's cultural influence continues to impact the United States, Latin America, and the Caribbean in the twentieth and twenty-first centuries. Since Michel-Rolph Trouillot's clarion call in *Silencing the Past* (1997) for historians and philosophers alike to acknowledge the significance of Haiti's revolutionary history, works like Nick Nesbitt's *Universal Emancipation* (2008) or Susan Buck-Morss's *Hegel, Haiti, and Universal History* (2009) have accepted the challenge of reminding the world of the contribution to modern political thought made by the most complete social revolution of the Age of Revolutions. In the wake of the bicentennial of the Haitian Revolution in 2004, a number of new academic collections appeared that further engage with this event. Collections that focus on how the revolution shaped other parts of the Atlantic world include *The Impact of the Haitian Revolution in the Atlantic World* (2001), *Reinterpreting the Haitian Revolution and Its Cultural Aftershocks* (2006), *Echoes of the Haitian Revolution, 1804–2004* (2008), *Tree of Liberty: Cultural Legacies of the Haitian Revolution in the Atlantic World* (2008), and *African Americans and the Haitian Revolution: Selected Essays and Historical Documents* (2010). Such a wealth of essay collections on the Haitian Revolution's international impact demonstrates the scholarly interest in Haiti and makes it possible to tell new stories about Caribbean, Latin American, and U.S. cultural and political history. The influence of the revolution—and the scholarship about its regional context—forms an important backdrop for the kinds of exchanges examined in *Haiti and the Americas*. For that reason, this introduction briefly surveys the Haitian Revolution's hemispheric reverberations before the rest of the book delves into subsequent interactions.

Saint-Domingue was an important center of regional trade and a model plantation economy during the eighteenth century. But the uprising among the enslaved that began in 1791 transformed the colony from an important node in hemispheric networks to the center of the battle between proslavery and antislavery forces that defined the Americas during this period. Fleeing planters, along with seamen involved in trade with the island, carried stories of the growing revolution to all corners of the Atlantic world.[1] France's other Caribbean colonies were most immediately and obviously affected. As Laurent Dubois's *A Colony of Citizens: Revolution and Slave Emancipation in the French Caribbean, 1787–1804*

(2004) argues, though Haiti may have been the only independent nation to emerge from the revolutions and wars of this period, these were none-theless regional events. Slave rebellions in Martinique in 1789 and Gua-deloupe in 1790, inspired by rumors of what was taking place in France, actually presaged the 1791 Saint-Domingue uprising. When the rebels in Saint-Domingue succeeded in forcing France to abolish slavery in its colo-nies in 1794, nowhere was this decree more enthusiastically implemented than in Guadeloupe; Victor Hugues's arrival there with the emancipation decree and the guillotine would later become material for Alejo Carpen-tier's 1962 novel *El siglo de las luces*. Napoleon was eventually able to rein-stitute slavery in these islands in 1802 and 1803, but the memory of this period remained alive not only in the 1811 slave uprising in Martinique but into the twentieth century in works like Daniel Maximin's novel *L'isolé soleil* (1981).

The islands that are today thought of as the English-speaking Carib-bean were also fundamentally shaped by the events of this period, as the British were able to take control of both Saint Lucia and Trinidad as a result of the chaos unleashed by the Haitian Revolution. At the outbreak of the uprising in Haiti, Saint Lucia was a French possession and thus experienced a parallel history to that of Martinique and Guadeloupe; by 1794, when the British launched a military campaign seeking to take control of the French islands, unrest among the enslaved and divisions among the whites had so undermined social cohesion in Saint Lucia that British forces were able to seize the island in twenty-four hours. But as word of the abolition of slavery in the French colonies was reaching Saint Lucia at just this moment, the British found themselves fighting insur-gent slaves and republican whites inspired by what had been achieved in Saint-Domingue. The British were driven from the island in 1795, their occupation lasting only a year. Fighting continued throughout the period as the British attempted to retake the island and reimpose slavery, which they finally succeeded in doing in 1803. But, as David Barry Gaspar argues, nearly a decade of freedom and rebellion surely shaped the consciousness of these newly British subjects. Trinidad also became a British possession during this period. The Spanish had tried to prevent a British takeover of Trinidad with their 1783 Cédula of Population encouraging Catholic slave owners to move to the island. By the 1790s, Trinidad thus became a prime location for planters fleeing the French islands, so that by the time the British did win control of the island in 1797, the ground had already been established for the French linguistic and cultural substrate that persists in Trinidad to this day. This influence can be seen in the creole spoken in Trinidad, in Trinidadian Carnival, and in the prominence of the free people of color in Trinidad during the nineteenth century.[2]

Even long-standing British possessions felt the influence of the slave insurrection in neighboring Saint-Domingue. Jamaica in particular was a destination for fleeing planters and soon became a site of rumors that freed Africans planned to export their revolution to other slave societies in the region. David Geggus notes that "in 1800, the year Toussaint Louverture became governor of Saint-Domingue, slaves sang in the streets of Kingston 'Black, white, brown. All de same'" (14). The planters meanwhile read anxiously of the events in Bryan Edwards's *An Historical Survey of the French Colony in the Island of St. Domingo*, published in London in 1797; Mimi Sheller argues that this "Haytian Fear" became a defining feature of the white Creole community beginning in the 1790s.[3] The British abolition of the transatlantic slave trade in 1807 clearly meant to respond to the fears unleashed by Saint-Domingue, and the next three decades before slavery's abolition were marked by constant unrest among the enslaved inspired by Haiti. *Hamel, the Obeah Man*, published in 1827 and arguably the first Jamaican novel, is centered on a slave rebellion; black and white characters in the novel all reference Saint-Domingue as a precedent and discuss the different lessons they draw from it.

Other European possessions in the Caribbean were equally destabilized both by the physical migrations of Saint-Domingue refugees and by the circulation of stories about the revolution. Curaçao was another site where Geggus finds French revolutionary songs being sung, in this case amid a major slave uprising in 1795 (12); Spanish-controlled Cuba meanwhile saw multiple rebellions throughout the 1790s, culminating in the Aponte conspiracy, centered around a free person of color who court documents revealed had a book of drawings including portraits of Toussaint, Dessalines, and Christophe.[4] Geggus also details how an uprising in Venezuela in 1795, led by a slave named José Chirino who had visited Saint-Domingue, resulted in demands by the rebels for "the law of the French" (11). These direct invocations show the extensive links between these slave societies and provide evidence of how central the rebel slaves in Saint-Domingue had become in these networks. Ironically, while the Haitian Revolution thus threw the slave system in these other sites into chaos, the rapid downfall of Saint-Domingue as a prime competitor in sugar production also led to an intensification of the import of slaves to some of the other colonies, especially Cuba.

Haiti came to embody the specter of radical antislavery not only for rebelling blacks but for planter paranoia; Sibylle Fischer's *Modernity Disavowed: Haiti and the Cultures of Slavery in the Age of Revolution* (2004) provides a masterful exploration of these two sides of what Haiti came to mean in the Spanish Caribbean. She begins with Aponte's trial and then examines subsequent white Cuban writers of the nineteenth century like José Antonio Saco, Domingo del Monte, and Cirilo Villaverde to show how their conflicted feelings toward black liberation are framed through their anxieties about the Haitian Revolution. The Dominican Republic's national identity and relationship to blackness are even more closely tied to its relationship with Haiti, since, as Fischer points out, "Dominicans nowadays celebrate the 1844 independence as the true beginning of the Dominican nation"; while this date "represents independence from Haiti . . . the Dominican Republic's colonial history would have pointed toward independence from Spain—either 1821 or 1865—as the more significant event" (133). In Fischer's reading, the Dominican Republic thus fits poorly into the New World story of growing nationalism or anticolonial overcoming; the disruption of these teleologies by the presence of Haiti leads Fischer to a methodology that emphasizes history as a never fully overcome trauma where identity becomes haunted by fantasies and submerged desires.

On the Spanish mainland, meanwhile, the renegotiation of Creole identity and the reconfiguration of colonial relations were refracted through the presence of Haiti as a newly free formerly colonial state. While in Europe the Spanish crown was in turmoil resulting from the French invasion of Spain in 1808, proponents of Creole independence like Francisco de Miranda and Simón Bolívar took not only philosophical inspiration but also logistical support from the Haitian republic. One of the first attempts to end Spanish rule in South America was launched by Miranda while he was in exile in Haiti in 1806. Karen Racine discusses how Miranda worked with printers in Haiti to produce propaganda in support of his expedition (161) and, with the model of Haiti in mind, even considered using nonwhite troops as part of his military forces (152–53).[5] Although Miranda's attempt to land in Venezuela was thwarted, he helped inspire the movement that led to independence there. Bolívar similarly used Haiti as a staging ground for his own military operations in present-day Colombia from 1815 to 1817, receiving support from Alexandre Pétion's government in return for a promise to end slavery in any liberated areas.[6] As much as these revolutionary leaders were affected by their relationships with Haiti, Marixa Lasso points to evidence that members of the lower classes—particularly free people of color—who fought for Colombian independence were directly inspired by Haiti. This kind of research, to which the essays in part I of *Haiti and the Americas* contribute, has made clear that Latin American independence was established in the shadow of not only the United States but also Haiti.

The relationship between Saint-Domingue and Britain's North American colonies predates the outbreak of the Haitian Revolution, becoming especially important during the U.S. War of Independence; the most notable example of the French colony's strategic importance is surely the participation of Saint-Domingue's military forces in the 1779 Battle of Savannah.[7] The Haitian Revolution drove large numbers of white refugees like Moreau de Saint-Méry to settle in Philadelphia, and free people of color created a new community in New Orleans;[8] *The Norton Anthology of African American Literature* credits a member of this community, Victor Séjour, with authoring the first published piece of fiction by an African American in the United States.[9] Enslaved blacks were brought to Philadelphia as property, challenging that northern city's gradualist approach to abolition and changing the composition of its African American community.[10] The new arrivals—who also ended up in Charleston, Richmond, and other locations—brought stories and images that intensified debates within the United States about slavery and the slave trade.[11]

U.S. foreign policy raced to keep up with the constantly shifting situation in Saint-Domingue. Toussaint Louverture's negotiations in 1798 with U.S. president John Adams resulted in a trade agreement that ignored the Quasi War in which the United States and France were engaged and showed Toussaint's willingness to craft a foreign and economic policy independent of colonial France; Adams eventually even offered military support to Toussaint in his battle for supremacy on the island with French and Spanish forces.[12] The policies of the young North American republic toward its aspiring black neighbor became a central issue in the U.S. presidential election of 1800.[13] Thomas Jefferson's victory over Adams meant a significant shift in U.S. policy: Jefferson's attitudes toward the slave revolution and declaration of Haitian independence were much more explicitly framed by his experience as a slave owner, leading him to go so far as to support Napoleon's plans to retake the island (and presumably reinstitute slavery). Leonora Sansay's novel *Secret History, or the Horrors of*

St. Domingo, published in Philadelphia in 1808, depicts the experience of the American wife of an exiled planter returning in the early days of the effort to take back the island and is one of the earliest fictional renderings of these events.[14] The expedition was a disaster: Napoleon's troops were routed as Haitians fought for an independence that would ensure their freedom. The final loss of the colony and the catastrophic costs of the expedition led to the sale of the Louisiana Territory to the United States, thus doubling the size of the young North American republic.[15] Yet the racist foreign policy initiated by Jefferson's refusal to recognize this neighbor's independence would hobble Haiti for many decades and anticipated Haiti's shift from French to U.S. domination.[16]

As U.S. planters and policy makers sought to come to terms with the threat of radical antislavery, black experience in the United States was transformed by the Haitian Revolution. Not only was the African American community significantly altered by the influx of nonwhite refugees, but the consciousness of blacks already in the United States was dramatically affected by what was happening in the Caribbean. As early as 1793, rumors of a slave revolt in Charleston showed the inspirational effect of the events in Saint-Domingue.[17] Haiti furnished inspiration for African Americans from the earliest days of the uprising, only intensifying with rumors that Toussaint planned to land forces to fight for black liberation on the mainland. Gabriel's Rebellion in Richmond in 1800 explicitly sought to replicate the successes of the enslaved people of Saint-Domingue, a connection fictionalized in the African American novelist Arna Bontemps's *Black Thunder* (1936). The 1811 Louisiana uprising that "turned out to be the largest slave revolt in United States history" was led by an enslaved man named Charles Delondes, who may have been from Saint-Domingue (Paquette, 218). Perhaps most famous was Denmark Vesey's elaborate conspiracy of 1822—whether as envisioned by Vesey himself or as invented by paranoid white slaveholders—which involved appeals to the newly independent Haiti and plans to escape to the black republic.[18] The memory of the Haitian Revolution would live on as a source of inspiration to African Americans throughout the nineteenth and twentieth centuries, to be evoked by William Wells Brown, Martin Delany, Frederick Douglass, and a whole generation of Harlem Renaissance writers;[19] the revolution maintained an almost equal grip on the white North American imagination, surfacing in abolitionist and planter discourse alike—especially in the lead-up to the Civil War—as well as in literary work like Herman Melville's "Benito Cereno."[20]

Beyond the Revolution

The Haitian Revolution's hemispheric reverberations have been documented in some detail by scholars in a variety of fields. Subsequent interactions between Haiti and the Americas have been much less thoroughly pursued, though, and it is to this history that our collection makes its most important contribution. One main exception to this dearth of research on Haiti's postrevolution influence has been work on how African Americans in the United States interacted with the early black republic. Sara Fanning and Leslie Alexander argue for the significance of president Jean-Pierre Boyer's advertising campaign inviting North American blacks to emigrate to the island, showing how throughout the 1820s thousands of free blacks emigrated to Haiti in response to these calls to build an independent black republic. Boyer's invitation thus created one of the earliest black nationalist and Pan-African projects. Jacqueline Bacon has also showed how the first African American newspaper, *Freedom's Journal*, gave Haiti a place of prominence in its imagined international black community. Millery Polyné's *From Douglass to Duvalier: U.S. African Americans, Haiti, and Pan Americanism, 1870–1964* (2010) looks at episodes such as Frederick Douglass's experience as consul general in Haiti to show the ongoing interactions between African Americans and the Caribbean nation.

As Polyné traces the interaction of African Americans and Haiti into the twentieth century, he points to the second crucial event, following the revolution, that defined Haiti's hemispheric significance: the U.S. occupation of Haiti from 1915 to 1934, which he calls a "watershed moment in U.S. African American and Haitian relations" (60).[21] Mary Renda's *Taking Haiti: Military Occupation and the Culture of U.S. Imperialism, 1915–1940* (2001) not only assesses this event in the context of Haitian interactions with African Americans in the United States but argues further that every aspect of U.S. culture was impacted by the occupation. Renda examines memoirs by U.S. marines, plays by Eugene O'Neill and Orson Welles, literary work by Langston Hughes and Zora Neale Hurston, and popular writing by Arthur Burks and William Seabrook to explore the multiple ways in which the occupation of Haiti shaped North American culture.[22] Renda's study thus adds to the work begun by J. Michael Dash's *Haiti and the United States: National Stereotypes and the Literary Imagination* (1988) in showing how U.S. imperial relations with Haiti have inflected and been enabled by the sensationalist discourse about the black republic. Renda and Dash help explain how images of Vodou (as voodoo) and zombies became part of U.S. popular culture alongside a foreign policy that was debating annexing the independent nation as early as the 1850s. The study of U.S. representations of Vodou and zombies, whether in the anthropological accounts of Hurston, the documentary film of Maya Deren, or Hollywood feature films like *White Zombie* (1932), has itself become an important subfield, with recent contributions by Joan Dayan, Peter Dendle, Mimi Sheller, and Bryan Senn.

While the U.S. occupation of Haiti framed the interaction of these two nations during the twentieth century, Haiti has continued to influence other parts of the Caribbean as well, even if scholarship on these exchanges has been more sporadic. The independent black state remained an inspiration to intellectuals from other islands. The Anglophone Caribbean's first major international literary figure, the Jamaican writer and poet Claude McKay, features Haitian characters prominently in novels like *Home to Harlem* (1928) and *Banjo* (1929); meanwhile Jamaica's first best seller, H. G. de Lisser's *The White Witch of Rosehall* (1929), involves a plot centered on the influence of Haiti.[23] O. T. Fairclough helped found Jamaica's first political party because of his experience in Haiti.[24] This generation of decolonization was deeply invested in applying the lessons of Haiti to their own anticolonial struggles: C. L. R. James's *The Black Jacobins* (1938) most obviously sought to deploy the example of the Haitian independence struggle to speak to his own colonial context, and Alejo Carpentier's *El reino de este mundo* (1949), Derek Walcott's *Henri Christophe* (1950), Édouard Glissant's *Monsieur Toussaint* (1961), and Aimé Césaire's *La tragédie du roi Christophe* (1963) all identify Haiti as key to understanding the Caribbean of this period.[25] These writers of decolonization returned to the Haitian Revolution as their point of engagement, and this tradition continues in works like Nalo Hopkinson's *The Salt Roads* (2003). Other recent Caribbean writers have moved past representing the revolution to incorporate the ongoing presence of Haiti in the region, whether in Mayra Montero's direct representations of Haiti in *Del rojo de su sombra* (1992) and *Tu, la oscuridad* (1995), in the depictions of Haitian culture in the Dominican Republic and Puerto Rico in Ana-Maurine Lara's *Erzulie's Skirt* (2006) and Ana Lydia Vega's short fiction, or in the almost invisible Haitians haunting the margins of Julia Alvarez's *How the Garcia Girls Lost Their Accents* (1991) and Zadie Smith's *On Beauty* (2005).

The Haitians who live in the shadows of Boston in *On Beauty* point to the most recent dimension of Haiti's transnationalism: just as the revolution first brought people from that island to the rest of the hemisphere, and just as the U.S. occupation put Haiti in the consciousness of its neighbors, so emigration from Haiti to the United States and other parts of the Caribbean during the last decades of the twentieth century and the early years of the twenty-first continues to give Haiti a central place in the imagination of the Americas. Alejandro Portes and Alex Stepick's *City on the Edge* (1993) describes how Haitian migration to Miami during the 1980s transformed the city, and New York, Montreal, the Bahamas, and Puerto Rico have become other sites of significant Haitian communities. International interventions in Haiti, in the form of the U.S. invasion in 1994, the United Nations' stabilization mission that began in 2004, and the relief effort following the 2010 earthquake, have all been framed by the presence of Haitians in neighboring countries and elite fears in those countries about further Haitian migration. These interventions have also been accompanied by a discourse, produced in media and popular culture, that continues to shape how Haiti is imagined.[26]

At the same time, a vibrant Haitian culture in North America has emerged both in cultural practices and in political organizing. Elizabeth McAlister's *Rara! Vodou, Power, and Performance in Haiti and Its Diaspora* (2001) and Jana Evans Braziel's *Artists, Performers, and Black Masculinity in the Haitian Diaspora* (2008) look at religious and musical performances as ways of negotiating migration; and Paul Farmer's *AIDS and Accusation: Haiti and the Geography of Blame* (1992) shows how Haitians in the United States responded to discrimination with demonstrations and rallies that became the basis of communal identity. This community has begun to be recognized by the mainstream, through Jean-Michel Basquiat's art in the 1980s, Wyclef Jean's successful musical crossover in the 1990s, and Edwidge Danticat's MacArthur fellowship in 2009. Along with Danticat, a new generation of Haitian American writers is charting the experience of this community; the anthology *The Butterfly's Way: Voices from the Haitian Dyaspora in the United States* (2001) shows the diversity of these writers. Similarly, the experience of migration to Canada has been recorded by writers like Dany Laferrière and Myriam J. A. Chancy. These authors write from within the interstitial network that links Haiti to the Americas; as transnational subjects transformed by their presence in the imperial center, they shadow and subvert the dominant narratives of Haiti that appear in Hollywood films or cable news broadcasts.

Haiti and the Americas

While the scholarly interventions made in edited collections about the Haitian Revolution or in monographs by Polyné, Renda, and Dash demonstrate the interest in the ways that Haiti remains an important part of the U.S. imaginary, we contend that scholars have only begun to understand the full scope of that relationship. The experience of an African American military attaché to Haiti, the effects of the U.S. occupation of Haiti on American art, and the emergence of transnational hip-hop identities are just a few of the topics that *Haiti and the Americas* adds to the existing scholarship on cultural exchanges between Haiti and the United States. Furthermore, the ongoing relationships between Haiti and parts of the Americas aside from the United States have scarcely been explored. Our examinations here of Simón Bolívar's relationship to Haiti, as well as the influences of Haitian thinkers like Anténor Firmin and Benito Sylvain on not just the African American W. E. B. Du Bois but also the Trinidadian Henry Sylvester Williams, point the way to areas brimming with promise for future research on Haiti's status as crossroads of the Americas.

Part I of *Haiti and the Americas*, titled "Haiti and Hemispheric Independence," opens up the investigation of Haiti's regional influence beyond the relationship with the United States. Essays by Sibylle Fischer and Matthew Casey look at the complex exchanges between Haiti and its Spanish-speaking neighbors, ranging from the pivotal time that Bolívar spent in exile in the newly independent Haiti to the political and cultural impacts of migrant laborers moving between Haiti and Cuba. Fischer refutes the common narrative that Bolívar saw Haiti only as a negative model for the independent Latin America he envisioned, arguing instead that his attitudes toward the Caribbean nation were much more complicated. Her chapter thus makes a case for the contribution of Haitian political thought to the hemisphere's emerging governmental institutions and philosophies via Bolívar. Haiti would continue to be a crucial staging ground for leaders of the struggle against Spanish empire throughout the nineteenth century, with Antonio Maceo, José Martí, and Ramón Betances all receiving support from the independent republic. Casey notes the connections these world-historical actors had with Haiti and adds a portrait of how economic migrants created cultural networks and political organizations that also managed to influence the course of Haitian and Cuban nation building. Despite the racialist fears of Cuban elites, alliances between working people on the two islands contributed support to the Cuban wars of independence in the nineteenth century, as well as opposition to U.S. occupation in the twentieth. These chapters thus track how the movements of people and ideas between Haiti and its neighbors shaped decolonization and independence in Latin America.

Fischer and Casey introduce the idea of Haiti's importance in the hemisphere's independence struggles and political formation; part II, titled "Haiti and Transnational Blackness," looks specifically at the complex relationship between Haiti and other communities of African descent in the Americas. Jeff Karem's chapter argues that while Caribbean contributions to Pan-Africanism have subsequently been downplayed, Haitian thinkers like Firmin and Sylvain crucially influenced the Anglophone Pan-African theorists Du Bois and Williams. David Kilroy's chapter looks at how the U.S. military deployed the African American Charles Young as envoy to Haiti just as North American imperial interest in the Caribbean was intensifying. These chapters show the two sides of the relationship between African Americans and Haiti, foregrounding how people of African descent in the United States negotiated loyalty to both U.S. imperial foreign policy and a transnational sense of blackness. At the same time, taking into account how the Trinidadian Williams's Pan-Africanism enters into the dialogue between Du Bois and Haiti shows how the intellectual exchanges within the hemisphere are not reducible to exchanges between the global North and South. These tensions complicate understandings of the histories that have formed fields like African American, black, or Africana studies.

The revolution that ended slavery in Saint-Domingue and created the second independent nation in the Americas was clearly the first event to place Haiti on the world stage. Part III of *Haiti and the Americas* looks at the next event to redefine Haiti's place in the hemisphere: the U.S. occupation of 1915 to 1934. During this period, images of Haiti came to the United States through newspapers, Broadway plays, painting, fiction, and film. Bethany Aery Clerico's chapter returns to the issues of blackness and American identity opened up in part II; in particular, she examines how African American writing composed during occupation, specifically Charles Chesnutt's novel *Paul Marchand, F.M.C.*, uses Haiti's spectral presence to destabilize mainstream versions of U.S. history and identity. Lindsay Twa places these African American responses to Haiti into the larger U.S. context, comparing illustrations by Aaron Douglas to those of Alexander King to think about how black and white artists and audiences in the United States imagined Haiti—and especially Haitian Vodou.

Part III ends with Nadève Ménard turning to how Haitians themselves responded to the U.S. occupation and the power disparities and gender dynamics it created. These chapters address the ways that Haiti entered the United States as U.S. troops entered Haiti, expanding the emerging body of scholarship in postcolonial and American studies that engages with the formation of U.S. empire.

Part IV, "Globalization and Crisis," turns to the new challenges that the globalized world of the twenty-first century presents for Haiti, especially after the governmental crisis of 2004 and the earthquake of 2010, contexts that scholars are only beginning to engage critically. Christopher Garland examines the film *Ghosts of Cité Soleil* to show how the film's ostensible documentary realism in fact uses the lenses of ghetto fiction and the hip-hop video to present a version of Haiti that confirms U.S. neoliberal narratives.[27] Myriam J. A. Chancy contextualizes the crisis ensuing from the 2010 earthquake by looking at the rhetoric surrounding U.S. aid and intervention in Haiti as she urges a reconsideration of what a more humane and human reconstruction of Haiti might entail. In this way, part IV investigates a context in which contemporary media and trade networks have made Haiti's positioning global, creating new and frequently precarious correspondences between the Caribbean and the rest of the world. Garland and Chancy thus place Haiti at the center of recent scholarship on globalization, communications, film, and media studies.

The book concludes with an afterword by the leading scholar in Haitian studies, J. Michael Dash. Capping off a collection that explores Haiti's influence internationally, Dash's essay returns to Haiti to consider how Haitian identity can be rethought in light of these transnational insights. Dash's afterword examines how Haitian intellectuals present competing visions of what it means to be part of the Americas; instead of tracing New World identity back to African or European roots, he makes the case that transnationalism, globalization, and diaspora have created a polyglot Haitian identity that makes any singular identification impossible. We close the book with Dash's essay to point to Haiti as an emblematically New World space, an ideal site for imagining American identity distinct from Europeanness or Africanness. Dash reminds us of what the status of geographic, cultural, and historical crossroads means for Haiti itself.

The range of topics explored and approaches employed by the contributors make *Haiti and the Americas* an exciting collection of cutting-edge scholarship on hemispheric relations. These essays complicate and contextualize our vision of Haiti, forcing us to confront our own biases and blind spots about the Caribbean nation. In bringing together scholars from a number of disciplines and a variety of interdisciplinary fields, we hope that this book occasions the kind of dialogue that allows for more nuanced representations of Haiti and fuller understandings of its place in the Americas. Scholars in African diaspora studies, American studies, Caribbean studies, Francophone studies, Latin American studies, and postcolonial studies can all read this book as an invitation to continue exploring the transnational cultural, political, and economic relationships that have shaped the Americas.

NOTES

1. Scott's "Afro-American Sailors" gives an excellent illustration of how seamen carried stories of the Haitian Revolution to other parts of the hemisphere.

2. Brereton focuses especially on free people of color in Trinidad in "Haiti and the Haitian Revolution," 127–29.

3. See Blouet, "Bryan Edwards and the Haitian Revolution"; Sheller, "The Haytian Fear."

4. Childs describes the many fascinating ways that Haiti appeared to inspire Aponte in "A Black French General."

5. For more on Miranda in Haiti, see Jenson, *Beyond the Slave Narrative*, 176–90.

6. See Lynch, *Simón Bolívar*, 97.

7. In "Catalyst or Catastrophe," Garrigus examines how the experience of fighting in the Battle of Savannah affected the consciousness of the Saint-Domingue free people of color involved. Oral history suggests that veterans of Savannah may have put military experience gained there to use during the Haitian Revolution and war of independence.

8. White focuses on the presence of the Saint-Domingue refugees in the United States to examine how different groups within the United States navigated the impact of the Haitian Revolution.

9. Hanger and Cartwright both discuss the community created in Louisiana by Saint-Domingue refugees. Brickhouse details the fascinating story of how Séjour, a Louisiana-born child of Saint-Domingue refugees, came in 1837 to publish his story "Le Mulâtre" in a Paris-based journal edited by a Martinican person of color.

10. For more on the experience of nonwhites from Saint-Domingue in Philadelphia, see Nash's "Reverberations of Haiti in the American North," as well as Branson and Patrick's "Étrangers dans un Pays Étrange."

11. Hunt's *Haiti's Influence on Antebellum America* remains a valuable discussion of the ways the Haitian Revolution influenced U.S. attitudes about slavery.

12. See Brown, *Toussaint's Clause.*

13. Egerton's "Empire of Liberty" argues that evaluations of the presidencies of Adams and Jefferson must take into account their divergent ideas about Haiti, and that one of the most important consequences of the election of 1800 was changes in U.S. policy toward Toussaint's government.

14. Drexler compares Sansay's representation of the Haitian rebels to that of Charles Brockden Brown in making the case for Haiti as a key influence on the political imagination of the early United States.

15. Paquette makes the case for Napoleon's defeat in Haiti as the catalyst for the sale of Louisiana in "Revolutionary Saint Domingue."

16. Jefferson's writings on Haiti are examined in Matthewson's "Jefferson and Haiti."

17. See Alderson, "Charleston's Rumored Slave Revolt of 1793."

18. For an extensive examination of Vesey's plot, see Egerton's *He Shall Go Free*. For the debate around the true existence of Vesey's conspiracy, see Johnson's "Denmark Vesey and His Co-Conspirators."

19. The volume edited by Jackson and Bacon provides an excellent exploration of the ways African Americans in the United States deployed the memory of the Haitian Revolution.

20. Clavin discusses the recurring imagery of Haiti during the Civil War era. See Beecher for more on the Haitian subtext of "Benito Cereno."

21. For historical background on the U.S. occupation of Haiti, see Schmidt, *The United States Occupation of Haiti*.

22. Renda omits from her study one of the more fascinating literary texts to come out of the United States during the 1930s, William Faulkner's *Absalom! Absalom!* Bongie explains how troubling and strange the representation of Haitian history contained in that novel is in *Islands and Exiles*, 189–217.

23. Rosenberg discusses the role that Haiti plays in *The White Witch of Rosehall* in *Nationalism and the Formation of Caribbean Literature*, 84–88. Smith looks at de Lisser's travel writing about Haiti in "H.G. and Haiti."

24. Hart recounts how Fairclough "had held a responsible post in the National Bank" in Haiti, but "returning to Jamaica in 1934, he presented his credentials to the managers of the two Canadian commercial banks then operating in Kingston" (xv). After being turned down because of his color, Fairclough "first conceived the need for a political party [in Jamaica], and . . . with some initial difficulty, persuaded Norman Manley to take the initiative" in forming the People's National Party, which would successfully advocate for a new constitution and eventually Jamaican independence during the 1940s and 1950s (xv).

25. Much has been written about each of these texts; for an overview of how the Haitian Revolution is deployed by the writers of decolonization, see Arnold, "Recuperating the Haitian Revolution in Literature," 191–98.

26. Potter presents an insightful analysis of U.S. news coverage of Haiti in "Voodoo, Zombies, and Mermaids."

27. Kaussen also critiques the film in terms of its complicity with neoliberalism.

WORKS CITED

Alderson, Robert. "Charleston's Rumored Slave Revolt of 1793." In *The Impact of the Haitian Revolution on the Atlantic World*, ed. David Geggus, 93–111. Columbia: University of South Carolina Press, 2001.

Alexander, Leslie. "'The Black Republic': The Influence of the Haitian Revolution on Northern Black Consciousness." In *African Americans and the Haitian Revolution*, ed. Maurice Jackson and Jacqueline Bacon, 57–79. New York: Routledge, 2010.

Arnold, James. "Recuperating the Haitian Revolution in Literature: From Victor Hugo to Derek Walcott." In *Tree of Liberty: Cultural Legacies of the Haitian Revolution in the Atlantic World*, ed. Doris Garraway, 179–99. Charlottesville: University of Virginia Press, 2008.

Bacon, Jacqueline. *Freedom's Journal: The First African-American Newspaper*. Lanham, MD: Lexington Books, 2007.

Beecher, Jonathan. "Echoes of Toussaint Louverture and the Haitian Revolution in Melville's 'Benito Cereno.'" *Leviathan: A Journal of Melville Studies* 9, no. 2 (2007): 43–58.

Blouet, O. M. "Bryan Edwards and the Haitian Revolution." In *The Impact of the Haitian Revolution on the Atlantic World*, ed. David Geggus, 44–57. Columbia: University of South Carolina Press, 2001.

Bongie, Chris. *Islands and Exiles: The Creole Identities of Post/Colonial Literature*. Stanford, CA: Stanford University Press, 1998.

Branson, Susan, and Leslie Patrick. "Étrangers dans un Pays Étrange: Saint Domingan Refugees of Color in Philadelphia." In *The Impact of the Haitian Revolution on the Atlantic World*, ed. David Geggus, 193–208. Columbia: University of South Carolina Press, 2001.

Braziel, Jana Evans. *Artists, Performers, and Black Masculinity in the Haitian Diaspora*. Bloomington: Indiana University Press, 2008.

Brereton, Bridget. "Haiti and the Haitian Revolution in the Political Discourse of Nineteenth-Century Trinidad." In *Reinterpreting the Haitian Revolution and Its Cultural Aftershocks*, ed. Martin Munro and Elizabeth Walcott-Hackshaw, 123–49. Mona, Jamaica: University of the West Indies Press, 2006.

Brickhouse, Anna. *Transamerican Literary Relations and the Nineteenth Century Public Sphere*. New York: Cambridge University Press, 2004.

Brown, Gordon. *Toussaint's Clause: The Founding Fathers and the Haitian Revolution*. Jackson: University Press of Mississippi, 2005.

Buck-Morss, Susan. *Hegel, Haiti, and Universal History*. Pittsburgh: University of Pittsburgh Press, 2009.

Cartwright, Keith. "Re-Creolizing Swing: St. Domingue Refugees in the *Govi* of New Orleans." In *Reinterpreting the Haitian Revolution and Its Cultural Aftershocks*, ed. Martin Munro and Elizabeth Walcott-Hackshaw, 102–22. Mona, Jamaica: University of the West Indies Press, 2006.

Childs, Matt. "'A Black French General Arrived to Conquer the Island': Images of the
     Haitian Revolution in Cuba's 1812 Aponte Rebellion." In *The Impact of the Haitian
     Revolution on the Atlantic World*, ed. David Geggus, 135–56. Columbia: University
     of South Carolina Press, 2001.
Clavin, Matthew. *Toussaint Louverture and the American Civil War: The Promise and
     Peril of a Second Haitian Revolution*. Philadelphia: University of Pennsylvania
     Press, 2010.
Dash, J. Michael. *Haiti and the United States: National Stereotypes and the Literary
     Imagination*. New York: St. Martin's Press, 1988.
Dayan, Joan. *Haiti, History, and the Gods*. Berkeley: University of California Press, 1998.
Dendle, Peter. "The Zombie as Barometer of Social Anxiety." In *Monsters and the
     Monstrous: Myths and Metaphors of Enduring Evil*, ed. Niall Scott, 45–57.
     Amsterdam: Rodopi, 2007.
Drexler, Michael. "Brigands and Nuns: The Vernacular Sociology of Collectivity after
     the Haitian Revolution." In *Messy Beginnings: Postcoloniality and Early American
     Studies*, ed. Malini Johar Schueller and Edward Watts, 175–200. New Brunswick,
     NJ: Rutgers University Press, 2003.
Dubois, Laurent. *A Colony of Citizens: Revolution and Slave Emancipation in the French
     Caribbean, 1787–1804*. Chapel Hill: University of North Carolina Press, 2004.
Egerton, Douglas. "The Empire of Liberty Reconsidered." In *The Revolution of 1800*,
     ed. James Horn, Jan Lewis, and Peter Onuf, 309–30. Charlottesville: University of
     Virginia Press, 2002.
———. *He Shall Go Free: The Lives of Denmark Vesey*. Lanham, MD: Rowman and
     Littlefield, 2004.
Fanning, Sara. "The Roots of Early Black Nationalism: Northern African Americans'
     Invocations of Haiti in the Early Nineteenth Century." In *African Americans and
     the Haitian Revolution*, ed. Maurice Jackson and Jacqueline Bacon, 39–55. New
     York: Routledge, 2010.
Farmer, Paul. *AIDS and Accusation: Haiti and the Geography of Blame*. Berkeley:
     University of California Press, 1992.
Fischer, Sibylle. *Modernity Disavowed: Haiti and the Cultures of Slavery in the Age of
     Revolution*. Durham, NC: Duke University Press, 2004.
Garrigus, John. "Catalyst or Catastrophe? Saint-Domingue's Free Men of Color and the
     Battle of Savannah, 1779–1782." *Revista/Review Interamericana* 22, nos. 1–2 (1992):
     109–24.
Gaspar, David Barry. "La Guerre des Bois: Revolution, War, and Slavery in Saint
     Lucia, 1793–1838." In *A Turbulent Time: The French Revolution and the Greater
     Caribbean*, ed. David Barry Gaspar and David Geggus, 102–30. Bloomington:
     Indiana University Press, 1997.
Geggus, David Patrick. "Slavery, War, and Revolution in the Greater Caribbean, 1789–1815."
     In *A Turbulent Time: The French Revolution and the Greater Caribbean*, ed. David
     Barry Gaspar and David Geggus, 1–50. Bloomington: Indiana University Press, 1997.

Hanger, Kimberly. "Conflicting Loyalties: The French Revolution and the Free People of Color in Spanish New Orleans." In *A Turbulent Time: The French Revolution and the Greater Caribbean*, ed. David Barry Gaspar and David Geggus, 178–203. Bloomington: Indian University Press, 1997.

Hart, Richard. *Towards Decolonisation: Political, Labour, and Economic Development in Jamaica, 1938–1945*. Kingston: Canoe Press, 1999.

Hunt, Alfred. *Haiti's Influence on Antebellum America: Slumbering Volcano in the Caribbean*. Baton Rouge: Louisiana State University Press, 1988.

Jackson, Maurice, and Jacqueline Bacon, eds. *African Americans and the Haitian Revolution*. New York: Routledge, 2010.

Jenson, Deborah. *Beyond the Slave Narrative: Politics, Sex, and Manuscripts in the Haitian Revolution*. Liverpool: Liverpool University Press, 2011.

Johnson, Michael P. "Denmark Vesey and His Co-Conspirators." *William and Mary Quarterly* 58, no. 4 (October 2001): 915–76.

Kaussen, Valerie. "Real Ghosts/Spectacular Hauntings: Containing Violence in Asger Leth's *Ghosts of Cité Soleil*." Francophone Caribbean and North America Conference, Florida State University, February 2010.

Lasso, Marixa. "Haiti as an Image of Popular Republicanism in Caribbean Colombia: Cartagena Province (1811–1828)." In *The Impact of the Haitian Revolution on the Atlantic World*, ed. David Geggus, 176–90. Columbia: University of South Carolina Press, 2001.

Lynch, John. *Simón Bolívar: A Life*. New Haven: Yale University Press, 2007.

Matthewson, Tim. "Jefferson and Haiti." *Journal of Southern History* 61, no. 2 (1995): 209–48.

McAlister, Elizabeth. *Rara! Vodou, Power, and Performance in Haiti and Its Diaspora*. Berkeley: University of California Press, 2001.

Nash, Gary. "Reverberations of Haiti in the American North: Black Saint Dominguans in Philadelphia." *Pennsylvania History* 65 (1998): 44–73.

Nesbitt, Nick. *Universal Emancipation: The Haitian Revolution and the Radical Enlightenment*. Charlottesville: University of Virginia Press, 2008.

Paquette, Robert. "Revolutionary Saint Domingue in the Making of Territorial Louisiana." In *A Turbulent Time: The French Revolution and the Greater Caribbean*, ed. David Barry Gaspar and David Geggus, 204–50. Bloomington: Indian University Press, 1997.

Polyné, Millery. *From Douglass to Duvalier: U.S. African Americans, Haiti, and Pan Americanism, 1870–1964*. Gainesville: University Press of Florida, 2010.

Portes, Alejandro, and Alex Stepick. *City on the Edge: The Transformation of Miami*. Berkeley: University of California Press, 1993.

Potter, Amy. "Voodoo, Zombies, and Mermaids: U.S. Newspaper Coverage of Haiti in 2004." *Geographical Review* 99, no. 2 (April 2009): 208–30.

Racine, Karen. *Francisco de Miranda: A Transatlantic Life in the Age of Revolution*. Wilmington, DE: Scholarly Resources, 2003.

Renda, Mary. *Taking Haiti: Military Occupation and the Culture of U.S. Imperialism, 1915–1940*. Chapel Hill: University of North Carolina Press, 2001.

Rosenberg, Leah. *Nationalism and the Formation of Caribbean Literature*. New York: Palgrave Macmillan, 2007.

Schmidt, Hans. *The United States Occupation of Haiti, 1915–1934*. New Brunswick, NJ: Rutgers University Press, 1995.

Scott, Julius. "Afro-American Sailors and the International Communications Network: The Case of Newport Bowers." In *African Americans and the Haitian Revolution*, ed. Maurice Jackson and Jacqueline Bacon, 25–38. New York: Routledge, 2010.

Senn, Bryan. *Drums of Terror: Voodoo in the Cinema*. Baltimore: Luminary Press, 1998.

Sheller, Mimi. *Consuming the Caribbean: From Arawaks to Zombies*. New York: Routledge, 2003.

———. "'The Haytian Fear': Racial Projects and Competing Reactions to the First Black Republic." In *Research in Politics and Society*, vol. 6, *The Global Color Line: Racial and Ethnic Inequality and Struggle from a Global Perspective*, ed. P. Batur-Vanderlippe and J. Feagin, 283–301. Greenwich, CT: JAI Press, 1999.

Smith, Matthew. "H.G. and Haiti: An Analysis of Herbert G. DeLisser's 'Land of Revolutions.'" *Journal of Caribbean History* 44, no. 2 (2010): 1–18.

White, Ashli. *Encountering Revolution: Haiti and the Making of the Early Republic*. Baltimore: Johns Hopkins University Press, 2010.

I

HAITI AND
HEMISPHERIC
INDEPENDENCE

1

Bolívar in Haiti: Republicanism in the Revolutionary Atlantic

—Sibylle Fischer

1816, Republic of Haiti. After the collapse of the First Republic in Vene-zuela in 1812 and the brutal reprisals that followed, Spanish American patriots had been arriving daily, by the boatload, in Haiti. Many had first sought refuge on the nearby islands of Curaçao, Trinidad, and St. Thomas, but eventually most of the refugees ended up in the coastal towns of Jac-mel, Jérémie, and Les Cayes in southern Haiti. In 1815 the fall of Cartagena set off another wave of refugees, with over six hundred Granadans taking to the sea. Under attack from royalist forces and ill equipped for the rough journey by sea, only four hundred of them ever seem to have made it to a safe haven. For most, this haven was Haiti. By early 1816, about two thou-sand residents from Venezuela and Nueva Granada were living in various Haitian towns on the southern peninsula and in Port-au-Prince.[1]

Facing the Caribbean Sea, the southern coast of Haiti had always had close connections to neighboring islands and the coastal towns of the mainland. Privateers and smugglers used Les Cayes as a base of opera-tions. A sizable community of foreign merchants had settled in Haiti's southern towns and left behind some remarkable accounts of their experi-ences, which often stress the urbanity and hospitality of the place (Verna, *Pétion y Bolívar*, 157–60). Among the Spanish American patriots who lived in Haiti were some of the important generals and *caudillos* of the early years of the military struggle against Spain, among them Carlos Soublette, José Padilla, Manuel Piar, Santiago Mariño, and José Francisco Bermúdez. Little is known about the early years of exile for Venezuelan patriots. For-tunately the record becomes thicker with the arrival of Simón Bolívar in December 1815. The president of the Haitian republic, Alexandre Pétion, a man of color and veteran of the revolutionary wars in Saint-Domingue, welcomed Bolívar and the group of insurgents who accompanied him, and directed the governor of the southern province to provide the refugees with rations of bread and salt fish. When Bolívar prepared his first invasion of the Venezuelan mainland from Les Cayes in March 1816, he did so with the funds and military support of the Haitian state. The invasion failed, and by August 1816 Bolívar was back in Haiti. In December he set sail again, this time from Jacmel, for a second, more successful attempt to retake Venezuela from the royalist forces.

Did some Granadan and Venezuelan families stay behind? How long did they live in Haiti? Did they ever leave, or did they eventually mix with the local population? In her memoir about the famous Jacmelian Carnival, the Haitian American writer Edwidge Danticat reminds us of a description we owe to the Haitian novelist René Depestre of men wearing multicolored "Bolívar hats" with bright feathers and long locks of hair. Danticat also points out that Jacmel's main street is to this day called Rue Barranquilla, after the Colombian harbor town. Why Barranquilla? Was the street named after Granadans who had settled there? Perhaps a nostalgic gesture by those who stayed behind? At least for a few years, Haiti was, it seems, a rather cosmopolitan place, with its southern coast figuring as a gathering point for populations that were swept up in the insurgencies on the mainland and were not welcomed by the colonial governments of the other Caribbean islands.[2]

I suspect that this picture of a cosmopolitan Haiti with close ties to revolutionary movements in the Atlantic will come as a surprise to many readers. According to most accounts, Haiti was an island cut off from its surroundings through diplomatic embargoes, a pariah in the hemisphere, set on its own eccentric loop. Did Haiti not represent all that white Creoles feared—a state that had grown out of race war, that was now run by former slaves and their allies, a state where whites, despite promises to the contrary, had been brutally massacred even after the end of warfare? Why did the Venezuelan and Granadan patriots and their families, most of them white Creoles, go to Haiti, of all places?

I think that the situation on the ground in the early years of the new Haitian republic may have been more complicated than many historical and contemporary accounts let on, and we should not simply assume that Haiti was merely a figure of fear and abhorrence in the Creole imagination. Haiti's diplomatic isolation by the imperial powers and its erasure from public records need to be weighed carefully against its prominent place in the lived experience of those who had spent time in Haiti or had otherwise been in contact with residents of the French-speaking Antilles. As Ada Ferrer shows in her important new work on the young republic's politics of "free soil," political ideas in the colonies, particularly among the enslaved, often took shape in dialogue with Haiti, and the new Haitian state clearly saw itself as making a "decisive intervention in the debate over freedom and rights." The problem is that this intervention was not necessarily recognized by the other participants in the debate. The scarcity of records is, among other things, a reflection of power relations in the slaveholding Atlantic. A similar picture emerges when we look at the relationship between republican Haiti and the Spanish American insurgency in the first two decades of the nineteenth century. Although often forgotten, Haiti played an important role in those early years by offering a safe haven to refugees from the mainland, providing military and financial support for the insurgents, and forcing the issue of slave emancipation onto the agenda. The question is whether Haiti's intervention had any noticeable impact on the political and intellectual discussions at the time.

As in the case of Haiti's radical antislavery politics, political debates that may have taken place in Haiti about republicanism and state building in a postslavery America are not well documented. I will show, however, that both textual and contextual evidence suggests that at least during the early years of the struggle for independence, the Haitian political experiments offered a kind of blueprint for the establishment of American republics and as such had a profound impact on the republican thought of Simón Bolívar. We can trace this impact only if we adopt a circuitous route and consider explicit textual evidence alongside indirect evidence regarding horizons of expectations, life experiences, and flows of communication. A full account of Haiti's place in the revolutionary Atlantic needs to consider a great number of factors, among them the strong presence of French-speaking residents in Venezuela's First Republic, the Haitian influence on early conspiracies on the mainland (e.g., the Coro conspiracy of 1795 or the conspiracy of 1797 in Guaira led by Gual and España), and the long Haitian exile of many Spanish American revolutionaries. Clearly, such a full account cannot be offered in the space of a brief essay. But even without such detailed contextualization, we can learn much if we consider the existential reality of the Spanish American insurgents in Haiti and superimpose the two chronologies of the young Haitian states and that of the Spanish American struggle for independence and their corresponding historiographies. What becomes clear rather quickly is that there are many points of contact and influence that have not been noticed in the existing literature. In light of the circumstantial and textual evidence, it seems unwarranted to assume that the Republic of Haiti was simply perceived as a monstrous aberration by Spanish American insurgents. No doubt the "specter of Haiti" tormented the Creole imagination and often shaped policies, but along with the specter there was also, importantly, the real Haiti, which during crucial years of the struggle against the Spanish empire played a remarkable role and offered important lessons for post-revolutionary state building.

The Disappearance of Haiti

The historiography of early nineteenth-century Spanish America is remarkably devoid of references to Haiti. The reasons for this are complex. The dearth of documentation on the early years of the Haitian republic and its policies is clearly an important factor, as is the national orientation of much earlier work on the independence period. This is compounded by an assumption of Haitian exceptionalism that should have been discarded a long time ago but continues to haunt nonspecialist scholarship. It remains difficult for some students of history to imagine Haiti as a modern republic, as the site of remarkably progressive asylum policies, or as a state with the resources to house and feed hundreds of refugees and provide supplies for two military expeditions. In fact, it is often assumed that there is a causal connection between Haiti's later troubles and its revolutionary antislavery origins: Haiti's "failure" must be rooted in the early nineteenth century. That is arguably not the case, or at least not in any simple way. When compared with the war-torn Spanish American states in the first decades after independence, Haiti looks rather like a success story. One wonders whether the refugees from the insurgent Spanish colonies, traumatized by brutal colonial warfare and grateful for having found a safe haven, might not have seen it that way.[3]

Ironically, the important critical historiography of the last two or three decades, which aims to contest a racially inflected historiography and to vindicate Haiti's place in history, has not contributed as much to rectifying this picture as one might have hoped. The scholarship continues to focus on the idea that Haiti was a nightmare for colonial powers and local Creoles, thereby neglecting to study Haiti's significant interventions in the slaveholding Atlantic. Haiti thus remains defined in purely negative terms: a spectral presence around which prejudices of color and early forms of racism coalesce and solidify. A distinction between fears regarding slave revolution and race war, on the one hand, and attitudes regarding the newly independent state of Haiti, on the other, is rarely made.[4]

A third important factor that has contributed to the disappearance of Haiti concerns recent changes in the way we understand the Spanish American independence movements. As the U.S. historian Jeremy Adelman has argued, the groundbreaking scholarship by historians like François-Xavier Guerra, José Carlos Chiaramonte, and Jaime Rodrígez O. has cast serious doubts on the liberal teleologies favored by an earlier generation of scholars as it tends to stress the continuity of social and political relations of European making in the American colonies. No doubt there is much that recommends this new wave of scholarship. However, shifting attention away from events and conflicts in Spanish America toward the imperial centers also has had some perhaps unintended effects: "The colonists have become peripheral players to their own story" (Adelman, 144). One would be hard-pressed to find a better way of describing what has happened to Haitian actors in the recent historiography.

Geographies of Reason

Simón Bolívar spent the better part of 1816 in the Republic of Haiti, where he was in close conversation with the leaders of the new postslavery state and received crucial support for his military expeditions against the royalist forces who had retaken key cities on the mainland after the collapse of the First and Second Republics in Venezuela. Yet most scholars of Bolívar's republicanism conform to the view that any modern intellectual influences need to be traced to non-Iberian Europe. Characteristically Bolivarian features are usually explained in reference to "pressures from American realities" and Bolívar's native "realism." The Haitian experience is rarely mentioned. Are there reasons for assuming that Bolívar never entertained any intellectual conversation in those long days in Haiti?

Clearly there are troubling aspects in Bolívar's handling of political issues relating to the demands of the people of color. His decision to have two powerful *pardo* generals, Manuel Piar in 1817 and José Padilla in 1828, executed for insubordination and sedition while sparing the lives of white *caudillos* who had been guilty of similar or worse offenses remains one of the more disturbing aspects of Bolívar's life. But we should not assume that just because Haiti's rulers were men of color, its role in the imaginary of the revolutionary Atlantic can be reduced to being an instantiation of what Bolívar called, derogatorily, *pardocracia* (literally, the rule of people of color). It is by now understood that the term *pardo* mixes considerations of class, color, and ethnicity. Neither Bolívar's attitude toward Haiti nor the established meaning of *pardo* justifies a purely racialist reading of the term. Haiti was arguably the site where questions of color, racial differences, and postcolonial state building entered the realm of republican thought for the first time. It was also the site where the challenges that confronted a society built on the ruins of the colonial plantation economy and slavery revealed themselves for the first time. Haiti was in many ways a laboratory of republicanism in postslavery America. It is hard to imagine that Simón Bolívar saw nothing but men of color making a mess of things without noticing the high political drama that was unfolding in front of his very eyes.

Still, most accounts of Simón Bolívar's life tell us that as the young scion of a rich Venezuelan family, he spent his formative years in France, where he absorbed the literary and philosophical canon of the Enlightenment.[5] We see him devouring the works of Montesquieu, Rousseau, and Locke and toying with the liberationist ideas of the Jacobins. We see him in Paris during the coronation of Bonaparte, and then again in Rome, profoundly moved by the ruins of the Roman republic and pronouncing his famous (if probably apocryphal) oath to liberate Spanish America from the Spanish yoke. Upon his return to Venezuela, he becomes involved in the struggle against colonial rule and slowly comes to believe that political and constitutional theories from Europe do not fit well with Spanish America's chaotic multiracial reality. The young Jacobin remakes himself as a moderate conservative and a realist. In a recent biography, John Lynch tells us that "his approach to knowledge was empirical, not metaphysical. . . . His realism always held back the full flow of ideas" (33). Others, perhaps less persuaded by the vision of a "pragmatic" Bolívar, stress the growing influence of classical republican thought, which, unlike Enlightenment republicanism, does not consider democratic governance as a necessary component of the republican state form.[6] Regardless of whether we think him to be moved by pragmatic concerns or by his readings of classical republicanism, however, a Bolívar emerges in these accounts who comes to believe that only a strong government can control the anarchic tendencies of an untutored populace with no experience in self-rule. This authoritarian tendency leads Bolívar to worry obsessively about *pardocracia*, eliminate insubordinate generals ruthlessly (especially when they belong to the class of *pardos*), and ultimately to assume military dictatorship in 1828.

A striking geography of reason is at work here.[7] Normative ideas about governance and state form come from Europe, particularly France and England, and ancient Greece and Rome. From America we get only a chaotic, unformed, mixed-race reality that resists theorization. When Europe can no longer answer the problems America poses, a pragmatic authoritarianism arises. Now, it would be foolhardy to deny, on account of some preference for deriving political thought from local traditions, the influence of European thinkers and traditions on Bolívar. Clearly, Roman republican thought, British monarchical traditions, and French republicanism left a deep imprint in Bolívar's mind. Still, the striking simplicity of this narrative that assumes a bipolar world—Europe and (Spanish) America—and a unidirectional transfer of ideas should give us pause.

We may in fact wonder whether some persistent puzzles in the historiography are not in part an effect of this somewhat reductive picture. Take, for instance, the claim that Bolívar's draft for a Bolivian constitution of 1828 was based on Bonaparte's 1799 and 1802 constitutions (Collier). On the one hand, there are indeed some similarities between Bolívar's drafts and Bonaparte's constitution, particularly that of 1802. Yet Bolívar's lifelong aversion to any comparison between himself and the French emperor is well documented, and the similarities between Bonaparte's constitution and Bolívar's are not such that they would place Bonaparte's influence beyond doubt. Regarding motivations, Bonaparte's autocratic measures and those adopted by Bolívar in postcolonial America are obviously quite different. Perhaps we need to think relations beyond the clichéd opposition between "enlightened Europe" and "savage America" if we really want to understand the ways in which the early Spanish American revolutionaries developed their political ideas.

There are other instances where the presumed geography of reason leads to puzzling questions. Take the insistence among recent biographers and intellectual historians that Bolívar should be considered a "realist" or even a "pragmatist." To be sure, as a general whose success depended largely on his ability to squelch local insurgencies and resolve the internal divisiveness among allied *caudillos*, Bolívar did not always conduct himself in accordance with high-minded principles. He was a military man convinced that his success ultimately depended on his ability to hold on to power. Perhaps that makes him a realist in the way that international relations theorists like to use the term. But on the face of it, there is little that speaks of pragmatism in the project of a young insurgent who, with no troops to speak of, haphazard sources of funding, and little support among local populations beyond the small circle of Creole elites, embarked from the outcast state of Haiti to "liberate" a territory that stretched from the Caribbean coast across the Andes to Peru. Little that suggests pragmatism, too, in the strikingly experimental aspects of some of Bolívar's constitutional thought: just take the idea to create, in addition to the executive, legislature, and judiciary, a *poder moral* (moral power) as a "fourth power." Or the idea to revive the Roman position of the censor in nineteenth-century Bolivia. The main justification for the label of realism is, I suspect, that Bolívar is taken to be refusing a "principled implementation" of European political projects.

Bolívar's famous invective in the Cartagena Manifesto (1812) against what he perceived as the weakly constituted first Venezuelan republic is an interesting example for the issue at hand. In a much-cited passage, Bolívar says:

> The operating codes our leaders consulted weren't those they might have learned from any practical science of governance, but those formulated by certain worthy visionaries who, conceiving some ethereal republic, sought to achieve political perfection on the presumption of the perfectibility of the human species. (Bushnell, 4)

At first sight, this may indeed be seen as a rejection of political theory and a call for a "realist politics." However, calling "the science of governance" "practical" is not the same as saying that only power matters or government is a merely pragmatic issue; after all, Bolívar adopts the term "science" for his idea of good governmental practice. Declaring some theoretical models unsuitable is not the same as saying that theoretical models are of no use. Bolívar's refusal to follow the principles of European state thinking does not appear to be the result of measuring European theory against American reality. In this early text, Bolívar merely takes issue with certain anthropological assumptions that he sees operating in some republican models. Later texts do not take up this particular argument but seem to be grounded in the comparative analysis of European republics and American republics. Bolívar had traveled in the new American republics in the north. He had experienced the collapse of the First Republic in Venezuela. By the time he wrote his important constitutional texts, he had witnessed the collapse of the Second Republic in Venezuela. But he had also spent almost a year in the Republic of Haiti, the second independent republic in America, where a constitutional regime sui generis had been created and in fact shown a resilience that had eluded the Spanish American first attempts at self-governance.

We have good reasons, then, to be skeptical about any simple picture of the flow of influences and the origins of theoretical thought. We have good reasons, too, for thinking that the Haitian experience might have had a significant impact on the political refugees from Venezuela and Nueva Granada, and thus ultimately on political thought during the struggle for independence. The argument that follows relies largely on Bolívar's published correspondence and major political statements, as well as on the few studies of the relationship between Haiti and the early struggle for independence in Venezuela and New Granada. It has to contend with the fact that the Haitian republic was careful not to be seen as interfering in the affairs of foreign countries, and exiled insurgents, mindful of Haiti's precarious status in the slaveholding Atlantic, were just as careful to avoid any close identification with the state that extended protection to them. This clearly affects the availability and legibility of sources and thus presents a serious methodological challenge. The exceptional circumstances call for a hermeneutics that moves gingerly between close textual reading and contextual considerations. While we have reason to be wary of readings that brush aside all but the most disparaging references to Haiti as "strategic," we do need to factor strategy and calculation into our accounts. At the same time, we should not discard all assumptions of common sense in favor of the more adventurous hypothesis that prejudice cancels out all other impressions. Rather, we should try to imagine, on the basis of the accounts we have, what the lived experience in Haiti may have been for boat people who had escaped the horrors of war on the continent and found safe haven in Haiti. There is a certain theatricality to the letters to and from Haiti that allows us to reconstruct the personal relationships behind the diplomatic formalities. Rhetorical features and implicit structures of dialogue and address can be important sources of information, especially when combined with extraneous knowledge we can gather from historiography and archival sources. I hope to show that a broadly hermeneutical approach can yield results that neither intellectual history nor textual criticism on its own can produce.

Horizons of Expectations

The first boats carrying refugees from Venezuela had begun to arrive in Haiti in 1812. The First Republic had collapsed, and Monteverde's royalist forces had quickly turned to brutal repression. There were random killings of detainees, the prisons were overflowing, and Creole property was being confiscated. Colonial bureaucrats were plainly unable to regain control of the situation. On June 15, 1813, Bolívar published a decree declaring "war to death." Patriot forces and royalists became locked in a campaign of terror. Whole villages were eradicated in extrajudicial executions, and military leaders gloated about their use of rape in terrorizing local populations. While the military struggle continued and Bolívar was trying to regroup his forces from the relative safety of Cartagena to the west of Caracas, many more people from the embattled towns along the coast fled and eventually made it to Haiti.

By the time Bolívar arrived in Haiti on December 24, 1815, two experiments in republican governance in Venezuela had failed. Fernando VII had been restored to power in Spain and had sent a large expeditionary force to restore the colonial regime. In his *Manifiesto de Cartagena* of December 15, 1812, Bolívar had singled out three factors as responsible for the failure of the republic: excessive leniency toward opponents and traitors, a lack of experience in governance by the citizens, and federalism. The relatively stable Haitian republic must have seemed like a remarkable example of postcolonial state building to refugees who had seen their own efforts collapse twice and who were fleeing the atrocities of colonial warfare. While the Haitian republic was certainly facing serious threats to its existence, these threats were likely perceived as caused by external forces—be it from France, which had not recognized Haitian independence at the time, or from the separate monarchical state Henri Christophe had set up in the north of the island. To refugees who had seen their own efforts collapse twice and were fleeing the atrocities of colonial warfare, the relatively stable Haitian republic must have seemed like a remarkable example of a postcolonial state embattled by outside forces but able to remain internally stable.

Despite official embargoes on any news from the postslavery state, most Venezuelans were probably familiar with Haiti's history long before they arrived in Haiti as refugees. A significant presence of French-speaking people in Caracas dated back to the 1790s, which is much commented on in diplomatic correspondence at the time (Gómez, "La revolución"; Soriano). While colonial authorities considered these French-speaking refugees—and it is often impossible to tell whether they were European French or Creoles from the French colonies—a potential threat to order and frequently accused them of spreading seditious ideas, they became an important support group for the government of the First Republic.

Francisco de Miranda, the president of the First Republic, was so fond of surrounding himself with French-speaking supporters that his detractors often denounced him as a *afrancesado* (Frenchified or Francophile).

From what can be gleaned from the record, the Franco-Antilleans were quite a heterogeneous group. Some were white plantation owners who had fled Saint-Domingue with their slaves in the early years of the uprising. Many of them arrived in Venezuela via other islands or the United States and thus belong to the same migration that affected the Oriente province in Cuba, New Orleans, and the eastern seaboard of the United States. Another wave of Franco-Antilleans arrived in Venezuela when Spain joined England in its attempt to put down the insurrection in Saint-Domingue and seize the island. When Spain captured some seven hundred French republicans and two hundred slaves from the ranks of the insurgents, they were taken to Venezuela (McKinley, 128–29). Then a significant migration took place from Saint-Domingue after Toussaint Louverture's defeat of the forces of André Rigaud in the south of the island in 1800. Many of the men of color who formed Rigaud's army either fled to neighboring Caribbean islands to join the ranks of Caribbean privateers or settled in other areas of the Caribbean, especially the Venezuelan coast, where they soon took up a trade, became involved in the sugar industry, or joined the republican military.[8] After Toussaint Louverture's occupation of the eastern part of the island, Dominican planters fled, often with their slaves. Many settled in Venezuela. Although not French, they too would have carried with them the stories and the language of the uprising in Saint-Domingue. And then there were, apparently (but here we are entering the territory of gossip and speculative attributions of intention, where one needs to tread carefully), veterans from the Haitian wars who arrived later, long after the declaration of independence of Haiti and after the proclamation of the embattled First Republic in Venezuela, and were keen to offer their services to insurgents on the mainland.[9] Due to this heterogeneity, it is not easy to develop a coherent picture of the Franco-Antillean population in Venezuela. However, most commentators at the time agreed that the Franco-Antilleans were in their vast majority republicans. It also seems to be the case—though harder to confirm—that they were for the most part people of color.

Horizons of expectation matter for our interpretation of events. What these refugees from Saint-Domingue and Santo Domingo told their Venezuelan hosts would have affected the way Venezuelans thought of Haiti and the way they experienced their subsequent exile on the island. We must be careful not to substitute the rumors, which are richly documented in communications between government agencies, spies, and diplomats, for a record of everyday conversation and popular expectations. Then, as now, inciting fear was an effective way for the authorities to justify security measures and extrajudicial actions, and the colonial authorities clearly had an interest in subsuming all forms of republicanism under the heading of "nightmare Haiti."

No doubt the stories of the French-speaking refugees varied, according to when and for what reason they fled the island. But let us imagine, at least, that the migrants from Saint-Domingue and other French islands would have told some part of their life stories and probably tried to explain how they ended up in Caracas. It is not difficult to guess what stories white planters who had lost their livelihood would have told: most likely, those white planters felt they had just escaped from the worst nightmare imaginable. More interesting is the question of what French republican soldiers and free men of color from Saint-Domingue might have told. We know from other sources that the social and political position of the free people of color in Saint-Domingue had been ambiguous: they had fought against the French colonial powers on account of their political rights, but also against Toussaint Louverture's army of mostly former slaves. For many free people of color, it would have been Toussaint, not the French, who drove them into exile. We also know that the antislavery commitments of the free people of color had not always been certain (Garrigus). Although their interests and ambitions were decidedly different from that of former slaves, they were clearly invested in notions of racial equality and the extension of political rights to free people of color. It is hard to imagine that these conflicts were not a topic of conversation in Venezuela, where in 1797 a multiethnic conspiracy in Guaira had been strongly influenced by Jacobin ideas and embraced abolition, and where royalist leaders were now trying to rally *pardos* and slaves for the Spanish side, taking advantage of the disappointment these groups were feeling about a republic that had failed to abolish slavery and created a two-tier citizenship system, which tied active citizenship rights to property. Did the refugees from Saint-Domingue identify with the Creole elite who established the First Republic and were not interested in abolishing slavery? Or did they warn their Venezuelan hosts about the dangers of owning slaves? It is probably less important to know what exactly was said than to give proper weight to the fact that some such conversations must have taken place, that it was highly likely that patriots in Caracas were more familiar with the concerns of the free people of color than with those of the former slaves under Toussaint Louverture. Let us remember, too, that the people of color had been defeated in a civil war, but by 1812 their social group could plausibly claim that they had recaptured the republic and brought peace to the war-torn island. The head of the republic was, after all, Alexandre Pétion, a former leader of the free people of color. For those who had fought in the wars, the idea that republican Haiti was ruled by former slaves would probably have seemed implausible.

Clearly these reflections have to remain somewhat speculative for now. The main point I would like to insist on, however, is a broad one and does not require any specious presuppositions: it is highly likely that Venezuelan and Granadan patriots, who had direct contact with refugees from Saint-Domingue and refugees from other French colonies in the Caribbean, would have drawn a clear distinction between "the nightmare" of the antislavery insurrection and the state that had come into being in the aftermath and brought relative peace to the island. Venezuelan patriots would have had a fairly sophisticated understanding of the racial, political, and social antagonisms that subtended the revolutionary wars and the new Republic of Haiti. It seems unlikely that they would have thought of the Republic of Haiti as synonymous with race war.

If we think that the horizon of expectations of the Venezuelan patriots was partly shaped by what migrants from Saint-Domingue reported, that they ended up seeking exile in Haiti seems both less surprising and more significant. Venezuelan patriots may still have thought that a repetition of the events we now call the Haitian Revolution needed to be avoided at all costs. But they might also have considered the final outcome a positive one: France, after all, had been defeated for good, the anarchy and violent conflict of the years of war had given way to relative peace and stability under a republican government, and the Haitian republic was, in fact, the only territory where the Spanish American patriots were truly welcome.

Bolívar in Haiti

On December 19, 1815, Bolívar sent a letter to the president of the Haitian republic, Alexandre Pétion, announcing his impending arrival in Les Cayes.[10]

Mister President:

For a long time I have hoped for the honor to enter into contact with Your Excellency and to offer proof of my profound esteem and recognition that your distinguished gifts and your countless good deeds on behalf of my unfortunate compatriots have inspired in me; however, I always feared to importune Your Excellency by distracting your attention for the briefest moment from the important matters that require your attention.

Fortunately for me, Mister President, circumstances oblige me to direct myself to the asylum of all republicans of this part of the world: I need to visit the country whose happiness is the result of Your Excellency's wisdom. . . .

I hope, Mister President, that the affinities between our sentiments regarding the defense of the rights of our common *patria* will gain me the effects of the inexhaustible benevolence you have extend towards all those who never appealed to it in vain. . . .

Your humble and obedient servant,

Simón Bolívar

On December 24, Bolívar arrived in Les Cayes. On December 31 he traveled to Port-au-Prince, accompanied by the governor of the southern province, Ignace de Marion. On January 1 he would have witnessed lavish festivities in celebration of Independence Day in the capital. Pétion received Bolívar on January 2. In a letter to his financial backer, the Curaçaoan merchant Luis Brion, on January 2, 1816, Bolívar gives a brief account:

I just paid him a visit, which was as pleasant as you can imagine. The President seemed to me, as in fact to everybody, excellent. His physiognomy reflects his character and the latter is as benevolent as it is well-known. I expect much from his love of liberty and justice. I have not yet been able to speak with him except in general terms. When it will be possible for me to delve deeper into matters, I will do it with all the reserve and moderation that befits our unfortunate situation. (Verna, *Pétion y Bolívar*, 162)

Despite its brevity, an interesting letter. Personal reactions are absent from the account, as is any sense of surprise. Instead the letter confirms what is "widely known" about Pétion's character: his benevolence and love of liberty and justice.[11] There is, possibly, a note of calculation here: Pétion's "love of liberty and justice" is introduced not as part of a quick character sketch but as a pawn in Bolívar's game plan. Bolívar's expectations must have been well settled by the time he arrived in Haiti. It is on the basis of the "well-known" facts about Pétion that Bolívar may have felt justified in expressing "expectations" after a single conversation that failed to go into any detail. There is a swiftness in all of this that makes sense only if we assume that much of what was on the table had been part of previous conversations among advisers and allies of, probably, both men.

We also see, in this first letter, the signs of a relationship that gains in substance and detail but never changes in its balance of affect. Bolívar arrived as a defeated military leader of a struggle that had twice failed quite miserably, and meets, for the first time, a president who had been a general in a war of independence, had been in exile, had weathered the storms, and had shown himself able to build a fairly stable and peaceful republic on the territory that had seen some of the most bloody warfare in recent memory. Bolívar, not otherwise known for his lack of self-regard, clearly assumes a subordinate position in face of the president of the Haitian republic.

Unfortunately we do not have any records for the conversations that took place between Bolívar and Pétion. We do not even know how many there were, and how long they lasted. Ardouin tells us that Pétion made himself readily available to the many exiled men, and at the time there were lively conversations taking place in Port-au-Prince (*Etudes*, vol. 8, chap. 5, p. 54). The only direct sources we have are the letters Bolívar wrote to Pétion—a total of nine—and a few others that pertain to his Haitian experience. From Pétion, only three letters have been found so far. Thus much depends on our ability to read these letters with a keen ear for any resonances with what we know about the political and diplomatic situation at the time.

On the basis of the letters, it seems that Pétion and Bolívar reached an understanding fairly quickly, and Pétion committed himself to supporting financially and militarily the Spanish American struggle for independence in exchange for a promise by Bolívar to abolish slavery in all liberated territories. When news arrived of the fall of Cartagena to the royalists, only a couple of days after this first conversation, Pétion immediately ordered that all agricultural exports to the Colombian harbor town be stopped. The exact form of the agreement between Pétion and Bolívar is not known, but judging from its implications and the swiftness of its implementation, one assumes that the agreement was fairly explicit. When Bolívar left from Les Cayes in March 1816, he had received several thousand rifles with bayonets and ammunition, vessels, soldiers, and a portable printing press.

The biographical literature often represents the pact between Pétion and Bolívar regarding the abolition of slavery as a last-minute cri de coeur on the part of a well-intentioned man of color deeply troubled by the suffering of his brethren. We read it over and over again: a final tearful embrace between Bolívar and Pétion, Bolívar bids him farewell, and then a last-minute plea:

> Shedding tender tears, Pétion answered: Que le Bon Dieu vous bénisse dans toutes vos entreprises! [May the Good God bless you in all your endeavors!]. With this gesture the magnanimous magistrate of Haiti demanded from Bolívar that he give liberty to the slaves when he arrived in Venezuela. . . . How can you found a republic while slavery exists, he said. Bolívar promised this to him, and added: do not ask me for this act of justice as compensation for your generosity, but rather as felicitous path of my fate.[12]

What is remarkable here is that a commitment that involved high stakes on both sides becomes the subject of a last-minute overflow of sentiment. This "foundational scene" is not just an outstanding piece of histo-kitsch; it is also a severe distortion of political realities. It recasts radical antislavery politics, with their significant diplomatic, military, and financial ramifications, in the teary language of metropolitan abolitionism. Haiti as a revolutionary political agent vanishes and is replaced by the depiction of two epic individuals linking arms in abolitionism's spontaneous embrace across color lines. This scene is highly unlikely. The Haitian republic had made it a constitutional commitment not to interfere in the affairs of foreign powers; without Haitian support, Bolívar's campaign to rid Spanish America of Spanish colonial rule might have ended in exile, in Les Cayes. High-risk promises like those on the table here are not made lightly, in the rush of emotion.

Indeed, later correspondence between Bolívar and Pétion suggests that the agreement was quite formal and explicit. In his letter to Pétion of September 4, 1816, written on the vessel that had taken him back from the mainland to Jacmel on the southern coast of Haiti, Bolívar gives an account of his military campaign and why his invasion had failed. In Verna's print edition of the letters pertaining to Bolívar's exile in Haiti, it amounts to a full six pages and contains a shot-by-shot rendition of the plans, battles, and strategic positionings.

> I declare, with my word of honor, Mister President, that I made the best use possible of the support that you extended to my fellow citizens,

and especially in favor of that unfortunate portion that was suffering in chains. . . . Can I, in the situation I am in, hope for your protection? I trust that Your Excellency will not abandon me to the fate that accosts me.

And then the postscript: "I have the honor to let you know, Mister President, that I have given Your Excellency exact accounts of my decisions and of the events during our expedition in all circumstances; I do not know whether these letters arrived in your hands since I have not received any replies" (Verna, *Pétion y Bolívar*, 489–90). We do not know whether those letters existed, and if so, whether they ever arrived in Port-au-Prince. They are not included in the collections I have been able to consult. Still, the decidedly defensive, almost abject tone of Bolívar's letter tells us something. Clearly Bolívar is trying to persuade Pétion that he has not violated the terms of their agreement and that Pétion has not wasted his resources on him. The lengthy letter is not a diplomatic note of the sort that tries to hide what it purports to explain. There are no grounds for reading this letter as "purely strategic": it recognizes Pétion as a superior to whom accounts must be rendered. Three days later, Pétion acknowledges receipt of the letter in a brief note full of good counsel and paternal support. He expresses his regret at the unfortunate outcome of the expedition and asks Bolívar to come to Port-au-Prince, where they would arrange for personal meetings (Verna, *Pétion y Bolívar*, 495). Thus begins Bolívar's second stay in Haiti.

The Bolivian Constitution

Bolívar left Haiti from Jacmel in December 1816 for his second, more successful invasion of the Venezuelan mainland. Like the first one, it was financed by the Haitian republic. Bolívar did not return to Haiti afterward, and judging from the letters that some of his Haitian friends sent over the years, he was not a good correspondent. Writing seven years after Bolívar's departure from Jacmel, the commander of Les Cayes, Poisson-Paris, complains, "This is the third letter that I have the honor of writing to you. The previous ones have remained unanswered" (Verna, *Pétion y Bolívar*, 500). Despite the unanswered letters and the discontinuous records, however, Haiti does not simply vanish.

Let us now turn to Bolívar ten years later. It is 1826. The great wars of independence are over, and Bolívar is at the height of his power. He is also increasingly worried about the prospects of the new American states.

Newly liberated Bolivia had charged him with writing a constitution. Bolívar considered the draft he presented to the Constituent Assembly his masterpiece and circulated the text to Peru and to Colombia.

Bolívar's address to the Bolivian Constituent Assembly is framed by a rather pessimistic assessment of recent history and the prospects of building free and peaceful societies after the collapse of the colonial regime. To be sure, the opening paragraphs fall well into the patterns established by classical rhetoric and combine hyperbolic statements of oratorical modesty with equally hyperbolic accounts of the challenges the orator faced, but Bolívar's apprehensions coincide with the concerns he expressed in his private correspondence. Although he summoned all his resources for the writing of the constitution, Bolívar insists, to find "the best way to deal with free men, based on the principles adopted among civilized people," "the lessons of experience" and the string of past disasters provide little encouragement for the future. "In the shadow of such sinister examples, what guides are there to follow?" What are the prospects for a country like Bolivia, "a tiny island of freedom that is perpetually pounded by the violence of the waves and hurricanes that seek unremittingly to sink her"? Bolívar ends with a warning: "Behold the sea you hope to traverse, the fragile boat's pilot utterly unskilled" (Bushnell, 54–55; translation modified).

The Andes are not prone to hurricanes, and Bolivia is practically landlocked. Bolívar was not a careless writer; what made him choose imagery that was so absurdly out of place? Faced with the challenge of writing his most complete and original constitutional text, Bolívar's mind appears to have slipped back to the Caribbean, to the early years of the struggle for independence. The history of violent struggles and the troubling question of political models—a question that had preoccupied Bolívar all his life—are captured here by images of Caribbean storms, fragile boats, and inexperienced pilots. It is difficult not to think of the hundreds of refugees from Venezuela and New Granada who took to the sea, entrusting their lives to rickety boats, hundreds of them dying on their way to Haiti, itself an embattled island under constant threat from outside forces.

These could, of course, simply be slippages of the unconscious mind and would have purely poetic significance were it not for the fact that a few pages later, Bolívar does indeed turn to Haiti, and this time he is perfectly conscious of it.

The island of Haiti (if you allow me this digression) found herself in a state of constant insurrection. After having tried every type of government known to man—empire, monarchy, republic—and a few never seen before, she had to resort to the distinguished Pétion to save her. The people put their trust in him, and the destiny of Haiti has not wavered since. Once Pétion had been named president for life with the power to choose his successor, neither the death of this great man nor the succession of the new president brought the least danger to the state: everything went forward under the worthy Boyer, as in the tranquillity of a legitimate kingdom. This is the triumphant proof that a president for life, with the power to choose his successor, is the most sublime innovation in the republican system. (Bushnell, 56)

Why does Bolívar invoke Haiti? Was it prudent to justify his highly controversial proposal of a presidency-for-life by referring to the most marginal of countries in his support? And even if Haiti seemed like a good example, he could have said something else—for instance, that the example of Haiti proved that black and mixed populations require strong governments. But no, he claims that Haiti "represents the most sublime republican order." The biographer Masur comments on this phrase by saying that it is plainly false and reeks of a guilty conscience. But why would the invocation of Haiti help assuage feelings of guilt? Still, unlike later historians, Masur at least notes the oddity of this line of argument.

In his address to the Constituent Assembly, Bolívar quite rightly points out that the Bolivian president is actually "denied all influence" in his constitution. "This reduction in executive power has never been tried in any duly constituted government" (Bushnell, 57). Later commentators have failed to note that Bolívar's self-interpretation is at odds with the conventional reading of the Bolivian constitution as an attempt to establish a quasi-dictatorial regime. To be sure, Bolívar may be trying to pull the wool over the eyes of the Bolivian conventioneers, but his affirmations are not altogether implausible in light of his draft proposals: the powers of the president are indeed rather limited and concentrated on issues of foreign policy and the military. We should note, too, that Bolívar characterizes his proposal as a defense against power-grabbing tyrants like Jean-Jacques Dessalines and Henri Christophe, both of whom he likens to Bonaparte in their ultimate failure to establish new imperial regimes. "There is no power more difficult to maintain than that of a new prince" (58).[13]

If Haiti indeed merely represented all that the Creole elites feared, if it indeed was an example of what Bolívar himself abhorred as an example of *pardocracia*, this invocation at such an important moment in his political career would plainly be inexplicable. So let us return one more time to 1816, the year Bolívar spent as a refugee in Haiti.

Pétion's Constitution of 1816

Bolívar's second stay in Haiti coincided with an important moment in the political history of the postrevolutionary state. In the spring of 1816—during Bolívar's first stay—Pétion had convened a constitutional commission and charged it with revising the 1806 constitution. Shortly after Bolívar's return to Haiti in September, this new constitution was proclaimed with republican pomp and circumstance. It was, unquestionably, *the* event of the year 1816 in Haiti. We do not know whether Bolívar read the text of the constitution, though it seems implausible that a passionate student of political theory and future author of constitutions would have ignored it. Did Bolívar and Pétion discuss the internal problems of Haiti and the reasons behind the revisions? Again, we do not have any record of their conversations. But we do know that Bolívar spent most of his time in Port-au-Prince during his second stay and that they had planned to meet.[14]

The circumstances that led to the new constitution would certainly have been intriguing to Bolívar, who had attributed the failure of the First Republic in Venezuela in part to constitutional problems, and who was already familiar with the difficulties of establishing stable authority in a postcolonial state. After the assassination of Dessalines in 1806—a plot in which Pétion played a key role—selecting a new head of state presented a dilemma. Henri Christophe, one of the most prominent veterans of the revolutionary war, had a powerful base in the military and a regional stronghold in the rich northern province and the Artibonite valley. Pétion, Christophe's main rival, had a power base in the less wealthy southwest. Christophe was clearly poised to assume power, but Pétion and his allies worried that Christophe's rule would be just as tyrannical as that of Dessalines. The 1806 constitution, largely drafted by Pétion, tried to contain the autocratic propensities of leaders whose instincts were shaped by years of warfare by creating a figurehead presidency, controlled by a powerful senate. Christophe, who was almost illiterate, but by no means stupid, quickly saw through this ruse and raised his troops. When the issue could not be resolved on the battlefield, Christophe retreated to his stronghold in the north and set up a separate state. In 1811 he turned his breakaway state into a hereditary monarchy.

But secessionist desires in Haiti were not limited to Christophe. Protesting Pétion's attempts to override the constitution and concentrate power in the hands of the chief executive after he assumed the presidency, André Rigaud, a veteran of the wars and leader among the former free population of color, set up a republic in the south of Haiti. That state collapsed after Rigaud's death in 1811, but Christophe's ally Goman continued to stir up trouble as the insurgent leader of a former Maroon community in Grand Anse, in the southwest. The former colony of Saint-Domingue, a territory covering barely twenty-eight thousand square kilometers, was threatening to break up into ever smaller sovereignties. The relations between the kingdom in the north and the southeastern republic never normalized, and Goman remained a threat throughout Pétion's rule. Bolívar, who had a taste for theatrical ruses, would certainly have derived some pleasure from hearing that when Pétion ordered Governor Marion to supply him with rifles and ammunition for the first expedition to the Venezuelan mainland, Pétion asked Marion to pretend that the supplies were needed for operations in Grand Anse.

The 1816 revision of the 1806 constitution clearly had a pragmatic purpose. It was, first of all, an attempt on Pétion's part to extricate himself from the trap he himself had set: unwilling to submit to the controls he had devised to curtail Christophe's power, Pétion had in fact ruled outside the constitution for several years, having forced the vast majority of senators to resign, and exercising tight control over those remaining in their seats. But the revisions were also, and perhaps more importantly, a constitutional response to the troubling issue of transfer of power and the continuing threat of territorial disintegration. Pétion was not in good health. Change in government in postcolonial Haiti seemed to be possible only through assassination, civil war, and territorial breakup. And as Haiti was splitting into ever smaller pieces, external threats were becoming more and more troubling again. It was probably no coincidence that just as the new constitution was being published, French agents arrived on the island with the charge to persuade the Haitian rulers to return to French rule.[15] The continuing disintegration of the state and descent into microsovereignties and warlordism could only have been an invitation for imperial adventures.

The question of whether the 1816 constitution of the Haitian republic creates an overly empowered presidency does not have an obvious answer. The constitution clearly shifts many rights and responsibilities from the senate to the first magistrate. It also gives the president the right to produce a roster of candidates for each senate seat, from which the Chamber of Representatives can then choose. So there is a definite concentration of power in the combined offices of the senate and the president. But this is arguably just an internal adjustment in the balance of power with little impact on issues of democratic governance compared to the previous arrangement. On the other hand, the 1816 constitution introduces a democratically elected Chamber of Representatives that is supposed to balance the power of the senate and the president and in that sense signifies democratic gains over the single-chamber arrangement of the 1806 constitution. Compared with Bonaparte's 1802 constitution, which scholars have identified as a source for both Pétion and Bolívar on account of its introduction of a lifetime appointment for the head of state and its heavy use of a highly controlled system of "electors," the Haitian charter seems much less geared toward securing presidential power and more concerned with avoiding a constitutional crisis every time a change of government occurs: unlike Bonaparte's 1802 constitution, it gives the president the right to choose his successor.

How much did Bolívar know about this situation? Bolívar himself never commented on Haitian politics in any direct way. However, on October 9, 1816, Bolívar sent the following letter to Pétion, congratulating him on having been elected president for life:

> Mister President:
> The quill is a faithful instrument for transmitting freely the honest feelings inspired by my admiration! If flattery is a mortal poison for lowly souls, well-deserved praise is nourishment for those who are sublime. I am taking the liberty to write to Your Excellency because I do not dare to speak what I feel for Your Excellency. Absence encourages me to express myself from the bottom of my heart. It is no doubt sweet to fulfill the obligations of recognition; but it is not obligation that dictates this respectful homage I desire to present.
>
> Twenty-five years of sacrifices, of glory, and of virtues have earned Your Excellency the unanimous vote of your fellow citizens, of all illustrious foreigners, and of the posterity that awaits you. Certainly, the most glorious attribute of authority a free people has bestowed upon Your Excellency is not power; nor is this authority Your Excellency's real merit. It is a power superior to all empires: it is that of charity. Your Excellency is the unique embodiment of this sacred treasure. The President of Haiti is the only one who governs for the people, the only one who governs his equals. The other

potentates are satisfied with being obeyed [and] scorn the love that has brought glory to Your Excellency.

Your Excellency has been elevated to the perpetual dignity of the chief of the republic by your fellow citizens' free acclamation, the only legitimate source of human power. Your Excellency is destined to eclipse the memory of the great Washington, clearing yourself a most illustrious path whose obstacles are superior to all means. The hero of the North only had to defeat enemy soldiers and his major triumph was that of his ambition. Your Excellency has to defeat everything and everybody, enemies and friends, foreigners and citizens, the fathers of the fatherland and even the virtues of his brothers. Still, fulfilling this duty will not be difficult for Your Excellency, because Your Excellency is superior to your country and your era.

I ask that Your Excellency accept, with the indulgence you have always shown me, the sincere expression of my unlimited admiration for Your Excellency's virtues, of your talents and of my gratitude for your favors. I am your very humble and obedient servant.
Bolívar

Certainly, an indulgent letter. But the heavy charge of flattery should not make us overlook the fact that this is also a very strange, opaque letter, a text that reads like a snippet of a conversation we otherwise missed. Why such extremes of flattery? And then, if Bolívar merely wanted to flatter Pétion, did he need to call him a visionary, ahead of his time? Why put him ahead of George Washington? And who are these friends that Pétion had to defeat?

Let us begin by noting that after an extensive *captatio benevolentiae*, Bolívar begins the letter proper by invoking the slave revolution: "Twenty-five years of sacrifices," he says. That takes us back to 1791, the year when the insurrection in Saint-Domingue began. In other words, Bolívar is taking stock of the revolutionary process in Saint-Domingue/Haiti. He recognizes Pétion not just as a head of state and potential supporter of Spanish American revolutionaries but as a former military man in the revolutionary war. This is quite remarkable, since we do know from other sources that for Bolívar the antislavery revolution of Saint-Domingue was not in itself an event to be celebrated. If Bolívar included the revolution among Pétion's achievements, it is, I suspect, for deeply personal reasons. Like Bolívar himself, Pétion had begun his career as a military leader, had suffered serious setbacks, had lived in exile, and had in the end established an independent, relatively stable postslavery republic. Bolívar had been treating Pétion as a figure of military authority and superior experience all along, and it seems likely that he saw in Pétion what he himself aspired to: a man who had successfully fought a war and then created a postcolonial state. Bolívar would have seen Pétion at the end of a struggle he was just embarking on, the embodiment of a transition that would actually elude Bolívar to the end of his life. What appeared as excessive flattery at first sight was, I suspect, more likely an expression of deeply felt filial identification.

The letter's most mysterious moment is the passage where Bolívar puts Pétion ahead of Washington, because he had to "defeat not only his enemies, but his friends and the fathers of the fatherland." Who are these friends and fathers of the fatherland that Pétion had to defeat? The only way I can make sense of this passage is as a reference to the endemic secessionism after independence, perhaps to André Rigaud, but particularly to Henri Christophe, the king in the north, and the intellectual elite he had gathered around himself—many of them former revolutionaries, military leaders, fathers of the fatherland, friends in a sense. There are good reasons for thinking this may be so: in his diagnosis of the failure of the First Republic in Venezuela, Bolívar had identified regional fragmentation, and the failure to put down the rebellion in the coastal town of Coro, as key factors. It seems very likely that in his conversations with Pétion, the threat of fragmented sovereignty and regional power bases to state building would have been an important issue, one around which the two men found a lot of common sentiment.

Far from being a mere example of strategic flattery, the letter of October 9 displays an opacity that can only stem from shared knowledge and emotional investment. Bolívar seems to have been well informed about Haitian politics and took up threads of conversation from earlier moments. The overall assessment of Pétion is the result of taking stock of the revolutionary/postrevolutionary process in its entirety, from 1791 to 1816, and his praise for Pétion is based on his handling of the postrevolutionary quagmire and the various separatisms that eventually arose.

In more abstract terms, we might say that it was in Haiti that the internal link between a change in government and fragmenting sovereignty had shown up for the first time. Before his Haitian experience, Bolívar had focused his concerns on federalism as an unsuitable constitutional arrangement for Spanish America. Postindependence Haiti offered a slightly different picture, one in which transition in the executive branch became the key issue, and regional fragmentation a potential effect of a fragile political process that had not fully emerged from revolutionary warfare. Bolívar's adoption of a lifetime presidency for the Bolivian constitution very likely reflected Haiti's postcolonial experience, not a leaf taken from Bonaparte's regime in France. As such it signified not, or not necessarily, a shift toward military dictatorship but a turn away from a republicanism that placed the alternative of federalism and centralism at the center, and toward a republicanism that would constitutionally preempt the recurrent crises associated with transitions in government and thus remove the incentives for tyrannicides, assassination plots, and secessionism.

Conclusion

Bolívar's extensive experience with postrevolutionary politics in Haiti had a powerful and long-lasting impact on his thought. In 1826, at the height of his power, yet deeply troubled by Spanish American future prospects, he returned to this formative experience. Far from representing the "spectre of race war," postrevolutionary Haiti actually provided Bolívar with a concrete political model for a solution to the postrevolutionary quagmire. What Bolívar saw in Haiti in 1816 was not a failed *pardocracia* but a republic threatened by the breakaway states that competing warlords were trying to set up. Ten years later, in 1826, when Bolívar was desperately conjuring all his political experience and philosophical knowledge in trying to devise a constitution for Bolivia that would prove more resilient than those he had seen failing, he turned to the one country that had gone through the postcolonial turmoil and emerged intact and in fact strengthened. Pétion had died within two years of the publication of the 1816 constitution, but his successor, Jean-Pierre Boyer, who is included in Bolívar's praise in the 1826 address to the Constituent Assembly of Bolivia, not only unified the territory of the former colony but incorporated Spanish Santo Domingo into Haiti through a negotiated settlement. Bolívar never opposed the annexation of Santo Domingo by Haiti.

Contrary to what many commentators have assumed, it seems that the main influences on Bolívar's 1826 constitution were not Bonaparte's constitutions. Quite the opposite. Bolívar appeals to Pétion's 1816 constitution as an alternative genealogy to that of Bonapartism—a genealogy where the issues of regime change and succession are at the heart, and where a *dirigiste* solution to those issues does not necessarily lead to a "strong presidency." Far from being a spontaneous digression of an associative mind, the turn to Haiti in Bolívar's 1826 address plays an important role in the argument, and we have no good reasons for assuming that this appeal was issued in bad faith.

It seems, then, that for Simón Bolívar, and perhaps also for some of the refugees who spent years in exile in Haiti, the Haitian republic was a blueprint for the problems the new Spanish American states had to resolve if they wanted to survive. The nightmare was not, or not just, slave revolution, though no doubt Haiti also exemplified the isolation that would result from such a revolution in the slaveholding Atlantic. But the most fearsome future in Bolívar's mind appears to have been that of the vast expanses of Spanish America broken down into countless microsovereignties, all cut off from the flows of Atlantic Enlightenment and international diplomacy: an apocalyptic nightmare, a descent into the private hells of ambitious kings and adventurers like Boves or Aguirre, the insane conqueror; a nightmare of civil wars where heads were boiled in oil and delivered to the enemy by men driven crazy by their lust for power and booty. The Haitian republic may have seemed like a peaceful haven indeed after those horrendous years of colonial warfare that had destroyed all remnants of the state and left the civilian population utterly unprotected.

NOTES

1. In *Bolívar y los emigrados patriotas en el Caribe*, Paul Verna gives a detailed account of the various emigrations from Venezuela and Nueva Granada to Haiti. His estimate of two thousand refugees in Haiti includes women and children. He also gives the names, with biographical summaries, for the male patriots who were known to have fled to Haiti. Unfortunately where the information comes from is not always clear, though it seems that Verna painstakingly worked through contemporary accounts. He also appears to have had collaborators in the National Archive in Port-au-Prince who provided him with information that is not collected anywhere else. Verna's little-known and little-cited research has been foundational for this article. With the exception of the Bolívar texts included in Bushnell's edition of Bolívar's writings, all translations are mine.

2. The nineteenth-century Haitian historian Beaubrun Ardouin is one of the few authors to mention this "interesting spectacle of a meeting of men from diverse countries, having all come to seek shelter under its laws favorable to liberty" (*Etudes*, vol. 8, chap. 5, p. 54).

3. It is worth noting that an earlier body of scholarship assigned a slightly more prominent place to Haiti. There is *La expedición de los Cayos* (1928), a small but useful

book by the Venezuelan historian Vicente Lecuna that details Bolívar's first campaign financed by the Haitian republic. The biography of Bolívar by Gerhard Masur (1948), a German historian who found asylum in Colombia from the Nazi tyranny, dedicates a chapter to Bolívar's Haitian experience, though he does not consider it a formative experience. By far the most informative work on the topic of Bolívar in Haiti is by the Haitian Venezuelan historian Paul Verna, who devoted his scholarship to the relationship between Pétion and Bolívar and the revolutionary culture that sustained it. Verna's studies from the 1960s to the 1980s are extremely rich in detail and recover important texts that had not been known before. Clearly they bear a strong imprint of Verna's Bolivarist commitments and need to be understood in the framework of liberal nationalist historiography with its penchant for tales of heroes, epic struggles, and uplifting results. Still, it is difficult to comprehend why his original research is no longer cited in the contemporary literature on Bolívar and the early wars of independence.

4. See, e.g., Aline Helg's important work on the role of racial thinking in the independence period, especially her article on the Padilla trial, where she argues that Bolívar's views regarding the people of African descent "were rooted in the colonial past and the specter of the Haitian revolution" ("Bolívar and the Spectre of *pardocracia*," 471). See also the recent dissertations by Cristina Soriano and Alejandro Gómez. Both Soriano and Gómez have accumulated a wealth of fascinating new evidence that documents imperial policies and general hostility toward Haiti in the revolutionary Atlantic.

5. See, e.g., Lynch, 21–40; Collier, 15–21.

6. See especially Rojas, *Las repúblicas del aire*.

7. I am adopting a term coined by the Caribbean philosopher Lewis Gordon, who has studied similar phenomena at length in the realm of philosophy.

8. Gómez, "Le syndrome"; Verna, *Pétion y Bolívar*; Córdova-Bello, 100–115.

9. See, e.g., the probably false accusation that the notorious massacre of Capuchin monks in 1817 was the responsibility of "negros de Santo Domingo" (cited in Larrazábal). No evidence points to a Haitian presence among the patriots at that point.

10. In a letter to his ally Luis Brion, who had arrived in Les Cayes in the summer of 1815, Bolívar made it clear that Haiti was not his first choice, because, he says, "I did not want to lose the confidence of these gentlemen" [probably the English]: "their aristocratic obsessions are terrible" (Verna, *Bolívar y los emigrados*, 53; translation mine) But clearly Bolívar was running out of options, and many of his fellow insurgents had already settled in Haiti. The Bolívar literature nevertheless disputes whether Bolívar left Jamaica with the intention of going to Haiti or whether he had planned to go back to Cartagena and changed his mind midway when he found out about the fall of Cartagena. While this dispute seems unimportant when considered in the context of Spanish American wars of independence, it is not when Haiti's position in the early nineteenth-century Atlantic is concerned. Lynch sidesteps the question. Verna's evidence in favor of an explicit decision on Bolívar's part to go to Haiti (*Bolívar y Pétion*, 150–56), based on documents discovered in the 1950s, seems persuasive.

11. There is a puzzle that cannot be pursued here but should at least be noted. It concerns Pétion's reputation as a "beloved," "good-hearted," "charitable" man, and his much-cited nickname "Papa Boncœur": Pétion, like Bolívar, like Dessalines, like Henri Christophe, and like all the generals in the early campaign in Spanish America, was a military man who knew how to use force as well as betrayal; it was he who had plotted Dessalines's assassination, he who set up Christophe for a disempowered presidency, and then, when things did not quite work out, ruled outside the constitution he himself had drafted. Even if Pétion was much loved among the people, Bolívar was probably aware of this track record. I suspect there is a story to be told here.

12. Larrazábal, *Correspondencia general*.

13. Of course, Pétion's constitutional commission drew on French precedents, including Bonaparte's constitutions, which can make it difficult to establish unequivocally the origin of specific provisions in the 1826 text. However, it seems that Bonaparte's lifetime appointees to "electoral bodies" are conceived in a way that gives them very little independence. Both the Chamber of Representatives in the Haitian republic and the three chambers in the Bolivian constitution are at least in theory capable of assuming the role of democratic representation and are removed from the orbit of presidential power.

14. The most detailed account of Bolívar's stays in Haiti is in Verna, *Bolívar y los emigrados patriotas*. Verna claims that Pétion was quite sick in the fall of 1816. It is entirely possible that Bolívar came to understand Haitian politics in conversation with other dignitaries and refugees who had gathered in and around the house of the Port-au-Prince–based merchant Sutherland. On the basis of later correspondence, it seems that Bolívar was quite close to Marion, the governor of the southern department, the official who actually supplied Bolívar with the military equipment for his expeditions. For the purpose of my argument, it does not matter whether Bolívar got his information from Pétion or someone else, though it would be interesting to establish in greater detail who was at the center of the circle of refugees in Port-au-Prince.

15. For the details on this truly bizarre story, see Ardouin, vol. 8, chap. 5.

WORKS CITED

Adelman, Jeremy. *Sovereignty and Revolution in the Iberian Atlantic*. Princeton: Princeton University Press, 2006.

Ardouin, Beaubrun. *Etudes sur l'histoire d'Haiti*. 11 vols. 3rd ed. Port-au-Prince: Fardin, 2005.

Bushnell, David, ed. *El Libertador: Writings by Simón Bolívar*. Trans. Frederick Fornoff. New York: Oxford University Press, 2003.

Collier, Simon. "Simón Bolívar as Political Thinker." In *Simón Bolívar: Essays on the Life and Legacy of the Liberator*, ed. David Bushnell, 13–34. Lanham, MD: Rowman and Littlefield, 2008.

Córdova-Bello, Eleazar. *La independencia de Haití y su influencia en Hispanoamérica*. Caracas: Instituto Panamericano de Geografía e Historia, 1967.

Danticat, Edwidge. *After the Dance: A Walk through Carnavel in Jacmel, Haiti*. New York: Crown Journeys, 2002.

Ferrer, Ada. "Haiti, Free Soil, and Antislavery in the Revolutionary Atlantic." *American Historical Review* 117, no. 1 (February 2012): 40–66.

Garrigus, John D. "Opportunist or Patriot? Julien Raimond (1744–1801) and the Haitian Revolution." *Slavery and Abolition* 28, no. 1 (April 2007): 1–21.

Gómez, Alejandro. "La revolución de Caracas *desde abajo*." *Nuevo Mundo, Mundos Nuevos* 8 (2008), http://nuevomundo.revues.org/32982 (accessed May 27, 2011).

———. "Le syndrome de Saint-Domingue: Perceptions et représentations de la révolution haïtienne dans le monde atlantique, 1790–1886." Ph.D. diss., Ecole des Hautes Etudes en Sciences Sociales, 2010.

Helg, Aline. "Bolívar and the Spectre of *pardocracia*." *Journal of Latin American Studies* 35, no. 3 (2003): 447–71.

———. *Liberty and Equality in Caribbean Colombia, 1770–1835*. Chapel Hill: University of North Carolina Press, 2004.

Larrazábal, Felipe. *Correspondencia general del libertador Simón Bolívar: Enriquecida con la inserción de los manifestos, mensages, exposiciones, proclamas, etc*. New York: Jenkins, 1871.

Lecuna, Vicente. *La expedición de los Cayos*. Caracas: Litografía y Tipografía Mercantil, 1928.

Lynch, John. *Simón Bolívar: A Life*. New Haven: Yale University Press, 2007.

Madiou, Thomas. *Histoire d'Haiti*. 8 vols. Editions Henri Deschamps, 1988.

Masur, Gerhard. *Simón Bolívar*. Albuquerque: University of New Mexico Press, 1948.

McKinley, Michael. *Pre-revolutionary Caracas: Politics, Economy, and Society, 1777–1811*. New York: Cambridge University Press, 1985.

Rojas, Rafael. *Las repúblicas de aire: Utopía y desencanto en la revolución de Hispanoamérica*. Mexico City: Taurus, 2009.

Soriano, Cristina. "Rumors of Change: Repercussions of Caribbean Turmoil and Social Conflict in Venezuela (1790–1810)." Ph.D. diss., New York University, 2011.

Verna, Paul. *Bolívar y los emigrados patriotas en el Caribe (Trinidad, Curazao, San Thomas, Jamaica, Haití)*. Caracas: INCE, 1983.

———. *Pétion y Bolívar: Una etapa decisiva en la emancipación de Hispanoamérica, 1790–1830*. Caracas: Ediciones de la Presidencia de la República, 1980.

2

Between Anti-Haitianism and Anti-imperialism: Haitian and Cuban Political Collaborations in the Nineteenth and Twentieth Centuries

—Matthew Casey

On June 23, 1930, the Port-au-Prince newspaper *Le Pays* began publishing a serial about the life of Antonio Maceo (1845–96), the slave-turned-military-hero who led Cuban separatists in battle against Spain during the second half of the nineteenth century.[1] The Cuban general was one of "the great figures" not only in the "history . . . of the peoples of Latin America" but also in the history of Haiti. As *Le Pays* noted, he had "interested himself much in our fate" and deserved "to be a little less ignored by us" ("Antonio Maceo"). A few years later, Enselmo Diaz del Villar, a Cuban diplomat in Haiti, made a goodwill speech in Port-au-Prince extolling the Haitian people for their contribution to Cuban independence in the nineteenth century. "It seems opportune to recall in this moment," he declared, "the support that my compatriots [Antonio] Maceo and [José] Martí found in this heroic and hospitable land in the course of the struggle for Cuban independence" ("Un nouveau diplomate"; "L'arrivée du nouveau ministre").

The content and contexts of these statements defy widely held notions about Haitian and Cuban relations in the late nineteenth century and the early twentieth. Given the negative associations between Haitians and race war in Cuba and the larger Atlantic world, why and how did Cuban independence leaders organize on Haitian soil without facing international scrutiny? How were these nineteenth-century collaborations against Spain invoked in the twentieth century in the context of renewed anti-Haitianism in Cuba and U.S. imperialism in both countries?

Cuba's wars for independence began formally in 1868 when a group of Cuban planters and their newly emancipated slaves, under the leadership

of Carlos Manuel de Céspedes, began a military campaign against Spanish rule. What came to be called the Ten Years' War (1868–78) ended with
the defeat of Cuban independence forces, who regrouped over the next
decade and renewed the military offensive in 1895.[2] Fighting had been
preceded by years of organizing by Cuban exile communities who had
established themselves throughout the Americas. Although one such
community existed in Haiti during the wars for independence, it has not
received as much scholarly attention as those in the United States and
other parts of the Americas.[3]

Since the Haitian Revolution's (1791–1804) radical challenge to slavery
and colonialism, the people of Haiti and the diaspora have been subject
to "complex expressions of anti-Haitianism" that have equated them vari-
ously with disease, primitivism, and racial revolution (Zacaïre and Reinhardt, 6). Historians have argued that the negative associations attached
to Haitians hindered their ability to organize politically with Cubans at
different moments in the nineteenth and twentieth centuries. In a study of
the 1895 meeting between José Martí and the Haitian politician and intellectual Anténor Firmin, Brenda Gayle Plummer argues that the racially
structured nationalisms of each country prevented Haitians and Cubans
from forming any long-standing alliance beyond the "shared elements of
a milieu, a sensibility, and a single encounter" between the two leaders.
Furthermore, "Martí's lessons on Haiti had been forgotten" as anti-Haitian sentiments resurged in twentieth-century Cuba amid renewed fears
of race war and mass Haitian migration to the island (Plummer, "Firmin
and Martí," 222).

During the first decades of the twentieth century, approximately two
hundred thousand Haitians traveled seasonally to work in Cuba's growing
sugar industry. They were greeted with disdain from the Cuban press, who
accused them of being primitive disease carriers who would start a race
war in Cuba. As recent scholarship indicates, Cubans' fears that Haitians
could bring race war to the island reached deep into the nineteenth century
(Fischer, pt. 1; Childs, 22, 76, 90). The charge was especially resonant after
Cuban independence, as many construed any autonomous black political
mobilization as a harbinger of a potential Haitian-style race war. Historians have argued that anti-Haitian racism, coupled with Cuban fears of a
race war led by Afro-Cubans or Haitians, closed off any possibilities for
Haitians to organize politically in Cuba (McLeod, 46–47; Chomsky, 10–13).

More recently, historians have identified moments when Cubans and
African Americans in the United States forged transnational political,

economic, social, and cultural links with Haitians. By employing the language and ideals of Caribbeanness or Pan-Americanism, individuals formed these bonds without appearing to threaten the social order or the sovereignty of their respective nation-states (Polyné, 9, 60, 71). In this regard, Philippe Zacaïre argues that Antonio Maceo's antiracism, humanism, and interpretation of history motivated the leader to visit Haiti and include the country in his vision of a Caribbean identity (Zacaïre, 57). One of the goals of this chapter is to contextualize Maceo's political project within the earlier actions of a larger and lesser-known group of Cuban political activists in Haiti.

This chapter builds on this recent scholarship by examining the manifestations of anti-Haitianism in the nineteenth century and the early twentieth in Cuba and tracing two moments when political activists, motivated by their opposition to imperialism, circumvented these ideologies. The first occurred during Cuba's initial independence war against Spain (1868–78), when Cuban exiles organized in Port-au-Prince and other Haitian cities with assistance from the Haitian government. The second was on Cuban soil, when Haitian migrants in Cuba formed a branch of l'Union Patriotique, an organization originally founded in Port-au-Prince to protest the U.S. military occupation of Haiti (1915–34). Though anti-Haitian discourses did not prevent political collaborations, they did shape the ways that such partnerships were framed and made known to the larger public. In the nineteenth century, Haitian and Cuban political cooperation was framed in terms of the countries' common history and the need for Pan-American unity. The Haitian government's actions, however, were deliberately kept silent from the wider public. In the twentieth century, on the other hand, this very aid was touted publicly by Haitian political activists who drew on their forebears' contribution to Cuban independence to carve out an organizing space in Cuba. While anti-Haitianism certainly drove a wedge between many Cubans and Haitians in the nineteenth and twentieth centuries, the anti-imperialism that emerged in each country from long-standing struggles against European and U.S. domination provided a common ideological ground where activists collaborated.

Haiti and the Struggle for Cuban Independence

The Haitian Revolution spread fears of radical antislavery and race war throughout the Atlantic world. These trepidations were especially prevalent in Cuba, though they were also coupled with economic opportunism by the country's planters. The vacuums in sugar and coffee production left by the destruction of France's most valuable colony were readily filled by Cuban producers. In the western part of the island, Cuban planters increased sugar production to take advantage of high prices and international demand. In 1791, Cuba exported 16,731 metric tons of sugar. By the end of the Haitian Revolution in 1804, sugar exports had more than doubled to 39,235 metric tons; they continued to increase during the nineteenth century (Moreno Fraginals, 43–46). Coffee production expanded in the eastern portion of the island as a result of the thousands of French planters and their slaves who fled revolutionary Saint-Domingue and settled in Cuba. In 1790, Cuba exported 7,400 quintiles of coffee. After 1804, production rose exponentially and peaked in 1833, when the country exported 641,589.75 quintiles (F. Pérez de la Riva, 8, 51, 74, 88).

This production was brought to fruition by a massive increase in the number of slaves imported to Cuba, a figure that quadrupled from the late eighteenth century to the early nineteenth. Cuban planters could not help but recognize that increases in slavery and large-scale agricultural production carried risks of slave insurrection like the one that had occurred in Haiti. Reprisals against real and perceived slave revolts increased during the period (Ferrer, "Speaking of Haiti," 225–28). During the first decades of the nineteenth century, as Spain's colonies fought for independence throughout South America, Cubans remained loyal to the Spanish crown, fearing that any type of popular mobilization on the island could transform Cuba into "another Haiti" (Ferrer, *Insurgent Cuba*, 2).

Almost three decades after the wars for independence ended in South America, Cubans began to organize for separation from Spain. Though a half century had passed since the Haitian Revolution had ended, the event figured in both Spanish and Cuban debates about the merits of slaves' participation in Cuban independence wars. As Ada Ferrer argues, references to Haiti "were standard ammunition in Spanish counterinsurgency," especially during the first decades of the conflict (*Insurgent Cuba*, 134). Spanish officials played on the very real fears of Cuban patriots that a social revolution would produce mass destruction and race war in Cuba. Cuban exiles who organized from the United States, and even some Afro-Cubans, warned that a mobilized Cuba could share "the fate of Haiti," thus leading many to distance themselves from the neighboring republic.[4]

By 1880, the "demagogic claim" that a mobilized Cuba would become another Haiti "had lost much of its force. The end of slavery and the expansion of a thoroughly multiracial rural workforce had undercut the stereotype of black Cubans as a subjugated mass, liable to volcanic eruption." Additionally, Cuban patriots declared that their new nation had transcended racial differences through the experience of cross-racial mobilization, allowing them to sidestep accusations of race war and leading to the creation of a powerful myth of racial harmony in Cuba (Scott, 131).

The anti-Haitian discourse of Spanish colonial officials did not prevent Cuban independence leaders from organizing on Haitian soil, even during the Ten Years' War (1868–78), when fears of a Haitian-style race war were regularly invoked. In early 1870, Manuel R. Fernández, a Cuban exiled in Kingston, Jamaica, was watching the political events of Haiti very closely.[5] In Haiti, a civil war between the Liberal and National parties was coming to an end. As he awaited its outcome, Fernández had "taken advantage" of the presence of an influential group of Haitians residing in Kingston to publicize the goals of Cuba Libre and ensure "that the victorious party sympathizes with Cuba." When Nissage Saget, a Liberal, consolidated executive power in Haiti, Fernández jumped at the chance "to travel to that Republic with the object of negotiating the recognition of Cuban independence by the governments of Hayti and Sto. Domingo" (Fernández, letter from Kingston). Saget did more than just recognize Cuba Libre; he formed "a central commission of assistance for Cuba" (Fernández to Presidente). By 1873, Fernández could confidently tell his superiors that "the Haitian government does not deny anything that may contribute to the independence of Cuba" (Fernández to Gral. Manuel de Quesada). Later in the decade, even Spanish officials in Haiti admitted that "sympathies" for the Cuban cause had "cast deep roots . . . in the Republic of Haiti."[6]

By the time Fernández arrived, Haiti already boasted a community of Cubans that would grow over the next decades and forge increasingly strong social and economic roots in the country. Between 1850 and 1871, ten marriages were conducted between Haitians and Cubans in Port-au-Prince (Burnham, 278). Others likely did not formalize their union through church or state. After Cuban independence, the Cuban consul in Haiti inquired about the citizenship rights of "illegitimate children" born in Haiti, "some of a Cuban father and Haitian mother, others of a Haitian father and a Cuban mother, and some whose parents are both Cuban" (Campuzano, 2; Salcedo, 3–5). By the 1890s, the number of Cuban immigrants in Port-au-Prince trailed only the Germans and the French. The Cuban community was economically active, as well. They had a reputation for being tailors and shoemakers. In 1885 a hair salon called La Cubana opened in Port-au-Prince. In 1930 its proprietor was Jean Rodriguez, of unknown, probably Cuban, origin ("Salons"; "Salon"). The community was large enough that well-known Cuban musicians and bullfighters regularly passed through Port-au-Prince in the 1890s (Corvington, 26, 29, 38, 93).

Like Fernández, many of the Cubans living in Haiti were proponents of self-rule. In the 1870s, Spanish officials complained that individuals passed their consular offices at night, yelling "Down with Spain!" and "Vive Cuba libre!" A Spanish flag had also been "trampled . . . by unknown persons" (Léger, 229–30). It was the existence and efforts of Fernández and other lesser-known actors that made later visits by Martí and Maceo possible. When Maceo arrived in Haiti for the first time in 1879, he was welcomed by a group of Cubans in Cap Haitien. They had formed the Club Segunda Campaña (Second Campaign Club) in his honor, "with the object of doing all within our power to help our heroic brothers in Cuba."[7]

While Cubans in Haiti raised money for the fight against Spain, the Haitian government actively provided material, logistical, and diplomatic support to the cause of independence. Between 1870 and 1877, three successive Liberal Haitian governments sold guns and ships to Cuban leaders for the war against Spain. Sometimes arms were supplied at no cost. Haiti also served as a convenient meeting point where soldiers could gather before embarking for eastern Cuba (Fernández to Miguel de Aldama, June 19, 1875). Within the first years after Fernández's arrival, a number of ships had left Port-au-Prince for Cuba, carrying weapons given by the Haitian government. "From here left the small expedition of Sr. Coronel Manuel Codina," which had received "all the military supplies and arms" that the Haitian government had to offer. Later a ship named the *Pioneer* left Port-au-Prince for Cuba with "a cannon, two thousand five hundred pounds of powder and . . . rifles" (Fernández to Manuel de Quesada).

As an officially recognized state, the Haitian government was able to interact with world powers that did not recognize Cuban or Puerto Rican anti-Spanish belligerents and would not negotiate with their leaders. For instance, in 1870 the Danish government seized a cache of "arms belonging to the Puerto Ricans" that had been hidden on the Caribbean island of St. Thomas. The weapons were being held "until they were claimed by a recognized government." Without revealing its ties to independence leaders, the Haitian government formally claimed the arms and later handed them over to the revolutionaries. They took the same actions with a stockpile of munitions in Curaçao (Fernández to Miguel de Aldama, June 16, 1870). Perhaps the most assertive manifestation of Haitian diplomatic aid to the Cuban independence movement was the government's protection of Cuban individuals and arms in the face of strong opposition from Spanish officials. One notorious case involved a ship called the *Hornet*, which flew a U.S. flag and had been purchased by Cuban insurgents to bring men and weapons from Haiti to Cuba. As the ship landed in the Haitian capital in 1871, "the Spanish consul [in Port-au-Prince] . . . directed an ultimatum to the Haitian government asking them to hand over the *Hornet* within thirty hours" on the grounds that it "had been declared a pirate by the Spanish tribunals in Havana." The Haitian government denied the Spanish request without admitting their closeness to Cuban exiles. According to Fernández, the "Haitian government . . . answered categorically 'that under no pretext would the ship be handed over'" (Fernández to C. Ramon Cespedes). Then Haitian officials "gave arms" to the ship's crew in case of an attack from Spain. Eventually a U.S. gunboat escorted the *Hornet*, which still flew a U.S. flag, out of Port-au-Prince harbor (Fernández to Manuel de Quesada; Léger, 218).

In contrast to dominant stereotypes that equated Haiti with savagery and race war, the collaboration between Cubans and Haitians was built on a recognition of the countries' shared histories of slavery and imperialism. Almost a decade before independence leaders like Maceo asserted Haitian-Cuban commonalities, lesser-known figures like Fernández made similar overtures to Haitians. Fernández sought to court public support in Haiti by publicizing the antislavery goals of the Cuban independence movement before the institution had been abolished by Spain. Upon arriving in Port-au-Prince, he requested "a certified copy of the decree of the abolition of slavery [and] another of the constitution of the Republic of Cuba" from movement leaders. He planned to present the two documents, which espoused individual and national liberty, to some "Haitian writers" who were founding a new newspaper and promised to publish "all that I judge favorable to our cause." Haitians also recognized these commonalities. President Nissage Saget drew parallels between Cuba's ongoing war for independence and the Haitian Revolution: "Directly or indirectly we will help the Cuban patriots: their cause is the same for which we have spilled our most precious blood during a fierce struggle." In an inversion of racist arguments that justified slavery, colonialism, and black disenfranchisement on the grounds that blacks (as exemplified by independent Haiti) were primitive, Saget described Haitian and Cuban struggles for independence and abolition as "the cause of civilization" (Fernández to Presidente).

The Cuban exiles' use of Haitian soil and their recognition of a shared history with the country were not unique. As an independent republic in close proximity to other Caribbean islands, Haiti served as an organizing hub for many of the region's political exiles fighting against Spanish colonialism or U.S. attempts to annex territories. Dominicans who opposed the annexation of their country to the United States found support from the Haitian government when they faced political repression in the early 1870s (Polyné, 37). As Fernández noted: "Hayti will give her last cartridge to impede the annexation of those countries to the United States" (Fernández to Aldama, June 16, 1870). In 1871 a Dominican political figure named Gregorio Luperon articulated Pan-American ideals from exile in Cap Haitien, Haiti; he referred to himself as a "soldier of emancipation for the South American world" (Luperon). In the previous year, Dr. Ramon Betances, the Puerto Rican independence leader, stopped in Haiti to pick up a large store of arms that the Haitian government had claimed on his behalf in St. Thomas in 1870 (Fernández to Miguel de Aldama, June 16, 1870). During his trip, he told a Haitian audience that the histories of Cuba and Haiti were intertwined in an effort to promote a larger sense of solidarity against imperialism (Zacaïre, 51).

Although anti-Haitian ideologies could not prevent Cubans from organizing with Haitians in the name of anti-imperialism, their collaborations were not immune to these negative stereotypes. Paradoxically, Cubans' efforts to cultivate popular support among Haitians during the Ten Years' War were matched by official secrecy from the Haitian government. Fernández repeatedly told other Cubans "absolutely not to divulge" any information about the Haitian government "with respect to Cuba." This posture was motivated by President Saget himself, who wanted to support "the Cubans, but . . . fears all kinds of international complications. He is ready to help us but asks that no publicity be given to what he does in favor of Cuban independence" (Fernández to Miguel de Aldama, August 23, 1870). For Saget, it was not just potential "international complications" that required surreptitiousness, but also Haiti's past experiences of "suffer[ing] so many humiliations from European powers."[8]

The Ten Years' War ended in 1878, and Cubans' space for political organizing in Haiti temporarily closed thereafter. Eighteen seventy-nine marked the end of a period of Liberal rule in Haiti and the beginning of the presidency of Lysius Salomon, who sided with Spain throughout his tenure out of fear that Cubans were allied with his political adversaries. In 1880, Salomon was even involved in an unsuccessful plot to assassinate

Antonio Maceo, who had been exiled to Haiti during the previous months. Cubans could not resume organizing in Haiti until Salomon left office in 1888 (Zacaïre, 62–66, 70). Soon afterward the Cuban community in Haiti regrouped, reorganized, and helped start the next independence war in 1895.

Cuba and the Struggle for Haitian Sovereignty in the Twentieth Century

Cuba's wars of independence were interrupted by the United States' military intervention in 1898, which hastened the defeat of Spain and decisively shaped the future of Cuba. Though nominally independent, Cuba's political and economic affairs were largely controlled by the United States through the Platt Amendment (Pérez). An influx of foreign capital sparked the expansion of the sugar industry in the eastern part of the country. In 1898, Cuba produced 259,331 metric tons of sugar. When U.S. troops left in 1902, production had already increased to 876,027 metric tons and steadily increased over the next decades (Moreno Fraginals, 38–39).

Increases in sugar production were powered by the labor of immigrant workers from Haiti and other parts of the Caribbean, precipitating renewed anti-Haitian discourses and fears of race war in Cuba. Between 1913 and 1929, official statistics recorded the arrival of 183,983 Haitians in Cuba (J. Pérez de la Riva, table vii). While planters depended on Haitians for their labor, journalists regularly referred to them as primitive disease carriers who would reverse the Cuban nation's march toward civilization, a project that many believed depended on white immigrants (McLeod, 25, 48–49; Chomsky, 1–4).

Fears of a Haitian-style race war were especially prevalent in Cuba because of events that occurred on the eve of the legalization of Haitian immigration. In 1912 an Afro-Cuban political mobilization was perceived as a provocation for race war by Cubans and their government. What came to be known as the Partido Independiente de Color (PIC) had been formed in 1910 by Afro-Cuban veterans who had become disillusioned with their inability to secure leadership roles in the postcolonial Cuban state. Their criticisms of racial discrimination in a country that claimed to have transcended such divisions were interpreted by many as a form of racism. Soon the Cuban congress passed the Morua law, which forbade the formation of any political party whose membership consisted of a single race. With their political party declared illegal, members of the PIC staged a public, armed protest in 1912, as other political groups had done before. The Cuban government responded with a wave of massive repression. Party members were killed, and untold thousands of Afro-Cubans, many unaffiliated with the movement, were murdered throughout the province of Oriente in 1912 (Helg, chap. 7; Scott, 229–48).

Some Cubans believed that Haitians were involved in the events of 1912. Even after the repression, fears of a race war remained in Cuba and were heightened by the arrival of immigrants, which one newspaper called "the Haitian Invasion" ("La invasión"; McLeod, 46; Chomsky, 5, 7, 13). Cubans' associations of autonomous black political mobilization and Haitian immigration with race war were expressed in a 1913 article in *Cuba Contemporánea*. The article opposed the entry of Haitians and all other "blacks" into Cuba, using census data to warn that they would soon overtake white Cubans numerically. The author implied that the Afro-Cuban leaders who opposed race-based immigration prohibitions were engaging in activities reminiscent of the PIC by trying to overwhelm the white majority. Finally, the article argued that the entry of foreign blacks would derail Afro-Cubans' attempts to achieve cultural parity with Cuban whites because Afro-Cubans would inevitably mix with the new immigrants, who "are not . . . so susceptible to modify their crude nature" (de Velasco, 74–77).

Among the Haitians who traveled to eastern Cuba during the first decades of the twentieth century were urban laborers and professionals who settled in Cuban cities like Santiago and Guantánamo. In 1919 there were 748 foreign-born adult males *de color* living in the city of Santiago de Cuba, and 507 in Guantánamo.[9] Haitians constituted an unknown but significant portion of them. In 1932 a Haitian newspaper estimated the "Haitian colony in Santiago de Cuba" to consist of "approximately 180 members" ("A propos de un cable"). Between 1902 and 1959, approximately one hundred Haitians residing in the urban areas of Guantánamo appear in the city's marriage records. In both cities, Haitians worked as *jornaleros* (unspecified laborers), carpenters, masons, shoemakers, machinists, tailors, musicians, watchmakers, merchants, *empleados* (unspecified low-level office positions), lawyers, and consuls. Women worked within their homes and in some cases as seamstresses.[10]

Like the previous generation of Cuban exiles in Port-au-Prince, the Haitians inhabiting Cuba's urban spaces developed extensive social networks. In Guantánamo, between 1904 and 1930, almost half of the forty-nine marriages of Haitians involved a spouse of another nationality.

Fourteen were with Cubans; nine were between Haitians and individuals from Guadeloupe, St. Thomas, Jamaica, the United States, St. Christopher, and Tortola (in the Virgin Islands).[11] In 1935, Louis Joseph Hibbert, the Haitian consul in Santiago, served as the godfather for the young Fidel Castro after marrying one of the boy's teachers (Ugás Bustamante, 65; Ramonet, 58–59).

These Haitians kept themselves informed of the political conditions in their home country. Regular steamship traffic carried people and goods between Haiti and the eastern regions of Cuba, facilitating the circulation of letters and printed materials between the countries. Newspapers from Haiti circulated in Cuban cities. In a letter to the Port-au-Prince daily *Haiti Journal*, Edmond Jansème, the acting Haitian consul in Santiago, Cuba, wrote "to remind you that our [Haitian] newspapers are read here" ("Les haitiens à Cuba"). "Despite the distance that separates it from you," one individual quipped to Haitian president Sténio Vincent in 1931, "the Colony [in Cuba] does not lose sight of you for even one minute" ("La colonie haitienne à Cuba").

One aspect of Haitian political life that did not go unnoticed by the Haitian community in Cuba was the formation of l'Union Patriotique. In 1915, as U.S. troops landed in Haiti to begin what would become a nineteen-year military occupation, a group of Haitian urbanites under the leadership of George Sylvain, a lawyer and former diplomat, founded l'Union Patriotique (UP-Haiti) in Port-au-Prince (U.S. Senate, 44; "Union Patriotique," *Le Nouvelliste*, August 11, 1915). The organization became particularly active in 1920. By 1921, it claimed a membership of "17,000 adherents, spread throughout all the important population centers" of the country. The group's stated goals were "to work to raise the restrictions placed by the United States of America on the plain exercise of independence and sovereignty of the Haitian nation." Unlike the military strategies of other anti-occupation movements, the UP-Haiti sought to achieve its goals through "pacific measures" ("Union Patriotique," *Bulletin Mensuel de l'Union Patriotique*, February 1921).

From its founding, the Union Patriotique's activities spread beyond Haiti's borders. The organization formed relationships with the NAACP and sent delegates throughout Europe and the Americas (Plummer, *Afro-American*, 131–32; Hector). Despite Cubans' widespread associations between Haitians and black autonomous mobilizations with race war, a branch of the Union Patriotique was formed in Santiago in 1926. The organization sought to keep members abreast of "the daily facts . . . of Haiti," to achieve "the unification of all Haitians," and to provide "instruction of their children born in this territory in the languages of French and Spanish." The UP-Cuba's educational plans included creating "a primary and secondary course, obligatory French class, as well as Haitian civic instruction, History and Geography of Haiti and Cuba" ("Reglamento," 16).

Although the UP-Cuba was founded by lettered Haitians in an urban setting, it enjoyed support from Haitian agricultural workers and Cuban newspaper editors. Of the thirty founding members, some had addresses that tied them directly to the Cuban sugar industry. Osner Prospere lived on the Central San German ("Lista"). The cross-class nature of the UP-Cuba's support is further indicated by the result of a collection it held for Joseph Jolibois fils, one of the organization's well-known traveling representatives. Jolibois was the editor of the *Courrier Haitien*, a Haitian newspaper that was shut down by occupation officials because its incendiary rhetoric was at odds with U.S.-imposed censorship laws in Haiti. After leaving jail, Jolibois took his anti-imperial message to other parts of Latin America and the world (Hector, 7; McPherson, 127). From February to April 1928, members of the UP-Cuba circulated within eastern Cuba to raise funds for Jolibois. The organization collected money ranging in increments from $1.00 to $46.00; the vast majority of collection sites were sugar plantations and farms. The collection yielded $397.55 and was featured in the Santiago newspaper *Diario de Cuba* ("Cerrada la suscripcion").

As in other moments when Haitians and Cubans organized politically, members of the UP-Cuba could not ignore larger currents of anti-Haitian racism or fears of race war in Cuba. Leaders of the UP-Cuba sought to circumvent these limitations by adopting techniques used by Afro-Cubans and other political activists in the African diaspora. This included invoking Haiti's previously silenced contribution to Cuban independence and framing their political goals in terms of Pan-Americanism.

The UP-Cuba represented a clear emulation of one of Afro-Cubans' most prominent political strategies. In republican Cuba, it was common for middle-class Afro-Cubans to organize into allegedly apolitical organizations that were registered with the government as social clubs. These clubs provided an autonomous space to socialize, educate members of the community, and engage in cultural and religious activities (de la Fuente, 15, 37–38, 140; Guridy, 73–75). Like Afro-Cuban clubs, the UP-Cuba registered with the government as a nonpolitical organization. Its constitution forbade "discussions of party politics" during meetings and was registered under the politically innocuous name of the George Sylvain Society for Recreation. The organization thus paid tribute to its original founder while staying within the bounds of Cuban political norms. Official stationery, however, included *Unión Patriotica* on its letterhead ("Reglamento," 13–17). The UP-Cuba opened its ranks to "foreigners, particularly the children of hospitable Cuba" as well, though member lists did not record individuals' nationalities, making it impossible to know how many joined ("Reglamento," 18).

The clearest example of the Union Patriotique's adoption of Afro-Cuban political strategies in Cuba was their references to José Martí, Cuba's "apostle" who perished on the battlefield during the Cuban wars for independence. Martí's words were used as the epigraph to an open letter written by the UP-Cuba and published in a Cuban newspaper: "Liberty is very expensive, and it is necessary to resign oneself to living without it or to decide to buy it at any price" ("Carta abierta"). Martí was a "signifier of social unity" in the first decades of Republican Cuba, invoked or silenced by groups trying to achieve their vision of the Cuban nation (Guerra, 3, 7). In the case of the UP-Cuba, this vision was one that tended toward Pan-American solidarity and anti-imperialism.

While the Haitian government's efforts to aid the cause of Cuban independence were necessarily kept silent in the nineteenth century, the UP-Cuba's own political viability required that these previous relationships be publicly invoked. When the UP-Cuba was criticized for its fundraising activities in Cuba, its leaders referred to Martí's 1895 sojourn in Haiti.[12] They claimed: "We are doing that which Cuba did when its Apostle Martí crossed the lands preaching and receiving donations to liberate his country" (President et al., 27–28). Through this analogy, the UP-Cuba's project of raising money and consciousness in Cuba became equivalent to Martí's and other Cuban exiles' similar actions in Haiti. Haiti's struggle against the U.S. occupation was related to Cuba's nineteenth-century wars for independence, just as those wars had been equated with the Haitian Revolution a generation before. In sum, Haitians' contributions to Cuba's nineteenth-century independence were touted at the same time that reciprocity was requested.

Despite their official apolitical stance, the UP-Cuba remained active in Haitian political affairs by using the language of Pan-Americanism. During the Sixth Pan-American Conference, held in Havana in January 1928, members of the UP-Cuba wrote an open letter to the official Haitian delegates. It was published in *Diario de Cuba* and asked them to join the chorus of voices who opposed the United States' imperial activities in Haiti and the Americas. The UP-Cuba made claims on the conference delegates "as the citizens of the Republic of Haiti that we are." They also invoked the memory of the Haitian Revolution to oppose the U.S. presence in Haiti. Haitian delegates were urged to "pull from the talons of the American eagle our liberty and our independence that our grandfathers bequeathed us at the price of a million sacrifices, and that they have signed over to us in their blood" ("Carta abierta"). As in the nineteenth century, the Haitian Revolution was invoked for its significance to the Americas as a whole, not just Haiti. Indeed, the letter's brand of nationalism was unequivocally Pan-American.

> We would feel very happy if these phrases . . . could stir up your patriotic sentiments and unconditionally place you on these worthy delegations that have denounced out loud, without any fear, the imminent danger that threatens the rights of Latin American peoples by the incessant Yankee interventions at the whims of Wall Street and in the name of Civilization. ("Carta abierta")

Thus members of the UP-Cuba, with the aid of Cuban journalists, publicly challenged U.S. imperial control over Haiti and the wider hemisphere and the pretensions to superior "Civilization" it entailed.

Like the Cuban exiles who organized in Haiti, the UP-Cuba depended on the larger political situation of their host country. In the late 1920s, the government of Cuban president Gerardo Machado was becoming increasingly dictatorial and began repressing many organizations in Cuba for political reasons. Cuban secret police interrupted a UP-Cuba meeting on January 2, 1928, and expelled Manuel Milanes, a Haitian-born man with Cuban citizenship, for unknown reasons, which the UP-Cuba described as "unjustified things" (President et al., 27–28; Corbea Calzado, 66–67). Later in the same month, Pierre Hudicourt, a member of the Haitian branch of the Union Patriotique, and Dantès Bellegarde, a longtime critic of Haitians' working conditions in Cuba, were barred from entering Cuba for the Sixth Pan-American Conference ("Cubans Bar Haitian"; Cook, 130–31).

The Union Patriotique's final political project was an attempt to cultivate support among Haitians in Cuba and the Dominican Republic for the Haitian election of 1930. After fifteen years of military occupation and puppet presidents appointed by the United States, the 1930 contest promised to be the first free election in occupied Haiti and a sign that U.S. troops would be leaving in the not-too-distant future (Schmidt, 107).

> We must insist . . . that the Haitians currently in Cuba and Santo Domingo will need only to register at their respective legations so that elector cards are emitted in their favor, [and] that they will reclaim them at the moment of their arrival in Haiti for their vote. This will assure us a formidable majority. (Séjourné)

It is unknown whether Haitians in either country participated in the 1930 election. Regardless, the "formidable majority" that the UP sought to build was achieved. Sténio Vincent, the nationalist candidate and onetime member of the UP-Haiti, was elected in the first presidential election of the occupation. Joseph Jolibois fils, the beneficiary of the UP-Cuba's fundraising activities, won a seat in the Chamber of Deputies ("Monsieur J. Jolibois"; "Le nouveau secrétaire"). After the election, Lamothe Azar, vice president of the UP-Cuba, traveled back to Haiti to represent "the Haitian colony in Cuba" in order to establish links with the new administration and assert the importance of the Haitian diaspora in Cuba ("La colonie haitienne").

Conclusion

The anti-Haitianism that spread through the Atlantic world in the aftermath of the Haitian Revolution manifested itself particularly strongly in Cuba. During Cuba's nineteenth-century wars for independence, Cubans across the political spectrum feared that their country's economic and demographic similarities to prerevolutionary Haiti could easily produce a Haitian-style race war. But for some Cubans and Haitians, the two countries' common experiences opposing imperialism and slavery provided an impetus for political collaboration. Indeed, a group of Cubans exiled in Port-au-Prince specifically invoked these and other historical commonalities in their successful petitions to the Haitian government for material and logistical support. Haitian government support for Cuban independence was kept silent to avoid international scrutiny, though such aid was hardly forgotten in the twentieth century.

By the first decades of the twentieth century, European formal colonialism was a memory in both Haiti and Cuba, though individuals in both places were experiencing direct and indirect forms of military, political, and economic domination by the United States. In the context of U.S. imperialism, thousands of Haitian laborers migrated seasonally to eastern Cuba to work in the island's sugar industry, prompting renewed anti-Haitian discourses and fears of race war. But as in the nineteenth century, anti-Haitian discourses coexisted with strands of anti-imperial thought. In eastern Cuba, Haitian activists organized politically against the U.S. occupation of their home country, invoking the two countries' experiences under foreign imperialism. They also called on Haiti's nineteenth-century contributions to Cuban independence to claim legitimacy in an otherwise hostile political climate. Though powerful, anti-Haitian discourses did not hold a monopoly over Cubans' ideologies or Haitians' transnational political and social relationships. By narrating Haitian and Cuban activists' struggles against imperialism, this chapter reconstructs the ideas that bound individuals across the Windward Passage and further accentuates the shared historical experiences on which they drew.

NOTES

1. I would like to thank Isaac Curtis, Natalie Kimball, and Lars Peterson for helpful comments on an earlier version of this chapter. Except for documents cited in other texts, all translations in the chapter are my own.

2. Between these two major wars was another, known as La Guerra Chiquita, in 1879. See Ferrer, *Insurgent Cuba*, chap. 3.

3. See, e.g., Luis-Brown.

4. *El Mulato*, April 8, 1854, cited in Luis-Brown, 442. See also Helg 50, 52.

5. Fernández was a Santiago-born educator and active member of the Freemasons who fled his hometown for Kingston when Spain cracked down on a number of patriots in eastern Cuba. Ibarra Martínez, 58–59; Pichardo Viñales, 169–70.

6. Commandant Autran, letter to the British Consul, December 17, 1877, cited in Léger, 229.

7. José Alvarez and Santiago Rojo to Antonio Maceo, September 30, 1879, reproduced in Maceo, 177–78.

8. Fernández to Presidente. In addition to the history of discrimination that Haitians experienced at the international level, Saget's anxieties were motivated by more recent moments when the Spanish government had demanded an indemnity from the Haitian government when it helped Dominicans fight against the 1861 Spanish occupation of the country. See also Fernández to Gral. Manuel de Quesada.

9. The term *de color* referred to people whom census takers identified as "black, mixed and yellow." *Census of the Republic of Cuba, 1919*, 454.

10. Compiled from the Registro del Estado Civil, Tomos de Ciudadanías, Provincial Archive of Santiago de Cuba.

11. Compiled from the Registro del Estado Civil, Provincial Archive of Guantánamo, Cuba.

12. This journey is chronicled in Martí, *Diarios de campaña*.

WORKS CITED

"Antonio Maceo: Nouvelle historique." *Le Pays*, June 23, 1930.

"A propos d'un cable de Cuba." *Haiti Journal*, February 29, 1932.

Burnham, Thorald M. "Immigration and Marriage in the Making of Post-independence Haiti." Ph.D. diss., York University, 2006.

Campuzano, Jorge A., Consul de la República de Cuba en Port-au-Prince, Haiti. Letter to Jefe del Despacho del Departamento de Estado en Habana, November 6, 1906, Secretario del Estado y Justicia, 23/711/2-5, National Archives of Cuba, Havana.

"Carta abierta a los delegados haitianos a la sexta Conferencia Panamericana." *Diario de Cuba*, February 10, 1928.

Census of the Republic of Cuba, 1919. Havana: Maza, Arroyo y Caso, 1920.

"Cerrada la suscripcion pro Union Patriotica haitiana: Resultado de la colecta." *Diario de Cuba*, August 9, 1928.

Childs, Matt D. *The 1812 Aponte Rebellion in Cuba and the Struggle against Atlantic Slavery*. Chapel Hill: University of North Carolina Press, 2006.

Chomsky, Aviva. "The Aftermath of Repression: Race and Nation in Cuba." *Journal of Iberian and Latin American Studies* 4, no. 2 (December 1998): 1–40.

Cook, Mercer. "Dantes Bellegarde." *Phylon (1940–1956)* 1, no. 2 (2nd Quarter, 1940): 125–35.

Corbea Calzado, Julio. "Historia de una familia haitiano-cubana." *Del Caribe* 44 (2004): 62–70.

Corvington, Georges. *Port-au-Prince au cours des ans: La métropole haitienne du XIXe siècle, 1888–1915*. 2nd ed. Port-au-Prince: Henri Deschamps, 1977.

"Cubans Bar Haitian." *New York Times*, January 13, 1928.

de la Fuente, Alejandro. *A Nation for All: Race, Inequality, and Politics in Twentieth-Century Cuba*. Chapel Hill: University of North Carolina Press, 2001.

de Velasco, Carlos. "El problema negro." *Cuba Contemporánea*, February 1913, 73–79.

Fernández, Manuel R. Letter written from Port-au-Prince to C. Ramon Cespedes, Comisionado Especial de la Rep. de Cuba en los E.U. de A, October 7, 1871. Donativos y Remisiones, 156/40-23, National Archives of Cuba, Havana.

———. Letter written from Port-au-Prince to Gral. Manuel de Quesada, October 20, 1873. Donativos y Remisiones, 156/40-25, National Archives of Cuba, Havana.

———. Letter written from Port-au-Prince to Manuel de Quesada, September 25, 1873. Donativos y Remisiones, 156/40-15, National Archives of Cuba, Havana.

———. Letter written from Kingston to Miguel de Aldama, Presidente de la Junta Central Rep. de Cuba, Puerto Rico, January 8, 1870. Donativos y Remisiones, 156/40-19, National Archives of Cuba, Havana.

———. Letter written from Port-au-Prince to Miguel de Aldama, Presidente de la Junta Central Rep. de Cuba, Puerto Rico, June 16, 1870. Donativos y Remisiones, 156/40-19, National Archives of Cuba, Havana.

———. Letter written from Port-au-Prince to Miguel de Aldama in Puerto Rico, August 23, 1870. Donativos y Remisiones 156/40-19, National Archives of Cuba, Havana.

———. Letter written from Port-au-Prince to Miguel de Aldama, June 19, 1875. Donativos y Remisiones, 156/40-21, National Archives of Cuba, Havana.

———. Letter written from Port-au-Prince to Presidente de la Junta Central Republicana de Cuba y Puerto Rico, February 15, 1870. Donativos y Remisiones 156/40-18, National Archives of Cuba, Havana.

Ferrer, Ada. *Insurgent Cuba: Race, Nation, and Revolution, 1868–1898*. Chapel Hill: University of North Carolina Press, 1999.

———. "Speaking of Haiti: Slavery, Revolution, and Freedom in Cuban Slave Testimony." In *The World of the Haitian Revolution*, ed. David Patrick Geggus and Norman Fiering, 223–47. Bloomington: Indiana University Press, 2009.

Fischer, Sibylle. *Modernity Disavowed: Haiti and the Cultures of Slavery in the Age of Revolution*. Durham, NC: Duke University Press, 2004.

Guerra, Lillian. *The Myth of José Martí: Conflicting Nationalisms in Early Twentieth-Century Cuba*. Chapel Hill: University of North Carolina Press, 2005.

Guridy, Frank Andre. *Forging Diaspora: Afro-Cubans and African Americans in a World of Empire and Jim Crow*. Chapel Hill: University of North Carolina Press, 2010.

Hector, Michel. "Solidarité et luttes politiques en Haïti: L'action internationale de Joseph Jolibois Fils, 1927–1936." *Revue de la Société Haïtienne d'Histoire et de Géographie* 49, no. 176 (June 1993): 7–53.

Helg, Aline. *Our Rightful Share: The Afro-Cuban Struggle for Equality, 1886–1912*. Chapel Hill: University of North Carolina Press, 1995.

Ibarra Martínez, Francisco. *Cronología de la guerra de los diéz años*. Santiago de Cuba: Instituto Cubano del Libro, 1976.

"L'arrivée du nouveau ministre cubain." *L'Action Nationale*, September 2, 1936.

"La colonie haitienne à Cuba." *Haiti Journal*, January 19, 1931.

"La invasión haitiana." *El Cubano Libre*, August 5, 1915.

"Le nouveau secrétaire d'État des Finances et des Travaux-Publics." *Le Pays*, November 29, 1930.

Léger, Jacques Nicolas. *Haiti, Her History, and Her Detractors*. New York: Neale, 1907.

"Les haitiens à Cuba." *Haiti Journal*, May 6, 1931.

"Lista de los miembros activos que formaron la Asamblea General . . ." December 4, 1926, Provincial Government, 2566/4/11, Provincial Archive of Santiago de Cuba.

Luis-Brown, David. "An 1848 for the Americas: The Black Atlantic, 'El Negro Mártir,' and Cuban Exile Anticolonialism in New York City." *American Literary History* 21, no. 3 (Fall 2009): 431–63.

Luperon, Gregorio. Letter written from Cap Haitien to Manuel R. Fernández in Port-au-Prince, January 30, 1871. Donativos y Remisiones 158/53-34, National Archives of Cuba, Havana.

Maceo, Antonio. *Papeles de Maceo, tomo 1*. Havana: Editorial de Ciencias Sociales, 1998.

Martí, José. *Diarios de campaña*. Havana: Centro de Estudios Maritanos, 2007.

McLeod, Marc C. "Undesirable Aliens: Haitians and British West Indian Immigrant Workers in Cuba, 1898–1940." Ph.D. diss., University of Texas at Austin, 2000.

McPherson, Alan. "Joseph Jolibois Fils and the Flaws of Haitian Resistance to U.S. Occupation." *Journal of Haitian Studies* 16, no. 2 (2010): 120–47.

"Monsieur J. Jolibois fils à ses electeurs." *Haiti Journal*, October 17, 1930.

Moreno Fraginals, Manuel. *El Ingenio: Complejo económico social cubano del azúcar, tomo 3*. Havana: Editorial de Ciencias Sociales, 1978.

Pérez, Louis A., Jr. *Cuba under the Platt Amendment, 1902–1934*. Pittsburgh: University of Pittsburgh Press, 1986.

Pérez de la Riva, Francisco. *El café: Historia de su cultivo y explotación en Cuba*. Havana: Imp. Marticorena, 1944.

Pérez de la Riva, Juan. "Cuba y la migración antillana, 1900–1931." *Anuario de Estudios Cubanos* 2 (1979): 3–75.

Pichardo Viñals, Hortensia. *Temas históricos del oriente cubano*. Havana: Editorial de Ciencias Sociales, 2006.

Plummer, Brenda Gayle. "The Afro-American Response to the Occupation of Haiti, 1915–1934." *Phylon* 43, no. 2 (2nd Quarter, 1982): 125–43.

———. "Firmin and Martí at the Intersection of Pan-Americanism and Pan-Africanism." In *José Martí's "Our America": From National to Hemispheric Cultural Studies*, ed. Jeffrey Grant Belnap and Raúl A. Fernández, 210–27. Durham, NC: Duke University Press, 1998.

Polyné, Millery. *From Douglass to Duvalier: U.S. African Americans, Haiti, and Pan Americanism, 1870–1964*. Gainesville: University Press of Florida, 2010.

President, Vice President, and Secretary General of the Union Patriotica Haitiana Georges Sylvain. Letter to José R. Barceló, Provincial Governor of Oriente, January 6, 1928, Provincial Government, 2566/4, Provincial Archive of Santiago de Cuba.

Ramonet, Ignacio. *Fidel Castro, My Life: A Spoken Autobiography*. New York: Scribner, 2009.

"Reglamento de la Sociedad de Recreo y de Instruccion 'Georges Sylvain.'" December 4, 1926, Provincial Government, 2566/4, Provincial Archive of Santiago de Cuba.

Salcedo, Pedro C., Jefe interino del Departamento de Estado, August 20, 1908. Secretario del Estado y Justicia, 23/711/2-5, National Archives of Cuba, Havana.

"Salon de coiffure: La Cubana." *Haiti Journal*, January 27, 1930.

"Salons de coiffure." *Haiti Journal*, June 22, 1931.

Schmidt, Hans. *The United States Occupation of Haiti, 1915–1934*. New Brunswick, NJ: Rutgers University Press, 1971.

Scott, Rebecca J. *Degrees of Freedom: Louisiana and Cuba after Slavery*. Cambridge: Belknap Press, 2005.

Séjourné, Georges. Letter to Perceval Thoby, September 15, 1929. Box 3, fol. 16, Kurt Fisher Haitian Collection (Additions), Manuscripts, Archives and Rare Books Division, Schomburg Center for Research in Black Culture, New York Public Library.

Ugás Bustamante, Gloria. *Haití: Vivir entre leyendas*. Havana: Pablo de la Torriente Editorial, 2002.

"Un nouveau diplomate cubain accrédité près notre gouvernement." *L'Action Nationale,* September 9, 1936.

"Union Patriotique." *Le Nouvelliste*, August 11, 1915.

"Union Patriotique." *Bulletin Mensuel de l'Union Patriotique* 3 (February 1921).

U.S. Senate. Inquiry into Occupation and Administration of Haiti and Santo Domingo: Hearings before a Select Committee on Haiti and Santo Domingo, volume 1. Washington, DC: Government Printing Office, 1922.

Zacaïre, Philippe. "Haiti on His Mind: Antonio Maceo and Caribbeanness." *Caribbean Studies* 33, no. 1 (January–June 2005): 47–78.

Zacaïre, Philippe, and Catherine Reinhardt. Introduction to *Haiti and the Haitian Diaspora in the Wider Caribbean*, ed. Philippe Zacaïre, 1–10. Gainesville: University Press of Florida, 2010.

II

HAITI AND TRANSNATIONAL BLACKNESS

3

Haiti, Pan-Africanism, and Black Atlantic Resistance Writing

—Jeff Karem

Following the Spanish-American War, many Caribbean writers developed intensive plans for resisting U.S. hegemony and preserving cultural and political autonomy, with Haitian authors leading the vanguard. Anténor Firmin and Benito Sylvain, in particular, established a critical discourse that examined both the local threat of U.S. dominion and the global implications of expanding Euro-American power. Firmin's and Sylvain's responses to expanding U.S. power advanced the development of both Pan-American and Pan-African ideologies and established a foundation for the intellectual work of subsequent generations of Caribbean and U.S. authors alike. The history of Haitian contributions to anti-imperialist resistance discourse during this period reveals that Pan-Africanism, along with the unified sense of cultural resistance that would culminate in the New Negro Renaissance, was the product of collaborative and dialogic relationships throughout the black Atlantic, born of mutual exchanges among U.S. and Caribbean writers.

Firmin and Sylvain were especially vital in fostering a multilingual, cosmopolitan Pan-Africanism, and their contributions formed crucial turning points in the development of the movement and its discourse. For example, in 1897 Henry Sylvester Williams (from Trinidad) founded the African Association in London to call attention to the problems of British colonialism in Africa, but after starting a dialogue with Sylvain and hearing of Firmin's ideas, Williams expanded the scope of the association to address the plights of all African-descended peoples under colonial hegemony throughout the world, including African Americans in the United States. The partnership of Sylvain and Williams culminated in the first Pan-African Conference in London in 1900, where Caribbean intellectuals presented philosophical, cultural, and political arguments alongside a broad range of African and African American participants. In the same

year, Firmin organized and presented a significant exhibit for the Exposition Universelle in Paris titled *De l'égalité des races humaines* (On the
Equality of the Human Races) (taken from his anthropological study of
the same name). W. E. B. Du Bois was a key participant at both the conference and the exposition exhibit, and his collaboration with Firmin and
Sylvain contributed key components to Du Bois's subsequent global anti-
imperialist vision, though he would ignore this collaborative history as he
laid claim to the role of father of the Pan-African movement in the 1920s,
a vision that many scholars continue to endorse.[1] In contrast to such a
model of exclusive paternity, this essay will examine the shared historical
provenance of Pan-Africanist discourse, with particular emphasis on the
transformative role of Haitian contributions to the movement.

Anténor Firmin's Proposal for a Haitian-U.S. Hemispheric Partnership

In the wake of U.S. imperial ascendance after the Spanish-American
War, black Caribbean writers feared that their region's racial politics
would be redrawn along harsh U.S. lines if the Caribbean became merely
a satellite to its northern neighbor. Foremost among these was Anténor
Firmin, a Haitian in exile who published widely in anthropology, history,
and politics. By 1889, Firmin had already secured himself a substantial
place in European intellectual circles as one of only two black members
of the French Société d'Anthropologie. In 1885 Firmin published a landmark anthropological study titled *De l'égalité des races humaines*, which
was an explicit rebuttal to Comte de Gobineau's racist tract *Essai sur
l'inegalité des races humaines* (Essay on the Inequality of the Human
Races). Firmin's refutation of Gobineau was outstanding in its time for
relying not on abstract a priori theoretical suppositions but on a rich
range of historical evidence and sociopolitical data. Firmin argued for
the basic equality of potential among all races: "Human beings everywhere are endowed with the same qualities and defects, without distinctions based on color or anatomical shape. The races are equal; they are
all capable of rising to the most noble virtues, of reaching the highest
intellectual development; they are equally capable of falling into a state
of total degeneration" (450).

Firmin's positivist methodology formed an apt precursor to the rigor-
ous sociology that Du Bois employed in landmark studies like *Black Reconstruction in America* (1935). Firmin's work also anticipated Afrocentric

and Pan-Africanist thought in arguing for a monogenic (single-origin) narrative of human civilization, with a crucial role played by black African culture, particularly via Egyptian civilization and its connection to the Greeks. Unlike many subsequent Pan-Africanists (particularly Marcus Garvey), who validated the "purity" of Africa as an anodyne to the white race, Firmin was skeptical not only of the value of racial purity but even of its possibility: "Observing that human beings have always interbred whenever they have come in contact with one another . . . the very notion of pure races becomes questionable" (64).

On the Equality of the Human Races shows a hemispheric awareness of the vital interactions between the United States and the Caribbean. Firmin cites both Stowe and Douglass in making his case that New World slavery enforces an inferior social status on African peoples rather than reflecting their existing potential (331). In one of the later chapters, "The Role of the Black Race in the History of Civilization," Firmin points to Haiti's successful war for independence from Europe, as well as his nation's support for the Latin American liberator Simón Bolívar, to argue that black Haitians played a crucial part in promoting liberty in the New World.

Following the U.S. victory over Spain, Firmin took an active role in engaging with the United States in both politics and writing. As Carolyn Fluehr-Lobban notes, in his role of minister of foreign affairs for Haiti, Firmin worked with Frederick Douglass (U.S. minister resident and consul general to Haiti at the time) in 1891 on the question of granting specific harbor rights to the United States at the town of Môle Saint Nicolas. The plan fell through because neither Douglass nor Firmin seemed willing to create a beachhead for U.S. imperialism on the island (xl–xli). Indeed, the entire episode, in which the USS *Philadelphia* lay anchored offshore, awaiting the chance to take possession of the harbor, anticipated in miniature the U.S. occupation that would take full force in 1915. Firmin also met with José Martí in 1893 in Cap Haitien to discuss how the Antilles might fit into Martí's Pan-Americanist visions, an exchange that Brenda Gayle Plummer explores in her comparison of Firmin's Pan-Africanism to Martí's Pan-Americanism.[2] In the wake of his awkward diplomatic exchange with Douglass, Firmin resigned his post. He was reassigned to Paris in 1900 but returned to lead an insurgency that called for a reduction of foreign interests in the island and a diminished role for the Haitian military. Firmin was unsuccessful and fled to St. Thomas, where he produced his final body of writings, which engaged directly the questions of U.S.-Caribbean relations in the New World.

When Theodore Roosevelt became president after the assassination of William McKinley, Firmin wrote a mammoth study (five hundred pages) about the future of relations between the United States and Haiti, titled *M. Roosevelt, président des Étas-Unis et la République d'Haïti* (Monsieur Roosevelt, President of the United States and the Republic of Haiti) (1905). This text, although little studied today, provides not only a complex portrait of how a progressive Caribbean intellectual viewed the United States but also a prophetic vision of Haitian-U.S. cooperation that could lead the hemisphere into the twentieth century. In *M. Roosevelt* Firmin advises Haitians to strengthen their military to preserve their sovereignty while arguing simultaneously that his nation should partner with the United States to lead the hemisphere. Firmin grounds his case in a careful renarration of U.S. history in the first half of the volume, followed by an equally systematic account of Haitian history. Firmin argues that the United States and Haiti are parallel nations that, while disparate in power, could stand shoulder to shoulder as revolutionary republics that have protected the New World from European intervention.

Firmin begins his volume by referring to "la question americaine," which is itself an effective retroping of a phrase usually applied by Europe and the United States to their "problem" zones. Firmin acknowledges a fear that "the advent of a new host at the White House [means] a threat to our national autonomy" (iii) but also aims to educate Haitians about "a great people with whom we have so many points of contact, material and moral" (iv; English quotations from *M. Roosevelt* are my translations). In tandem with this generous estimation of his northern neighbor, Firmin recognizes that a central challenge in understanding U.S. history is that a nation founded in the name of liberty could be simultaneously committed to militaristic expansion (and hence to the subjugation of others) from its earliest days—a paradox that would not be substantively explored by U.S. historians until much later in the twentieth century. A crucial goal of *M. Roosevelt*, according to Firmin, is "to grasp how a people given to the dignity of liberty and of equality put their energy into conquering others, empowered by these enlightened ideas, seeing them as the source of all social well-being and progress" (v). For Firmin, it is this peculiar combination of idealism and imperial ambition—which he sees as reaching its apogee in Roosevelt—that makes the United States such a formidable neighbor. Firmin argues that reckoning with that imposing possibility will be beneficial for his country: "And it will be a new merit for Roosevelt if his beautiful and healthy energy, after having inspired in us a salutary fear, makes us find our way again after having long abandoned our national destiny" (x).

As the language of "destiny" suggests, Firmin aims to complicate, and perhaps co-opt, the U.S. claims to Manifest Destiny. He notes that much as the United States declared its independence and sought to offer a model republic in contrast to European monarchy, Haiti also fought to achieve its own sovereignty and could serve as a model of black autonomy for the world: "For Haiti this ideal is the sublime effort of a small nation to rehabilitate an entire race" (ix). Firmin views these apostolic missions of the United States and Haiti not as simply parallel but as mutually intertwined, particularly insofar as the United States had failed fully to enfranchise African Americans and had thus compromised its own ideals.

As Firmin elaborates his historical comparisons across the volume, he finds both shared values and shared problems that would benefit from mutual aid between the nations. Firmin pays careful tribute to the highest ideals treasured by the United States, even as he subtly suggests parallel lessons that the United States should learn from its own history. For example, in recounting the history of U.S. independence, Firmin honors the founding fathers, especially Washington ("the immortal name that will always awaken in our spirit sentiments of respect and of admiration"), and refers to the Declaration of Independence as "a sacred thing" (103, 105). Firmin couches his appreciation of the American Revolution in a discourse of natural justice that suggests the rectitude of past and future defenses of Haitian sovereignty: "No one will recoil before the sacrifices necessary for the defense of a cause in which one has recognized justice" (103).

Almost immediately after concluding his discussion of the Revolutionary War, Firmin turns to the so-called Negro Question in U.S. history. While giving credit to the United States for abolishing slavery, Firmin argues that the nation needs to resolve its own issues of race prejudice and segregation before it can truly become a leading force in the civilized world: "Undoubtedly, a problem remains to be resolved, before the American people can really assume the leading role among civilized nations. I must speak of the troubling question of granting Afro-Americans the prerogatives of citizens and social equality, which are so ardently contested throughout all of the South of the United States" (131). Firmin corresponded with Booker T. Washington and had traveled through the United States, so he was well aware of the unequal treatment of African Americans there. Perhaps because he offers such admiration for the nation's ideals elsewhere in the book, Firmin is particularly scolding when

the United States fails to live up to them. Firmin contends that the preju-
diced whites of the South are unpatriotic, and that it is they, not African
Americans, who threaten the integrity and potential of the country: "It is
impossible to create, in white South Carolina or Alabama, for example, the
sentiment of national solidarity capable of suppressing racist repulsion.....
The brain of this descendant of the ancient slaveholders is now held in the
tight circle of the superannuated doctrines of Morton and Gliddon" (207).
By implicating racial scientists like Morton and Gliddon in this problem,
Firmin skillfully reveals that it is not simple regional ignorance that results
in race prejudice but antiquated and irrational dogmas circulated within
the United States.

No doubt because of his awareness of the power of prejudice in shaping
policy, Firmin feared that the Monroe Doctrine might be applied unjustly
to invade Haiti. Firmin comments that "the question of race dominates
fatally the problem of Haiti's destiny" (vii), and he notes that "after that
famous doctrine, what interests Haitians the most in their relations with
the United States, is the question of race or color prejudice" (193). Perhaps
surprisingly for contemporary scholars, Firmin does not object to the
Monroe Doctrine per se; as he declares, "I will gladly repeat the words of
the President of the United States, 'I believe with all my heart, in the Monroe Doctrine'" (192). Instead he objects to its improper application. For
Firmin, the U.S. invasion of Cuba was not in accordance with the Monroe
Doctrine because the United States was not protecting the hemisphere
against new European intervention but seizing a part of the Americas for
itself. Firmin satirically represents McKinley's intervention as a misguided
romantic quest, with the president fancying himself a Wagnerian hero:
"He must have felt that he was a good man, a loyal knight, Lohengrin, pro-
tector of the weak, calling for help for desperate Cuba" (165).

In discussing future relations between Haiti and the Roosevelt administration, Firmin expresses great admiration for the president as a man of
both action and ideas, and offers a sense of cautious optimism that the
relationship can be one of partnership rather than domination. Commenting that "the true American has never had a fear of pursuing risks,
when the prize to be won has been sufficiently worthy" (181), Firmin pre-
dicts that it would be difficult to prevent U.S. incursion if the president
set his mind to it, given Roosevelt's forceful character, "a combination of
intellectual initiative, of sporting discipline and moral development, all of
which are hard to find in the same individual" (182). More philosophically,
Firmin observes that Roosevelt has deployed a noble but highly mutable

ideal for governing U.S. foreign policy: "le plus grand bien" (the greatest good) (182). Firmin offers a brief mention of the U.S. hegemony over the Philippines as a cautionary example of how difficult it can be to check U.S. expansion under this ideal: "Who could deny that 'the greatest good' for the citizen of the Philippines is liberty, with political franchise, and that he should prefer it to independence under the malfeasance of a national oligarchy?" (182).

This seemingly straightforward rhetorical question has multiple layers of meaning and aptly embodies Firmin's complex views regarding U.S. policy. At one level, it pays tribute to the "greater good" effected by the U.S. intervention. At another, the possibly ironizing quotes around "the greatest good," as well as Firmin's sense that the U.S. intervention cannot effectively be "denied," suggest the dangerous inevitability of intervention under those idealistic auspices. Firmin also makes clear that this "greatest good" is problematic because it comes at the price of independence. What would make U.S. intervention so potent and dangerous was that Roosevelt possessed both great military force and an idealistic narrative to justify the use of that force. In the context of Haiti, the last phrase—"independence under the malfeasance of a national oligarchy"—seems to be a jab at the Haitian government that had sent Firmin into exile, a government he perceived as a corrupt oligarchy itself. In this light, Firmin's cautionary citation of the Philippines suggests that if Haitians do not maintain an effective government and military presence for themselves, the United States will have not only the military means but the ideological justification to invade their nation.

Turning away from specific discussions of Roosevelt and the hemispheric geopolitics of his day, Firmin devotes the second half of *M. Roosevelt* to recounting Haitian history, which he develops in parallel to his previously elaborated version of U.S. history. Citing each country's revolutionary history and republican origins, Firmin perceives "déstinées dependant" (dependent destinies) (285). Returning to the language of exceptionalism used at the start of the book, he argues that each nation has a responsibility to protect sovereignty in the hemisphere and to share in furthering the development of "les deux Ameriques" (216)—a formulation that echoes Martí's formulation of "nuestra America" but also draws those Americas closer together. Although Firmin observes many continuities in the second half of his book, he also notes the radically different origins of each revolution. After suggesting that scholars should treat the revolutions in parallel, he also suggests that there should be a degree of "proportion" in estimating the subsequent successes or failures of each nation (287). The founding fathers of the United States were highly educated landowners trained in the Enlightenment traditions of humanism and science who made a conscious choice to leave Europe to found colonies of their own design. In Haiti, however, "one finds all the conditions of those predecessors exactly reversed" (289). The black population of Haiti came from a slave trade that forced people away from their native countries and combined them with foreign peoples, "strangers forced together from diverse places in Africa, often as distant as the space that extends from Portugal to the Ural mountains" (233). Firmin argues that it is a tribute to the Haitian people that they founded a republic under conditions that were the reverse of the privileged opportunities afforded to Europeans in North America. Firmin makes this case not only to give proper credit to the extraordinary achievement of Haitian independence but also to offer a bulwark against claims that the subsequent political turmoil on the island constituted evidence of racial inferiority or an inability of Haitians to govern themselves.

As Firmin moves toward the conclusion of *M. Roosevelt*, he calls for a cooperative relationship between the United States and Haiti, grounded in mutual interest, investment, and shared democratic history. He asserts that neither nation has yet reached its full potential: "But Haiti is nothing more than the leading nation of the blacks and the United States still has not seized its destiny within the Western hemisphere" (291). Rather than abridging Haiti's autonomy, the United States and Haiti should work "cote à cote" (side by side) to develop both their nations and the American hemisphere and should recognize that each has something to offer the other (478). Haiti, most obviously, needed its sovereignty to be respected and could benefit from an influx of U.S. investment and capital. In turn, Haiti could provide the United States with an example of black democracy and integrated society that could transform the U.S. South into a patriotic part of the nation once again. Cooperation between African Americans and Haitians would ensure that "the states of the South will be filled with a larger civilization" (481). In this regard, Firmin cites his relationship with Frederick Douglass as evidence of the fruitful possibilities of cooperation between African Americans and Haitians.

Firmin was certainly not the first to advocate for partnering between African Americans and black West Indians—Edward Blyden and Martin Delany each did so, as well—but he skillfully placed his proposal in a mutually pragmatic context to make it palatable to a skeptical U.S. audience.

Clearly recognizing that expanding the influence of African Americans through such a partnership would offend "les blancs du Sud" (the whites of the South) and thus strengthen the Democrats, Firmin reassures Roosevelt and politically like-minded readers that black solidarity, enhanced by Haitian influence in the United States, would solidify the legacy of Lincoln and guarantee the future success of the Republican Party. Such astute awareness of the internal complexities of U.S. electoral politics shows not only Firmin's considerable (albeit optimistic) acumen but also the wide range of rhetoric he employs to solidify a U.S.-Haitian partnership. In the book's closing pages, Firmin argues that an intervention would be contrary to the interests of the United States, cautioning that one must balance "the benefit of such acquisition . . . in comparison with the considerable expenditures, in human lives and in money" (471–72). Beyond cautioning the U.S. reader, he advises the Haitian people to prepare themselves for the possibility of invasion and to remember the tactics and traditions that brought them victory against the French: "Hand in hand, we will press our backs against the slopes of our protecting mountains, putting our shoulders together, united for the common prosperity, as for the common defense" (496). Unfortunately, Firmin's less-optimistic predictions regarding the necessity for Haitian defenses would prove truer than his vision of partnership. He may have been correct to note that "Haïti n'a rien a craindre de M. Roosevelt" (Haiti has nothing to fear from M. Roosevelt) (463), but Haiti would have much to fear from M. Wilson, as history would show.

Henry Sylvester Williams and the Pan-African Conference of 1900

The case of Henry Sylvester Williams is particularly illustrative of the collaborative emergence of Pan-African discourse from the Caribbean in tandem with other contributors from the black Atlantic. Owen Mathurin and Marika Sherwood have each well illustrated Williams's contributions to Pan-Africanism in their biographical studies, but most critical understandings of the movement have still neglected Williams and the first Pan-African Conference, which he organized. As Sherwood observes, "Williams has been virtually written out of history" (xv). Williams's intellectual life at the turn of the century provides an apt model of the Haitian-American-Atlantic cultural crosscurrents I trace in this essay. Born in Trinidad, Williams trained as a teacher and served his community in that capacity for many years but gradually turned his attention to political and cultural activism. Specific details of his life are sparse before his arrival in London, but Sherwood has documented that Williams left Trinidad in the early 1890s, toured the United States and Canada (including enrolling as a student in Dalhousie University in Nova Scotia), and made contact with significant African American intellectuals and leaders. Sherwood convincingly argues that that these included Bishop Alexander Walters (a leader in the African Episcopal Methodist Church in the United States), T. Thomas Fortune (editor of the *New York Age*), and Bishop James Holly (an African American clergyman and scholar who became a leader in the Episcopal Church in Haiti) (14). Williams also corresponded subsequently with Booker T. Washington, which suggests that he had made some contact with him during his time in the United States. Holly and Walters would prove vital collaborators in organizing the Pan-African Conference, and Washington would provide a strong voice of encouragement for the endeavor as well.

Williams left Canada to seek greater professional opportunities in London; Sherwood documents that he enrolled in evening classes at King's College London in 1896 in preparation to take the bar exam. In London Williams joined political circles aimed at improving rights for England's colonial subjects in Africa, especially the heavily segregated South Africa. In 1897, Williams started a group of his own, the African Association, to advance the cause of African rights. The original charter of the association states that its mission was to combat the excesses of British imperialism, primarily within the African continent. Its purpose was "to encourage a feeling of unity and to facilitate friendly intercourse among Africans in general; to promote and protect the interests of all subjects claiming African descent, wholly or in part, in British Colonies and other places, especially in Africa" ("Aims and Objects"). The association's mission soon expanded, however, as Williams enlarged his circle of interlocutors to include other black intellectuals from the United States and Francophone colonies. The record of correspondence is incomplete, but Sherwood has shown that Williams was in substantial dialogue with Booker T. Washington and Benito Sylvain from 1898 to 1899, and Sylvain's discourse seemed to have particular import for Williams.

Both Mathurin and Sherwood suggest that as his career in London developed, Williams looked to Firmin and Sylvain as inspirations for his political activism (Mathurin, 49; Sherwood, 70). After developing a dialogue with Sylvain and encountering the ideas in Firmin's *De l'égalité des races humaines* (a text for which Sylvain was a key exponent), Williams expanded the scope of the association's mission. A document reporting on the association's work in 1898 not only presented concerns about Africa but also explicitly addressed "the distressed condition of the West Indies" ("Brief Statement"). In a similar spirit, Williams turned his political activism directly homeward, and he published his first tract, "The People's Case" (1899), to advocate for Trinidadian self-rule and democratic government. Williams's expanding awareness of the shared oppression of African-descended peoples resulted in a parallel expansion of the mission of the African Association beyond its original boundaries. In 1899, Williams worked with Sylvain to organize the first Pan-African Conference, and Sylvain persuaded him to expand the scope of the conference beyond the problems of the British Empire to include the experience of all Africans and African descendants under European or American hegemony (Sherwood, 70). During this time, Williams also corresponded with Bishop James T. Holly, who was himself a leader of Caribbean-U.S. collaboration and had advocated black emigration from the United States to Haiti. Williams contacted Booker T. Washington about the prospective conference and proposed to Washington that there should be "a general union amongst the descendants of Ham" (September 27, 1898). Washington responded positively by endorsing the conference in a number of African American periodicals, including the *Indianapolis Freeman* and the *Colored American* (Sherwood, 50). Alexander Crummell, pastor of St. Luke's Episcopal Church in Washington, D.C., and first president of the American Negro Academy, was also enthusiastic about the gathering. After corresponding with Williams, Crummell recommended to W. E. B. Du Bois that he attend to represent African Americans and the United States at the conference.

The Pan-African Conference brought together a significant body of West Indian, African, and African American intellectuals to present and discuss philosophical, cultural, and political arguments about the status and future of African and African-descended peoples throughout the world. The roster of attendees was a veritable who's who of global black leadership at the turn of the century. Besides Williams, Du Bois, and Sylvain, the attendees included the famous composer Samuel Coleridge-Taylor, J. F. Loudin (director of the Fisk Jubilee Singers), Bishop Alexander Walters, and Firmin himself.[3] Bishop Walters presided over the proceedings and provides the most thorough account of the conference in his autobiography, *My Life and Work* (1917). Participants passed resolutions regarding labor conditions, civil liberties, and black property, including a

critique of U.S. segregation. A committee from Williams's African Association reported to the conference that the association, in keeping with
the global mission of the gathering, had voted to change its name to the
Pan-African Association (Sherwood, 91). Du Bois was elected to chair
a committee tasked with addressing the nations of the world on behalf
of the conference. He coauthored, along with Williams, Walters, and
the Reverend Henry B. Brown, a manifesto titled "To the Nations of the
World." It proclaimed that "the problem of the Twentieth Century is the
problem of the color line," which Du Bois famously reiterated in *The Souls
of Black Folk* (1903). While it is not possible to recapture all the details of
collaborative production that resulted in "To the Nations of the World," it
emerged from the conference as a document supported by multiple sides
of the black Atlantic. Although Du Bois's re-presentation of this idea in
his own work is now the most famous statement of the "problem of the
color line," it was a shared declaration in its textual provenance, and both
Walters and Sylvain described "To the Nations of the World" as a collaborative product.[4]

Overall, the West Indian presence at the conference was dominant.
Sylvain was the first keynote speaker, which reveals the high esteem in
which he was held by the organizers. Besides Sylvain and Williams, other
Caribbean contributors included C. W. French (St. Kitts), John E. Quinlan
(St. Lucia), William Meyer and Richard Phipps (Trinidad), and George J.
Christian (Dominica). Although full copies of their contributions are not
extant, the program listings are available, and the very titles reveal that
the West Indian intellectuals were especially global in their emphases and
were helping to develop a greater diasporic black community across varied
geographies. French's "Conditions Favoring a High Standard of Humanity,"
Sylvain's "The Necessary Concord to Be Established between Native Races
and European Colonists," and Christian's "Organized Plunder and Human
Progress Have Made Our Race Their Battlefield" each pointed toward a
globalized sense of blackness. Taken together, these presentations, along
with "To the Nations of the World," offered the first collaborative, globalized program of black uplift of its kind, and it preceded the New Negro
Renaissance and the Pan-African Congress of 1919 by almost two decades.

Walters's description of the reception of the conference reveals the
singularity of its historical moment. After submitting a petition to the
British government regarding abuses in South Africa, the conference officers received a reply from a ministry official named Bertram Cox, Esq.,
writing on behalf of Neville Chamberlain and the queen to reassure the

conference that "she [the queen] was graciously pleased to command him to return an answer to it on behalf of her Government" and that "Her Majesty's Government will not overlook the interests and welfare of the native races" (Walters, 257). The conference also received official invitations from many London dignitaries, including members of Parliament and the lord bishop of London himself (262–63). Walters also wrote that following their circulation of the conference resolution to other black leaders after the conference, the officers received "numerous letters . . . from different parts of the world commending the work of the Pan-African Association and the National Afro-American Council" (263).

Given these lively collaborations at the conference, one might expect Du Bois to acknowledge the shared production of this Pan-African vision, but that was not to be the case. In the wake of the first Pan-African Conference, Du Bois arrogated to himself the cultural capital of representing Pan-Africanism while distancing himself from debts to his Caribbean collaborators. Du Bois makes a passing reference to the first Pan-African Conference in *Darkwater*,[5] but he never substantively discussed his participation in the conference, nor did he describe the contributions of West Indian intellectuals to Pan-Africanism. In his *Autobiography*, Du Bois makes no mention of the conference at all. In reporting on his travels to Europe in 1900, he mentions only briefly his time at the Exposition Universelle in Paris and is entirely silent about his collaboration with Firmin and other Caribbean thinkers at that event. Du Bois gives the impression in his autobiography that he returned to the United States having invented the idea for a Pan-African gathering entirely on his own: "I had emerged with a program of Pan-Africanism, as organized protection of the Negro world led by American Negroes. But American Negroes were not interested" (184).

A need to maintain a fiction of paternity may have accounted for Du Bois's almost unbelievable silence about the West Indies and West Indian intellectuals in his own writing. Du Bois's silence was also likely rooted in a personal and nationalistic stake in "owning" Pan-Africanism, a movement that, in his words, should be "led by American Negroes." Scholars have contributed to this silencing as well. Many accounts of Pan-Africanism erroneously cite Du Bois's Pan-African Congress of 1919 as the first such gathering or treat him as the undisputed father of the movement.[6]

Du Bois did finally credit the conference for the term "Pan-African" almost forty years later, in *The World and Africa* (1946), but the tone of his description still insists on his legitimacy as the effective originator of

Pan-Africanism. Du Bois did not mention any of his colleagues by name, and he minimized the importance of the conference itself:

> This meeting attracted attention, put the word "Pan-African" in the diction- aries for the first time, and had some thirty delegates, mainly from England and the West Indies, and a few colored North Americans. . . . This meeting had no deep roots in Africa itself, and the movement and the idea died for a generation. (5)

Du Bois's last sentence could more properly be restated as "died for me for a generation," as he did not return his attention to the matter until 1919, when he called his own Pan-African Congress.

Benito Sylvain's Global Vision from the Caribbean

After the 1900 conference, Williams, Firmin, and Sylvain each worked to spread Pan-African ideals, and they planned future meetings in the United States and Haiti. Williams published a new journal to further the aims of the conference, *The Pan African*, and traveled extensively to found new chapters of the association in the Americas, including visits to Jamaica, Trinidad, and the United States, where he addressed the Afro-American Council in 1901. *M. Roosevelt* advanced the case for Haiti as the exemplary republic to lead African and African-descended peoples into the twentieth century. Inspired by the conference and Firmin's work, Sylvain developed an extensive treatise on the future of African-descended peoples in the twentieth century, *Du sort des indigènes dans les colonies d'exploitation* (On the Fate of Indigenous Peoples under Colonial Exploitation) (1901). This text provided a crucial line of continuity between nineteenth-century Pan-African thought (in both the United States and the Caribbean) and the much-acknowledged flowering that would emerge in the New Negro Renaissance. In fact, the comparative anthropological and political works of Firmin and Sylvain presaged the postcolonial discourse that would emerge during the 1960s, as they diagnosed and classified the effects of varied colonial practices throughout the non-Western world. As much as Du Bois is rightly credited for his role in rethinking the centrality of Africa to geopolitics (especially in *The World and Africa* [1946]), he was relatively silent during most of his career on the full range of the black Atlantic, especially in comparison to Sylvain and Firmin.

Sylvain was committed to comparing the experiences of colonized peoples in Africa with those in the Caribbean and Latin America. Toward this end, *Du sort des indigènes dans les colonies d'exploitation* builds on Firmin's anthropological argument for the equality of human races to analyze the history of U.S. and European colonization of Africa and the American hemisphere. Maintaining a commitment to Firmin's anthropological, positivist perspective on race, Sylvain positions himself in this volume as a defender against the "calmonié" (calumny) of black inferiority. Sylvain's study offers a series of comparative histories exploring European and U.S. colonial practices, with particular emphasis on how these nations have systematically suppressed the potential of African-descended and indigenous peoples in their colonized territories. He classifies colonizers into three categories: "(1) conscious enslavers . . . [who] are vampires more or less disguised as men; (2) unconscious enslavers who, without mistreating the indigenous out of prejudice, intend to keep them perpetually in the condition of social inferiority; (3) the rare apostles of true civilization, who have the just and generous conception of the role of colonizers" (326; English quotations from Sylvain are my translations). Perhaps the sharpest barb in this critique, beyond the comparison to vampires, is the suggestion that colonizers who support systems of social inferiority are just as much "enslavers" as those who are explicitly exploitative in their systems.

Recognizing that the refusal to allow African-descended peoples access to tools of uplift and education would relegate them to subservience or to the status of "une souvenir ethnographique" (an ethnographic souvenir) (253), Sylvain is emphatic that colonizers not withhold their resources from the colonized: "Pour bien coloniser, il faut civiliser" (to colonize well, one must civilize) (327). At the same time, he skillfully suggests that the task of civilizing also applies to the colonizers themselves. "Pour bien coloniser, il faut civiliser" is an ambiguous maxim because of its grammar: who is to be civilized, the colonizer or the colonized? Indeed, when Sylvain enumerates the vices that "civilisateurs" need to extirpate, he lists some of the expected tropes applied to native peoples, such as "backwards or barbarous customs" and ignorance, but also "pride" and "greed" —traits more aptly associated with the colonizers themselves (327).

Much like Firmin, Sylvain drew on positivist science and evolutionary theory to defend equality and to counter the racist science of Herbert Spencer. Sylvain's rebuttal of Spencer anticipated Du Bois's refutation in *Dusk of Dawn* (1940) by almost forty years. Countering Spencer in his own Darwinist terms, Sylvain argues that recognizing the equal rights of all peoples is a necessary step in humanity's evolution. To attempt to stop this process is both unethical and unnatural: "Civilization is the state of evolution, an essentially dynamic state, which permits organized societies to ensure the moral perfection of man" (327). Consequently, for Sylvain, color prejudice is not only irrational but also an impediment to the evolution of world civilization: "Therefore, what is the obstacle that hinders the application of these principles of equity and of wisest politics? The most stupid and hateful of social prejudices: what we call the prejudice against color" (417).

Sylvain used the United States as a primary example of how color prejudice inhibits progress. He mentions Stowe in his study to remind his readers that the debilitating effects of slavery have already been well established: Stowe "has sufficiently dramatized the horrible scenes of slavery that we can cease to insist on the depressing effects of servitude" (245). Sylvain cites Douglass's writings extensively, notably his struggle with the "slave breaker" Covey in the *Narrative*, to demonstrate that degradation is a reversible process. Moreover, he uses Douglass's ascent as evidence of a bounty of potential within African Americans, West Indians, and Africans that ought to be developed. While crediting Douglass as "the greatest orator from the United States," Sylvain wonders what he would have been able to achieve "if instead of having spent the most fertile years of his youth in the heart of slavery, he had been sent to the University of Cambridge, Oxford, or West Point" (246). Sylvain thus argues that the segregationist tendencies in white colonialism reveal a fundamental hypocrisy: if U.S. and European whites were really so confident of black inferiority, then they would not feel obliged to bar the way to higher education or other opportunities. That they uphold those barriers shows that white colonizers are more dedicated to suppressing civilization than to spreading it: "The fears of the civilizers give the lie to their promises" (246).

As Sylvain's case draws to a close, the United States becomes more fascinating for his vision, as it embodies extremes of opportunity and oppression without equal in Sylvain's experience. Sylvain extensively describes the means by which southern states, post-Reconstruction, tried to suppress black votes—physical intimidation, poll taxes, literacy tests (418–19)—all of which show a fear of black political action rather than a true belief in African Americans' racial inferiority. Sylvain also notes that the United States is the only nation in the world with a substantial number of lynchings, a shameful case of American exceptionalism: "Nowhere in the world manifests a character of violence more hateful than the United

States: lynchings, which occur almost daily, with scenes of incredible savagery" (470).

Sylvain struggles to explain how such savagery in the South could coexist with a body politic that produces figures like Washington and Douglass. The best explanation he can offer is that the South was not founded by religious men or by descendants of the Enlightenment but "by criminals, by freed or escaped convicts, and by prostitutes" (420), a theory that, while not wholly correct, effectively renders the white South, not African Americans, as the problematic "other" that the United States must struggle to assimilate. Even with these criticisms, Sylvain argues, perhaps overly optimistically, that most of the United States, which had previously consigned African Americans to slavery, now embraced them as citizens: "In a generation, contact with Americans has made them into citizens" (420). Sylvain marvels at the paradox that, while racial violence is subjugating blacks in the U.S. South, African Americans and Africans are gathering in New York City to learn from American democracy: an "assembly of Africans comes, to the heart of New York, in a popular meeting room aimed at teaching American democracy, to vindicate the rights of citizens" (420).

African American writers during the New Negro Renaissance would also explore this contradiction, noting the dramatic contrast between the opportunities in New York and intensive oppression elsewhere in the United States. But whereas those writers would strike a decidedly nationalistic, even exceptionalist, note in positing Harlem as the "Zion" for global black culture, the works of Sylvain, Williams, and Firmin showed a more nuanced awareness of the complex global dialectics that produced Pan-Africanist discourse. Their writings and activism give the lie to Du Bois's claim that Pan-Africanism lay dormant for a generation after the first Pan-African Conference. While the ideals of Pan-Africanism reached a crucial flowering in the United States during the Harlem Renaissance, the seeds were planted collaboratively two decades earlier, with Haitian colleagues like Firmin and Sylvain breaking vital ground for their Pan-African brethren throughout the Americas.

More broadly, the leadership of these Caribbean figures in developing Pan-Africanism reveals that this movement was not the product of a unitary father figure or the property of any one nation. Haitian intellectuals played a crucial role in initiating and fostering this discourse, and they served not as points of origin but as catalysts for activism and debate that spread throughout the Americas and across the Atlantic. Pan-Africanism at the end of the nineteenth century and the beginning of the twentieth was the product of a multinational and multilingual dialogue and was as transformative for its contributors as it was for the political discourse of the time. More broadly, the role of Haiti and other West Indian islands in advancing Pan- Africanism reveals the crucial place of the Caribbean in both American and world literatures.

NOTES

1. Most scholars in the United States have positioned Du Bois as the father of Pan-African and related postcolonial discourses in the American hemisphere. John Carlos Rowe, for example, cites Du Bois's early writings like *The Souls of Black Folk* and *Darkwater* as "forerunner[s] of contemporary cultural and postcolonial criticisms" (*Literary Culture and U.S. Imperialism*, 177). Kenneth Mostern credits Du Bois with anticipating the whole of twentieth-century postcolonial theory and cites 1903 as the dawn of that era: "*The Souls of Black Folk* fulfils the entire definition of postcolonialism in nearly identical ways as *The Location of Culture* itself" (259). While I agree with aspects of each of these assessments, they underrate the role of Caribbean contributions by treating Du Bois as the sole originator of American postcolonial critique.

2. See Plummer, "Firmin and Martí."

3. According to Carolyn Fluehr-Lobban, Firmin attended, though not as a signatory or presenter (xxxix). Sherwood also finds evidence for a connection between Williams and Firmin in London because Firmin was listed as vice president for the Haitian chapter of the Pan-African Association after the conference (99).

4. See Walters, *My Life and Work*, 255. See also Benito Sylvain, *Du sort des indigènes*, 510.

5. Du Bois mentions the conference in passing: "We were in London in some somber hall where there were many meeting, men and women called chiefly to the beautiful World's Fair at Paris; and then a few slipping over to London to meet Pan-Africa. We were there from Cape Colony and Liberia, from Haiti and the States, and from the Islands of the Sea." Du Bois, *The Oxford W. E. B. Du Bois Reader*, 581.

6. For example, the chronological appendix to the new edition of Du Bois's *Autobiography* confuses these two gatherings and credits Du Bois as the convener of the first Pan-African Conference (248). The most comprehensive Du Bois biographer, David Levering Lewis, credits him as the paterfamilias of Pan-Africanism and ignores the contributions of Haitian and Caribbean colleagues, commenting that Du Bois returned to the United States "with the satisfaction of having fostered a new movement" (251).

WORKS CITED

African Association. "Aims and Objects" (1897). In *Origins of Pan-Africanism: Henry Sylvester Williams, Africa, and the African Diaspora*, by Marika Sherwood, 40. New York: Routledge, 2011.

———. "Brief Statement" (1898). In *Origins of Pan-Africanism: Henry Sylvester Williams, Africa, and the African Diaspora*, by Marika Sherwood, 55. New York: Routledge, 2011.

Du Bois, W. E. B. *The Autobiography of W. E. B. DuBois*. New York: Oxford University Press, 2007.

———. *The Oxford W. E. B. Du Bois Reader*. Ed. Eric J. Sundquist. New York: Oxford University Press, 1996.

———. *The World and Africa*. New York: Oxford University Press, 2007.

Firmin, Anténor. *The Equality of the Human Races*. Trans. Asselin Charles. New York: Garland, 2000.

———. *M. Roosevelt, Président des Étas-unis et La République de Haiti*. Paris: V. Pichon et Durand-Aurias, 1905.

Fluehr-Lobban, Carolyn. Introduction to *The Equality of the Human Races*, by Anténor Firmin. New York: Garland, 2000.

Lewis, David Levering. *W. E. B. Du Bois: Biography of a Race*. New York: Henry Holt, 1993.

Mathurin, Owen. *Henry Sylvester Williams and the Origins of the Pan-African Movement, 1869–1911*. Westport, CT: Greenwood Press, 1976.

Mostern, Kenneth. "Postcolonialism after W. E. B. DuBois." In *Postcolonial Theory and the United States*, ed. Amritjit Singh and Peter Schmidt, 258–76. Jackson: University Press of Mississippi, 2000.

Plummer, Brenda Gayle. "Firmin and Martí at the Intersection of Pan-Americanism and Pan-Africanism." In *José Martí's "Our America": From National to Hemispheric Cultural Studies*, ed. Jeffrey Belnap and Raúl Fernández, 210–27. Durham, NC: Duke University Press, 1998.

Rowe, John Carlos. *Literary Culture and U.S. Imperialism*. New York: Oxford University Press, 2000.

Sherwood, Marika. *Origins of Pan-Africanism: Henry Sylvester Williams, Africa, and the African Diaspora*. New York: Routledge, 2011.

Sylvain, Benito. *Du sort des indigènes dans les colonies d'exploitation*. Paris: L. Boyer, 1901.

Walters, Alexander. *My Life and Work*. New York: Fleming H. Revell, 1917.

Williams, Henry Sylvester. Letter to Booker T. Washington, September 27, 1898. In *Origins of Pan-Africanism: Henry Sylvester Williams, Africa, and the African Diaspora*, by Marika Sherwood, 50. New York: Routledge, 2011.

4

"Being a Member of the Colored Race": The Mission of Charles Young, Military Attaché to Haiti, 1904–1907

—David P. Kilroy

Rising to the rank of lieutenant colonel by the time of his forced retirement from the U.S. Army in 1917, Charles Young served much of his career in uniform as the only black commissioned officer in the American military. As such he posed a persistent dilemma for both the military command structure and the political authorities in Washington, who shared a commitment to preserving segregation in the army. There were occasions, however, when Young's race was seen as an asset by senior officers and politicians alike. Young spent a combined total of nine years serving as U.S. military attaché in what were then the world's only two independent black republics, Haiti and Liberia. Young was chosen for these assignments almost entirely for racial reasons. His two separate appointments to Liberia came at the request of the U.S. State Department, where his primary role was to train Liberian defense forces. His mission to Haiti was conceived by the Military Information Division of the U.S. Department of War, and his goal was to gather military intelligence to be used in building a contingency plan for a possible U.S. occupation of Haiti.

Young's 1904 mission is illustrative of a number of different representations of Haiti in the United States in the early twentieth century. From the perspective of the U.S. government, Haiti was a weak and unstable state, vulnerable to European intervention and thus a danger to American hegemony in the Caribbean. It was in this context that the contingency plan for invasion was deemed prudent. From the perspective of the U.S. Army, Haiti was an exotic, tropical, and entirely black environment, a place where no white officer could be expected to succeed in gathering intelligence. As the sole black commissioned officer in the army, Young's superiors determined that, "being a member of the colored race," he was the ideal candidate for the post. From Charles Young's perspective as a member of the African American middle class, Haiti, the oldest black republic in the world, was a source of inspiration and pride, and he was determined to do his part to help preserve it from the clutches of European imperial powers, even if that meant facilitating a U.S. occupation. During his stay in Port-au-Prince, Haiti took on new meaning for Young, awakening in him a Pan-African identity that would prove increasingly influential over the course of his life.

In 1904, Captain Young became the first U.S. military attaché ever posted to Haiti and the Dominican Republic. Since the United States began sending military attachés overseas, the majority had been posted to the capitals of the major powers in Europe and Asia. After the Spanish American War, however, the United States began to consistently post military attachés to the countries of Latin America and the Caribbean. Much of the impetus for these new postings came from the Roosevelt Corollary to the Monroe Doctrine, which unilaterally sanctioned U.S. intervention in the affairs of Latin American and Caribbean nations to preserve U.S. hegemony in the Western Hemisphere and fend off European intervention. The undertaking of the construction of the Panama Canal in 1904 greatly enhanced U.S. security concerns in the region (Vagts, 33; Kilroy, 60).

As opposed to the more traditional diplomatic function of those who served in Europe and Asia, military attachés in Latin America and the Caribbean were charged with gathering military intelligence and compiling geographic surveys. This intelligence was critical to the successful implementation of the practice of "gunboat diplomacy," whereby the United States intervened regularly in the affairs of its southern neighbors. Military attachés thus played a pivotal role in securing U.S. dominance in the region in the first quarter of the twentieth century. Young's posting to Haiti and the Dominican Republic was designed to gather relevant intelligence to be used in the event that Washington determined a U.S. invasion of either island nation was warranted. The U.S. government perceived both Haiti and the Dominican Republic as perennially weak states, prone to internal disorder, and thus vulnerable to European intervention. Washington was determined to prevent any such intrusion into what since 1898 it had come to regard as its exclusive sphere of influence. According to the *Army and Navy Journal*, the unofficial voice of the U.S. military establishment, "the chaotic conditions of political affairs [on Hispaniola] . . . may yet require the intervention of American influence" (939). With insufficient intelligence to develop viable contingency plans for military action in Hispaniola, the army impressed upon the War Department the necessity of dispatching an attaché to the island (Kilroy, 60).

Haiti's deteriorating image in Washington in the early twentieth century makes clear that developing such a contingency plan was viewed with a degree of urgency. The historian Brenda Gayle Plummer writes that the racist ideology of the imperial age cemented the image of Haiti in the minds of many Americans as an exotic, sinister mix of "voodoo, cannibalism, [and] political brutality" (79). Western social Darwinist theories posited that Haitians, like people of color everywhere, were degenerating and needed white benevolence to save them. The official U.S. view of Haiti was of a country sliding into political chaos, and a mix of geostrategic concern and racial prejudice led to a growing temptation to intervene to "clean house" (Plummer, 8). President Theodore Roosevelt, whose administration dispatched Young to Haiti, worked from the assumption that order was the basis of all civilization and disorder bred tyranny. The Roosevelt Corollary was issued with a view to fending off European competition in the Caribbean while extending American order throughout the region. It was against this strategic and philosophical backdrop that U.S. policy toward Haiti in the first decade of the twentieth century moved from a position of relative detachment to an increasingly interventionist bent.

This policy shift coincided with growing U.S. concern over the commercial and strategic interest shown by the British, French, and Germans in Haiti. The intervention of German warships in Haitian affairs in 1897 and again in 1902 had been a cause of particular alarm in Washington. Berlin acted ostensibly in support of private German interests threatened by an increasingly unstable political environment in Haiti, but Washington, having used the same cover for the dispatch of U.S. warships and marines to Haiti on several occasions at the turn of the century, feared that such pretexts masked a broader German ambition to gain control of the National Bank of Haiti and to establish a coaling station at Môle Saint Nicolas. The Roosevelt administration placed the blame for this challenge to American hegemony not on German imperial ambition but on political instability in Haitian politics and what the president referred to as the "crying disorders at our very door" (Jessup, 554).

Roosevelt felt strongly that the United States should exercise "some kind of supervision" over Haiti, not just for geostrategic reasons but also out of a broader sense of mission (554). Writing in 1908, Roosevelt lamented that but for domestic opposition, which he attributed to a lack of understanding on the part of the American public regarding the situation in Haiti, "I would have interfered . . . already, simply in the interest of civilization" (555). Roosevelt's secretary of state, Elihu Root, wrote in the same year that U.S. intervention was likely to occur, but the United States must wait for the right "psychological moment." Root decried as "densely ignorant" the suspicion of the Haitian people that the United States wanted to "gobble up their country," but at the same time he acknowledged that "they have some pretty good reasons for doubting the advantages of too close an association between the United States and a black man's government." Root clearly anticipated that when U.S. intervention came, it would be in the interest of imposing American order, not in facilitating more effective self-government in Haiti. For officials in the Roosevelt administration, racial prejudice precluded the prospects for the success of Haitian democracy. According to Root, popular self-government was in fact one of the primary "elements which have brought ruin to Hayti" (Jessup, 306).

For the U.S. government, Haiti was an important piece of a larger Caribbean geostrategic puzzle, but the Roosevelt administration lacked solid intelligence on the conditions in the republic. Unable to provide the General Staff with requested information on Haiti and the Dominican Republic, the Military Information Division of the War Department suggested in 1904 that "a suitable officer" be dispatched to Hispaniola to gather intelligence. Young met all of the War Department's suitability criteria for the job. It was undoubtedly a high point of his career and clearly reflected the War Department's confidence in his capabilities. His service in the Philippines and his knowledge of French and Spanish were no doubt significant factors in his selection. Above all else, however, he was chosen for the assignment because he was the most senior black officer in the U.S. Army, and his superiors expected that by virtue of his race, he would "command the immediate confidence and good will" of the Haitians and be far less conspicuous than a white officer and thus more effective in gathering intelligence (*Army and Navy Journal*, 939). That Young was designated as military attaché to both Haiti and the Dominican Republic clearly reflects Washington's relative ignorance of the political (and physical) geography of the island. From the beginning there was a good deal of confusion about whether Young was to present his credentials in both Port-au-Prince and Santo Domingo, and less than a month after his arrival, the secretary of war canceled Young's appointment to Santo Domingo, citing the inexpediency of serving in the two capitals at the same time (William Powell to John Hay, June 8, 1904, DUSMH; Powell to Hay, June 4, 1904, DUSMH; Hay to Powell, June 28, 1904, DIHSD).

Young quickly got to work in Port-au-Prince and proved highly adept in his new role. During his first week, he met in quick succession with President Pierre Nord Alexis and leading cabinet officials. According to U.S. legation reports sent to Washington, Young gained immediate celebrity status among the Haitian elite. As the highest-ranking black officer in the U.S. Army and the first American military attaché posted to the country, Young had an obvious cachet. He was also an extremely cultured and erudite individual, multilingual, musically talented, well traveled and well connected in the United States, all of which added to his attraction. Young's popularity in Port-au-Prince provided a solid foundation for his mission, as the goodwill of Haiti's powerful and influential elite was a necessary prerequisite for him to carry out his orders to compile an original study of the island. In late summer Haitian officials granted him permission to travel into the interior, and in September 1904 he undertook the first of many reconnaissance missions that would take him to the remotest corners of the republic. Over the next two years, Young traversed the length and breadth of Haiti on horseback and made numerous excursions across the border into the Dominican Republic. Usually absent from the capital for two to three weeks at a time, Young would return to Port-au-Prince laden with information that he then compiled into detailed reports forwarded to the Military Information Division in Washington (W. H. Furniss to Elihu Root, DHL; Powell to Hay, June 8, 1904, DUSMH; Murville Ferere to Powell, June 3, 1904, DUSMH).

The results of Young's labors were manifold. In addition to numerous detailed reports on the topography, communications, fortifications, and military preparedness of Haiti and Santo Domingo, Young compiled a 294-page monograph on Haiti analyzing all aspects of the republic, from its government and laws to its culture and language. He drafted a series of detailed maps of the regions he had toured, many of which were previously uncharted, and in the process created the first systematic cartographic record of the island of Hispaniola. Young also displayed his skill as a linguist by compiling a detailed French-English-Creole dictionary and grammar. The U.S. legation sent glowing reports to the State Department commending the quality of Young's work and also noted that his cordial relationship with Haitian government officials was the key to much of his success (Heinl, 31; Powell to Hay, April 5, 1905, DUSMH; Powell to Root, October 20, 1905, DUSMH; Furniss to Root, March 7, 1906, DUSMH).[1]

This relationship came under mounting strain, however, as Young's operations became increasingly covert in nature. Beginning in January

1905, Young had been authorized by the Military Intelligence Division to begin traveling incognito. There was a limit to the scope and content of the information that Young's hosts were willing to share. Secrecy was required to gather information on leading Haitian individuals and their movements, photograph buildings and structures of military or political importance, and survey potential "landing places" and encampments for occupying troops (Military Intelligence Division to Charles Young, January 26, 1905, MID; Young to Military Intelligence Division, February 3, 1905, MID). By the spring of 1906, Young's welcome in Haiti was beginning to wear thin, and he was finding it increasingly difficult to "obtain desired information" (Young to Military Intelligence Division, April 28, 1905, MID). Word reached the U.S. legation in Port-au-Prince of accusations of spying leveled against Young for sketching fortifications and gathering information on the government, and a rumor circulated, which both Young and the legation strongly denied, that he had been detained and mistreated by a contingent of Haitians (Powell to Hay, April 5, 1905, DUSMH; Furniss to Root, March 1, 1907, DHL).

In April 1907, while he was away on a reconnaissance mission to Cap Haitien, Young's clerk broke into his office and stole a monograph on the Dominican Republic (which subsequently ended up in Santo Domingo) that Young had been preparing. This breach of security and the theft of classified documents not only jeopardized Young's personal safety but also undermined his future effectiveness as an intelligence agent in Haiti. U.S. minister William Furniss informed the State Department that in his opinion the whole affair had been instigated by the Haitian government to embarrass Young and have him recalled (Furniss to Root, March 1, 1907, DHL). Despite Furniss's pleas that recalling Young now might serve to encourage the already widespread belief that the United States was planning an invasion of Haiti, the War Department concluded that it had little choice (Furniss to Root, March 13, 1907, DHL). In March 1907, Young received orders to return to the United States.

Young's three-year stay in Port-au-Prince would have important implications for U.S. policy toward Haiti. President Roosevelt took a personal interest in Young's work, reading many of his reports and heaping praise on the military attaché for "the admirable character" of his work (William Loeleb to Young, May 2, 1907, NAMCC). Roosevelt had Haiti very much in mind when he issued his corollary to the Monroe Doctrine, noting that the "chronic-wrong doing" and "impotence" of such states might "force the United States . . . to the exercise of an international police power."

Chief of staff Major Franklin J. Bell commended Young's monograph as a work of particular value to the U.S. Army (Lieutenant Colonel Jones to Charles Young, October 30, 1907, CFC). When American military intervention in Haiti finally occurred in 1915, it was executed with relative ease. This, together with the ability of the United States to occupy the republic for nineteen years thereafter, was due in no small measure to the maps, reports, and monographs so painstakingly compiled by Charles Young. A key player in the occupation, Marine Major Smedley Butler, who took charge of the Haitian gendarmerie, reportedly relied heavily on Young's maps and reports to carry out his operations in the interior (Lawson, 14). Although the occupation of Haiti resulted in widespread charges of racism and imperialism from black leaders, including Young's close friend W. E. B. Du Bois, and newspapers in the United States, Young never expressed any misgivings about his role in facilitating U.S. policy.

Young's perception of Haiti, and of his own role there, was largely consistent with the ideological underpinnings of U.S. policy. As a West Point graduate, Young was imbued with the spirit of "duty, honor, and country" and felt a deep sense of loyalty "to the country that educated me [and] put shoulder straps on me" (Young to Senator Atlee Pomerene, August 20, 1918, CFC). Young's career coincided with the dramatic rise of the United States as a world power, and in addition to his years in Haiti, his service in the Philippines, Mexico, and Liberia reflected the expanding reach of American interests. He remained convinced throughout his career of the essential goodness of the United States and routinely contrasted the altruism of American foreign policy with the selfishness of the European powers. He regarded Teddy Roosevelt as the greatest man of his age (Roosevelt in turn praised Young as the epitome of black manhood) and shared many of TR's convictions about order and civilization, convinced that countries lacking such virtues must have them imposed from the outside. As far as Haiti was concerned, Young believed that its record since independence compared favorably with neighboring republics in Central America and the Caribbean, but it "could have done better, and must and will do better in the future" (Young, *Military Morale*, 240). In his mind, the gravest danger to Haiti's future success was the greed and self-interest of the European powers, while the United States was a disinterested force for good capable of providing a regenerative boost to the flagging fortunes of the republic.

Young, however, also brought a distinctly African American dimension to his thinking about U.S. foreign policy. He believed that all true

American patriots must recognize that racial prejudice was a cancer in American society. Heavily influenced by his close friend and confidant W. E. B. Du Bois, Young embraced the concept of the Talented Tenth and the perception that as a member of a small but growing black professional class, he had a duty to lead the struggle for racial equality in America. He carried this commitment to racial equality and elite leadership with him into his service overseas, and though he embraced the paternalist mission of American foreign policy, he rejected notions of racial hierarchy that most of his white compatriots harbored. Young held that people of all races had the same "natural capacity and aptitude," but civilization was a product of contact with "superior people," by which he had in mind an educated, rather than a racial, elite (Young, *Military Morale*, 208). Just as Young was convinced that the black middle class would open the door for the integration of the African American masses, so too was he convinced that the educated, professional African American middle class had a duty and obligation to transpose the virtues of the American Republic to the sister black republics of Haiti and Liberia. In essence, Young blended Du Bois's vision of the Talented Tenth with his own conviction in the paternalist mission of American foreign policy.

Young's faith in the power of elite leadership is evident in his fascination with, and deep admiration for, Toussaint Louverture. Young had grown up in an age when no black leader had a greater international reputation than Toussaint, who, more so than Jean-Jacques Dessalines, personified the Haitian Revolution in the minds of most African Americans. As a military man, Young was drawn to what he saw as Toussaint's unsurpassed leadership abilities, most clearly evident in his ability to rout "the best troops of Napoleon Bonaparte." Toussaint, like Haiti, held symbolic significance for Young and for African Americans in general; the achievements of this "pure negro and slave until after fifty years" were a testament to the innate abilities of all people of color and an example of the transformative power of elite leadership (Young, "The Negro Officer"). Young was deeply disappointed to arrive in Port-au-Prince and find no memorials or monuments to his hero, and so, on top of his official duties, he undertook research for a drama on the life of Toussaint. On his tours, he visited battle sites from the Haitian Revolution and made frequent research visits to the College of St. Martial in Port-au-Prince. "Love for a true patriot" and "race pride" in the "enlightenment, magnanimity, statesmanship, and military prowess of the full blooded African slave" fueled Young's ongoing fascination with Toussaint, and he would finally complete a draft of the drama while stationed in Liberia in 1921 ("Biography of Charles Young," CFC; Young to Furniss, March 15, 1906, DHL).

During the three years he was stationed at Port-au-Prince, Young developed a deep and genuine interest in Haitian culture and society. Initially he had a hard time adjusting to "the customs of an always peculiar people," and soon after arriving in 1904, he wrote to a friend back home, "Give me my own U.S. if this liberty run to seed is the alternative" (cited in Shellum, 179). However, by the time he left three years later, he had developed a deeper understanding of the Haitian people and their culture. He drew a stark contrast between what he saw as the political corruption and "viciousness" of Port-au-Prince on the one hand and the towns and villages of the interior on the other, which he characterized as "jewels" inhabited by "kindly, simple and industrious people" (undated notes, CFC). His travels in the interior of Haiti also brought him into contact with the widespread practice of Vodou, which he recognized as critically important in shaping the culture of Haiti's largely peasant population to the extent that he devoted a whole section of his monograph to the subject. Young came to appreciate that Vodou and its practitioners constituted one of the most direct links to Africa in the Americas that he was likely to encounter. This exposure to the culture of the Haitian interior awakened in Young a deep interest in Pan-African identity that was largely absent before his arrival in Haiti. Pan-Africanism became an increasingly important theme in his life and was a key factor in his decision to accept two tours as military attaché to Liberia, even though the second tour occurred after his forced retirement from the army on grounds of ill health. His home in Wilberforce, Ohio, became a veritable museum of Africana, full of art and artifacts from Haiti, Liberia, Jamaica, and Nigeria, and the music he composed, most notably for Du Bois's extravagant 1915 pageant *Star of Ethiopia*, experimented to some critical acclaim with the rhythms of Africa. It was during a fact-finding mission in search of the "truth about the black man" to the ancient city of Kano in Nigeria that Young would fall ill and die in 1921 (Kilroy, 153).

From the time he left Haiti, his thinking about the status and condition of black people in the Americas was informed by his newly awakened interest in the history of slavery and the heritage of Africa. He now came to the firm conclusion that slavery had upset the equilibrium of the people who were its victims, and not enough time had elapsed since emancipation to restore a sense of balance ("Notes on Jamaica," NAMCC). Young's overseas experiences, first in the Philippines and then in Haiti, exposed him to a broad range of issues of race and ethnicity. From the capacity of Filipinos for self-rule to the legacy of slavery and Western paternalism in the Caribbean, he struggled to find meaning in a world where people of color appeared always to be subject to white rule or to be laboring under the legacy of that rule. Taking his cue from the increasing popularity of the sociological studies in Western intellectual circles at the turn of the century, Young worked on a monograph while in Haiti, seeking to explain the relative strengths and weakness of disparate ethnic and racial groups spanning the globe.

Borrowing heavily from the writings of European sociologists and psychologists, the resulting work, *The Military Morale of Nations and Races*, with its heavy emphasis on the primacy of the nation-state and its propensity to engage in racial stereotypes, is in many respects conventionally Victorian. In it Young continued to express his pride in the role of the United States as an emerging world power, which he attributed primarily to the nation's democratic traditions and advanced industrial economy. However, he departs from the standard script on the issue of race, pointing to racial prejudice as the United States' Achilles' heel and refuting European claims of racial primacy and the White Man's Burden. In this regard there are echoes of *De l'égalité des races humaines* (1885), by Anténor Firmin, the Haitian intellectual and political revolutionary. Firmin, whose revolutionary movement was crushed by his onetime ally Nord Alexis during Alexis's march to the presidency, challenged Western sociological racism and portrayed Haitians, and blacks in the Americas in general, as victims of the slave trade and plantation system. Firmin also contended that given the right leadership and freedom from outside interference, blacks throughout the world were poised for a cultural renaissance that would rival the significant contributions to world civilization made by black people during the classical age. In a 1905 work on U.S. foreign policy, Firmin empathized with the Monroe Doctrine and U.S. concerns regarding disorder in the Caribbean (Plummer, 74–76). While there is no evidence that Young met Firmin, some evidence suggests that Young actively sought out the work of the Haitian intellectual, and strong echoes of Firmin's work are present throughout *Military Morale*. Young writes, for example, that in Haiti, despite the existence of a liberal constitution, the president is able to exercise autocratic powers because generations of slavery left the people predisposed to being ruled rather than ruling themselves. Like Firmin, Young sees hope on the horizon and argues that all that is lacking in Haiti is "progressive . . . leadership," the example for which Young was convinced could come from the United States, and its citizens of African descent in particular (Young, *Military Morale*, 209, 240).

From the perspective of the army in which he served and the government that sent him there, Young's mission was a success. His detailed maps and meticulous country study proved invaluable to the U.S. occupation in 1915 and thus to the broader policy of securing U.S. hegemony in the Caribbean. Young would continue to see his role as an agent of positive change rather than a stool of imperialism, as his some of his critics contended. When he returned to Liberia in 1920 for this second tour as military attaché, there were widespread claims on the streets of Monrovia and in the black newspapers in America that Liberia was poised to fall victim to U.S. occupation as Haiti had done in 1915. Young despaired that all the "Haiti" talk was undermining the U.S. mission in Liberia. He remained convinced that both Haiti and Liberia should be willing to sacrifice part of their sovereignty to the United States to preserve their long-term independence as black republics (Kilroy, 148–53). While his own experience in Haiti and the subsequent U.S. occupation had done little to shake his faith in the benevolence of U.S. foreign policy, Haiti had transformed his views on race and identity. Haiti awakened in him an interest in "the black man the world over," and in addition to serving the United States, he now came to see his overseas postings in the broader context of "uniting blacks in 2 continents together in sympathy and friendship" (undated notes, CFC). This was certainly the subtext for his decision to come out of retirement to return to Liberia in 1921 and the rationale for undertaking the trip to Nigeria, where he died a year later.

NOTES

1. Only a fraction of Young's work on Haiti and the Dominican Republic is still extant. His intelligence reports and monograph were destroyed in the early 1920s when the War Department cleaned out its "dead" files. His French-English-Creole dictionary is housed in the library of the Army War College in Carlisle, Pennsylvania, and some of his maps survive in the National Archives, II, in College Park, Maryland. Young's cable communications with the Military Information Division (see MID) and the dispatches of the U.S. minister to Haiti to the State Department (see DUSMH) only hint at the voluminous and detailed nature of his reports and monograph.

WORKS CITED

Archives cited in the text have been identified by the following abbreviations:

CFC   Charles Young Papers, Coleman Family Collection, Akron, OH.

DHL   U.S. Department of State, Dispatches from the Haitian Legation, Record
         Group 84, National Archives II, College Park, MD.

DIHSD   U.S. Department of State, Diplomatic Instructions of the Department of
         State, 1801–1906, Haiti and Santo Domingo, Record Group 59, National
         Archives II, College Park, MD.

DUSMH   U.S. Department of State, Dispatches from U.S. Ministers to Haiti,
         1862–1906, Record Group 59, National Archives II, College Park, MD.

MID   U.S. Department of War, Military Information Division, 1904–6, Office
         of the General Staff, Army War College, Record Group 165, National
         Archives, Washington, DC.

NAMCC   Charles Young Papers, National Afro-American Museum and Cultural
         Center, Wilberforce, OH.

Army and Navy Journal 41 (May 7, 1904).

Heinl, Nancy Gordon. "Colonel Charles Young: Pointman." *Army Magazine* 27 (March
     1971): 30–34.

Heinl, Robert Debs, and Nancy Gordon Heinl. *Written in Blood: The Story of the
     Haitian People, 1492–1995.* Lanham, MD: University Press of America, 1996.

Jessup, Philip C. *Elihu Root.* Vol. 1. New York: Dodd, Mead, 1938.

Kilroy, David P. *For Race and Country: The Life and Career of Colonel Charles Young.*
     Westport, CT: Praeger, 2003.

Lawson, E. H. "One Out of Twelve Million: Unrevealed Facts in the Life of Charles
     Young, West Pointer." *Washington Post*, May 26, 1929, 11, 14.

Morrison, Elting E., ed. *The Letters of Theodore Roosevelt.* Vol. 7. Cambridge, MA:
     Harvard University Press, 1954.

Plummer, Brenda Gayle. *Haiti and the United States: The Psychological Moment.*
     Athens: University of Georgia Press, 1992.

Shellum, Brian G. *Black Officer in a Buffalo Soldier Regiment: The Military Career of
     Charles Young.* Lincoln: University of Nebraska Press, 2010.

Vagts, Alfred. *The Military Attaché.* Princeton, NJ: Princeton University Press, 1967.

Young, Charles. *The Military Morale of Nations and Races.* Kansas City, MO: Franklin
     Hudson, 1906.

———. "The Negro Officer." Letter, *New York Evening Post*, April 5, 1919.

III

THE U.S.
OCCUPATION

5

Haiti's Revisionary Haunting of Charles Chesnutt's "Careful" History in *Paul Marchand, F.M.C.*

—Bethany Aery Clerico

Nevertheless, the awful example of San Domingo, where the land, for its sins,
had been drenched in blood, was always before the eyes of those just across the
Gulf of Mexico who still fostered the institution of slavery.
—Charles Chesnutt, *Paul Marchand, F.M.C.*

In 1921, African American writer Charles Chesnutt was concerned about the U.S. occupation of Haiti. The press was reporting an increase in violence between Haitian Caco insurgents and U.S. Marines; the soldiers, ostensibly on a stabilizing mission, were accused of massacring the resistance fighters daily. Chesnutt had kept a close watch on the events since 1920, and he eventually began drafting letters to lawmakers that called for the removal of troops.[1] He argued that the U.S. administration's "possession" of Haiti was "without right" and urged the administration, if it was in fact interested in "orderly government," to turn its attention away from Haiti and toward the lynchings in the U.S. South (*An Exemplary Citizen*, 166). During this time, Chesnutt was also writing and seeking publication for *Paul Marchand, F.M.C.*, a historical novel about a quadroon man living in 1820s New Orleans who discovers that he is legally white. The title character struggles with the implications of this surprising turn, and the text concludes when Marchand renounces his place as a white American and moves to France. The novel unfolds against the backdrop of the southern United States' uneasiness about the recently successful Haitian Revolution, and its plot twists are generated by Haitian-identified characters who have made their way into Louisiana. In 1921, then, it would seem that Haiti was on Chesnutt's mind.

What is startling about these details is that critical conversation has thus far failed to address the novel's preoccupation with Haitian events or its position within a contentious age of U.S.-Haitian relations. It is extremely hard, in fact, to not see Haiti's presence in *Paul Marchand*. And yet, despite Haiti's ubiquity, criticism has focused on the nation's worsening race relations as the novel's primary historical context. For example, the novel was denied publication during the author's lifetime and has received less-than-laudatory reviews since its 1998 release by the University Press of Mississippi. Scholars argue that *Paul Marchand*'s concluding rejection of the United States as a home for its racially complex characters and the novel's pastiche local-color style of writing are likely pessimistic and anachronistic responses to U.S. race relations, which had grown increasingly violent by 1921.[2] What value scholars attribute to the novel lies in their ability to use the text to reconstruct a particularly bleak moment in African American literary history. Publications by African Americans during this period, which Chesnutt termed "post-Bellum, pre-Harlem," were scant.[3] The texts that have emerged are often read in comparison to the advances made during the Harlem Renaissance, where literature was both artistically innovative and ideologically engaged in the fight for African American enfranchisement.[4] As a result, discussion of the post-bellum, pre-Harlem period often looks to the struggles occurring within national boundaries to contextualize a writer's artistic and social vision, that is, between North and South, between black and white, between Old and New Negro.[5]

These readings centered on the United States have had a deleterious effect on *Marchand*'s reputation, and they illuminate some central problems in American literary and cultural studies with respect to Haiti. Looking closely at the critical tendency to temper disappointment over *Marchand*'s form with concessions for the period, I suggest that the charges against Chesnutt of failed artistry and vision are the result of a strictly national conversation, which overlooks the ways that Haiti's presence in the novel acts as a transnational revision to the familiar, if outdated, genre of local color. I am thus interested in how we might emend the conversation by reading, as Chesnutt's narrator urges in the epigraph, with Haiti as a haunting presence "always before the eyes." In so doing, we see that Chesnutt's rather uninventive novel was working with a familiar genre to bring the unfamiliar, Haiti, into the scope of his narrative about New Orleans history.

Even the most cursory examination of the novel's plot is impossible to undertake without extensive reference to Haiti. Marchand's transformation from quadroon to son of New Orleans's wealthiest Creole family depends on a complicated backstory regarding that family's relationship to Haiti. When we first meet Marchand, he is suffering under New Orleans's strict caste system, one that allows the white citizens to abuse him despite his wealth and education. Marchand's reversal of fortune arrives when the patriarch of the Beaurepas family dies. Old Monsieur Pierre Beaurepas's will reveals that Marchand is his son, displacing the man's five greedy nephews from the fortune they imagined to be theirs. We learn that Pierre Beaurepas married his wife in a secret ceremony, and they conceived a child, Paul. However, they had to relinquish the child when his wife's first husband, presumed dead, returned to New Orleans. Consequently the child, Paul Beaurepas *ci-devant* Marchand, was sacrificed to "save the mother's good name." He was raised by a "discreet quadroon woman" who was "ignorant of his origin" (101). In the meantime, Pierre and his wife wait for her first husband to die; when he does, they marry in a public ceremony and plan to adopt their son.

Just as they are poised to reclaim Paul as their own, the Haitian Revolution interrupts. Pierre Beaurepas's brothers, René and Louis, own estates in Haiti and are "killed by insurgents, with tortures unnamable" (119). The only survivors of "the Haitian branch of the family" are five Beaurepas children, the family slave, Zabet Philosophe, and Zabet's grandson—who is the son of Zabet's daughter and René Beaurepas (37). The "refugees from that unhappy island" board a boat for New Orleans, undertaking the arduous crossing under Zabet's protection (102). Upon their arrival, Pierre and his wife feel they will be subjected to public criticism should they adopt a child just when they are burdened with the care of Pierre's nephews. Perhaps the most surprising plot twist in the story is that one of the five nephews is the son of a Haitian slave, for when one of her master's children dies during the journey from Haiti to New Orleans, Zabet passes her own grandson off as the fifth son. Not until the text's final pages does Paul reveal to his cousins that one among them is the secret Haitian child, transported into the United States and passed off by his Haitian grandmother as white.

Haiti's presence in the narrative as a persistent interruption to the white family's composition gains relevance when we also consider Haiti's prevalence in the moment of the text's composition. Chesnutt's lobbying efforts indicate that he was wrestling with what representative value Haiti might have for African Americans' struggle for social equality given its own forcibly subordinate position to the United States. *Marchand*'s narrator makes clear in the epigraph that Haiti has long been seen not as an inspiration but as an "awful example." This was particularly true in 1921. The violence between the marines and the Cacos had grown so pervasive that a senatorial inquiry was dispatched to assess the merit of the occupation (Renda, 33). Scholars theorize that this violence, which was ultimately downplayed in the official review, was in part a response to the memory of the Haitian Revolution.[6] For example, Eiko Owada argues that the Caco resistance would have "reminded Americans of slave revolts in the nineteenth century" and "recalled the Haitian Independence battles," and that the Marine Corps' subsequent massacre of insurgents was simply a continuation of the nation's suppression of any iteration of the eighteenth-century revolt (115–16). The Haitian Revolution's pervasive presence in *Marchand* opens up questions about how Chesnutt might have related this perpetual U.S.-Haitian discord to the worsening domestic racial conditions. In 1919 alone "there had been race riots in two dozen cities, towns, or countries, rampant lynchings and resurrection of the Ku Klux Klan, and a dismal falling off of jobs in the North for Afro-Americans" (Lewis, *When Harlem*, 23). This led to the "cultural sublimation of civil rights" and had a "cruelly decompressing impact" on African American life that persisted into the early 1920s (Lewis, introduction, xxii). Certainly, struggles for enfranchisement and the Caco struggles against the U.S. encroachment on Haitian sovereignty would have compounded for Chesnutt and other activists a picture of state-sanctioned racial violence at home and abroad.[7]

   Marchand's Haitian preoccupation is born out of this moment, and I contend that as Chesnutt observed the marines' crushing response to the Caco revolts, the Senate's refusal to withdraw troops, and the administration's failure to enforce the Fifteenth Amendment in the South, he was developing a sense that racial violence was in fact the prerequisite to the U.S. nation's notion of "orderly government."[8] Moreover, Chesnutt's overlapping creative and political writing endeavors indicate that he suspected U.S. ideals of "orderly government" have developed historically in response to its "awful" and blood-drenched neighbor. Yet these landscapes—the anxious United States of the 1820s, preoccupied with the aftereffects of the Haitian Revolution; and the anxious United States of the 1920s, whose violent reaction to the Caco insurgency is evidence of the nation's unease with any echo of the revolution—highlight a persistent desire in the United States to see Haiti as peripheral to its national project.

As I will demonstrate, Chesnutt's source material satisfies this desire, for it relegated the Haitian Revolution to the periphery of New Orleans history. In so doing, his sources formed a hegemonic narrative that I read as akin to what the Martinican poet and theorist Édouard Glissant calls "History with a capital H," a "highly functional fantasy of the West" (64). According to Glissant, totalitarian History derives its authority from a process by which the disempowered are subjected to what he terms a "nonhistory," an "ideological blockade" that occurs when a people's collective consciousness has been dislocated from History (62). Nonhistory, then, might be understood as an alternative historical space that is made up of what Glissant refers to as missed opportunities that need to be "repossess[ed]" (87, 62).

The novel pursues this repossession by working with Haiti as a revisionary tool to enact on the reader a haunting sense that the historical narrative of the revolution in the Americas is what Michel-Rolph Trouillot refers to as a "particular bundle of silences" (27). Chesnutt's sources represent one particular bundle, a local archive about New Orleans in which African Americans and Haitians are dislocated from a History that minimized the revolution's impact. A closer examination of *Marchand*'s historical details reveals a tension between this History and what I observe to be a second counterhistory, a narrative comprising Chesnutt's revisions, where he inserted Haiti back into passages that he has taken from his source material. This second narrative responds to Haiti's debased treatment within those late-nineteenth-century local-color writings, where the global impact of the revolution is stripped of meaning and, as Glissant theorizes, "deformed by dominant ideology" (88). *Marchand* imagines these points of deformation as moments when power dynamics in the city might have been challenged, thus acting as a repository for unacknowledged events and persons. The subtle nature of these revisions lends the counternarrative a spectral quality, for the novel depicts Haiti as lingering presence that haunts the margins of the narrative.

My reading of this haunting counternarrative draws from theories of spectrality by Jacques Derrida and Ian Baucom, both of whom propose a type of historical knowledge that is informed by a sense of the nonsynchronous and antiprogressive nature of time in the modern world, qualities that facilitate the ability of past events to haunt the present. According to these theories, a history is spectral to the extent that an event's (re)appearance

in the present signifies that event's resistance to chronological entrench-
ment, thus confounding histories that would interpret its significance by
relying solely on teleological narrativization. When an event does not
reside comfortably in that earlier moment, it disrupts what Derrida refers
to as the "reassuring order of the presents" (39). Baucom's theory also con-
ceptualizes the ghost's disruption as an opportunity to reconsider what
he terms the "elasticity" and very *existence* of the present" (324). Following these theoretical prompts, we might understand *Marchand* as a ghost
story insofar as it ruminates on the Haitian Revolution as a specter that
is always interrupting the readers' ability to see Haiti and New Orleans
as distinct from each other in the present moments that belong to this
novel: 1820 and 1920. In this sense, the narrative exhibits what Baucom
terms a "ghost-mindedness" (323) because neither landscape, as imagined
by Chesnutt, offers readers a stable present, one that concludes History's
march forward by arriving at an exceptional United States. As I will demonstrate, the specter of revolution unsettles the reassuring stories of the
United States' orderly constitution, both in 1820 as an expanding nation
and in 1920 as a hemispheric beacon of republicanism.

Consequently, as the novel accommodates Haiti, it reminds readers
that the revolution's impact echoes across the century; this reminder is
rendered in spatial terms, since the specter hangs above the watery expanse
between the two republics. For example, as we see in the epigraph, the
revolution's specter occupies a transnational expanse between Haiti and
New Orleans, where the Gulf of Mexico joins, rather than divides, the U.S.
city and the blood-drenched San Domingo. The ghost's haunting ground,
in other words, establishes that *Marchand*'s boundaries exceed those of
its source material, an archive of national historiographies that worked
to naturalize this "picturesque provincial French town" and its "strains of
alien humanity" to the story of U.S. growth and prosperity throughout the
nineteenth century (*Marchand*, 5). Therefore I contend that the implications of Chesnutt's hauntological inclinations lie with the ghost's ability
to repurpose these local narratives to suit what we should understand to
be the novel's hemispheric, not national, purview. The specter draws New
Orleans into a space that lies beyond both Haiti and the United States,
and I propose that Chesnutt is imagining for his narrative an entirely new
region, one produced by nonhistory that acts as a counterpart to the New
Orleans of local color. This region derives historical meaning not from
its subordinate relationship to the nation, where diverse regions contribute to, rather than challenge, the nation's sense of distinction, but from

its participation in a hemispheric network of movement, exchange, and influence that operates outside the domain of the nation-state.

Such an approach enlivens our understanding of the regionalism—not simply the local color—that undergirds the novel's historical effort. As my reading of *Marchand* indicates, Chesnutt's transnational perspective lends his regionalism a critical edge that other scholars have overlooked. I argue that his local-color sources serve to confirm national sovereignty, but the revisionary regionalism that *Marchand* exhibits is an opportunity to redress the national project's foundational logic that the United States has finite temporal and spatial boundaries, the very delineations that allow for the illusion of natural order. Indeed, it is this logic that has naturalized critics' reliance on national periodicity and geography to determine the novel's merit. If, however, we read for *Marchand*'s ghost-minded remapping of New Orleanian history, we find evidence that Haiti is not peripheral but essential to the U.S. national project, its nonhistory the very condition on which the present national fantasy of orderly government is assembled.

Given these details, I propose that we read *Marchand* not as a historical novel but as a literary quarrel with history.[9] The passages where Chesnutt argues with local color give us reason to consider what potential Haiti may have offered to African American writers who were struggling against an oppressive historical narrative. To that end, Chesnutt's novel offers us much more than a glimpse into how literature responds to a grim moment in U.S. history. In fact, it becomes paradigmatic for how the literary imagination can contribute to the work of repossessing future space within the U.S. historical narrative for the Haitian Revolution. Such a shift in vision counters the claims that *Marchand* is pessimistic and anachronistic; rather, we come to see the novel as a revisionary evisceration of the histories of postrevolution New Orleans.

The Local-Color Archive and Chesnutt's Too-Shiny Louisiana Tale

Chesnutt gathered historical information about Creole life in old New Orleans by turning to a well-regarded series of local-color narratives written in the late nineteenth century. During Reconstruction, northern editors embarked on a mission to create a new southern history, commissioning writers to produce what we now categorize as "local color," a postbellum literary genre whose sketches of southern life rendered the formerly seditious region an amusing, provincial, and romantic space. Local-color stories about New Orleans played a prominent role in this history by blanching from their accounts the city's slaveholding vices, its significance as a port city within the transatlantic slave system, its accommodation of one of the South's largest auction blocks, and its famous touristic trafficking in miscegenation. In the late nineteenth century, three writers dominated New Orleans local color: Charles Gayarré, George Washington Cable, and Grace King. Together, their depictions of the city's colonial and early national past helped to shape this emergent history.

Local color performed a significant nationalist function after the Civil War. As publishers took part in the United States' efforts to erase sectional difference from the national memory, their project produced a palatable form of fiction—a "'new' southern literature"—that rewrote southern history through the lens of nostalgia and the language of nationalism (Ladd, 45). Given its contrived origins in the North, local color was hardly an organic literary development; rather, it was a specifically engineered instrument of erasure. According to Kate McCullough, publishers selected writers who would display the "North's cultural monopoly" by "demonstrating that the South . . . had become entertaining rather than threatening" (189). To ameliorate the South's sectional associations, editors worked to cultivate portraits that were dissociated from, or inoculated against, the "threatening" histories of slavery and miscegenation. George Washington Cable's work illustrates this inoculation best. Although Cable's contributions to New Orleans history cannot be underestimated, Barbara Ladd argues that his historical material was largely dictated by his editors, who outlined "certain areas in which he was asked not to work . . . in the history of slavery and the color line and the growth of U.S. nationalism upon the foundation provided by that history" (46).[10] As they sought to render the South familiar and quaint, editors manipulated New Orleans's notoriously diverse racial history. For this reason, we can begin to read early local color as analogous to History, rather than simply as a minor literary genre.

We see the relationship between local color and History developing best in the intertextual sniping between Gayarré, Cable, and King; their literary conversation produces a particular version of New Orleans history that stems from contentious debate over how to represent the region's racial complexity and manipulates local details to maintain a singular focus on the region's white, European ancestry. Gayarré inaugurates this conversation, and he is commonly known as both the "official historian of French

Louisiana" and a "confirmed white supremacist" (Kreyling, xii–xiii). In the 1870s, Cable was inspired by Gayarré's *Romance of the History of Louisiana* (1848), as well as his expanded *History of Louisiana* (1866). Cable went on to produce *Old Creole Days* (1879) and *The Grandissimes* (1880), works that were both immensely popular and immensely "indebted to" Gayarré.[11] However, Gayarré famously objected to Cable's portraits of Creole society and spent a great deal of time trying to discredit him.[12] King, who was Gayarré's student and was also ideologically opposed to Cable, began writing her own history, *New Orleans: The Place and the People* (1895), "to defend the old order against Cable's criticisms" (McWilliams, notes, 188). One of their central areas of disagreement concerned the relevance of New Orleans's black population to their histories. According to Violet Harrington Bryan, black subjects "did not exist" for Charles Gayarré and Grace King (103). On the other hand, Cable's histories were more inclusive of black subjects (to many Creole readers' chagrin), but, according to critics, such subjects generally existed in the narrative only as silent characters or social problems (Foote, 99).[13] While each writer's representation of race is quite nuanced, it is not too much to say that, given their shared preoccupation with containing "threatening" representations, these writers offer evidence that local color was an ideological battleground over southern history. Together, Cable and "the Charles Gayarré–Grace King New Orleans literary *ancien régime*" (Bryan, 95) produce a body of work that derives from northern editors' manipulations and white supremacist assumptions and goes on to inform mainstream historical knowledge of the city well into the twentieth century.

To grasp the complexity of Chesnutt's revisions to this body of historical knowledge, we have to trace his reliance on the local-color archive to generate his study of New Orleans in the 1820s. The novel's foreword tells readers that the writer has made "free reference" to Cable and King. In fact, extended portions of *Marchand* are paraphrases of, or direct quotes from, Cable and King.[14] However, from the text's opening lines, Chesnutt invites readers to see that these histories form a problematic narrative for the enraced American writer. While his foreword asserts that the novel's details are "historical incidents" that he gleaned from "Miss Grace King and Mr. George W. Cable" (3), he also implies that such details are problematic because King's and Cable's "careful studies of life in the old Creole city" have not accounted for the lives of people like Marchand: "If there was not a Paul Marchand case in New Orleans, there *might well have been*" (3; italics mine). This pronouncement regarding the historical elusivity of his title character calls into question the accounts by Cable and King, suggesting that a "careful" history can never be known precisely because the lives of racial subjects were precluded from the record. However, Chesnutt revises these details by inserting Haiti back into the incidents, where it functions as a ghostly ancillary to the text's local-color sources.

Perhaps the most pronounced example of this insertion is the character of Zabet, the Haitian slave who passes her grandson off as one of Pierre Beaurepas's nephews. Zabet is a staple in New Orleans local color. King argues that "no relation of the city in the first quarter of the century is complete without Elizabeth, or 'Zabet Philosophe'" (341). Chesnutt clearly agrees, since Zabet figures extensively in his novel. However, it is significant to note that King locates Zabet's origins in New Orleans; she writes that Zabet was born "in the house of the widow of an officer who had served under Bienville" (341). In *Marchand*, though, Zabet is not born in New Orleans but lived in Haiti first.[15] Chesnutt establishes that she arrived in New Orleans via "San Domingo, from which she had fled, with her master's children, during the insurrection of 1793," and *then* came to New Orleans, where she became "a public institution" (9). By resituating Zabet, Chesnutt complicates our understanding of her as a traditional local-color figure. His revisions map her (and the local-color history she represents) within a hemispheric system, and she emerges from the violence of the revolution with information that could undermine transfers of power as the Beaurepas family's fate unfolds. Zabet, then, allows Chesnutt to position Haiti in the text, like Marchand, as a what "might well have been." Haiti's presence in his regional history draws attention to lives that have been obscured by local color's superficial treatment of the quadroon class as a charming feature of Creole life. Although Chesnutt's novel attends to local color's picturesqueness, it is decidedly more interested in the many conceivable ways that a character like Marchand might have "acted" (3). Consequently his regionalism distinguishes itself from local color, since he focuses on critical action, not provincial submission; from this perspective, Chesnutt can imagine that local color's historical figures might have been not merely docile scenery but active participants who took advantage of the revolution's tumult to, in Zabet's case, save future generations from disenfranchisement.

These nuances are lost on *Marchand*'s critics. Focusing myopically on Chesnutt's indebtedness to local color, critics have categorized the novel as an uninventive continuation of that tradition, one that scholars argue was anachronistic by the 1920s. For example, Matthew Wilson wonders if readers could have seen past Chesnutt's use of the "old-fashioned conventions of local color to its bitter disillusionment," both of which, Wilson argues, are the result of Chesnutt's position within an "intolerable" United States (198). This sentiment is echoed in Arnold Rampersad's review of *Marchand*'s publication in 1999; while he enthusiastically surveys the novel's social vision, he notes that Chesnutt's "art was outmoded" because he "reached arthritically into the past of local-color writing for a too-shiny Louisiana tale of French Creoles, alabaster maidens, haunted octoroons, desperate duels, miraculous wills and letters, and the like" (33). However, Chesnutt's foreword is evidence that he knew the genre would undoubtedly produce a "too-shiny Louisiana tale." Yet *Marchand* is more than a Louisiana tale. As it revises the local-color archive, it repossesses historical space for actions that may have been inspired by insurgency—such as Zabet's opportunistic swap—but were silenced within the *régime*'s carefully assembled record.

A Careful History of Slave Insurrection in New Orleans

To observe how Chesnutt's novel makes visible History's deformation to Haiti, I focus on the novel's treatment of one historical incident, a slave insurrection in New Orleans in 1811. The text's brief reference to this singular insurrection appears to be little more than a passing detail that contextualizes the reader's understanding of New Orleans's social environment in 1820:

> Negro insurrections were ever the nightmare of slavery. . . . Under the strict repressive discipline of the pioneer French and Spanish slaveholders, such few risings as had ever been attempted, were small and easily suppressed, and the single one which took place in Louisiana after the American occupation, had proved a costly failure for the rioters. (82)

In this passage, Chesnutt's description of insurrection spans the century between the novel's setting and its authorship by calling attention to occupation as a prerequisite to racial unrest. The passage implies that slave insurrection in New Orleans is facilitated by the uneasy power dynamics that followed the Louisiana Purchase: Yankee influence lacked "repressive discipline," thus encouraging the enslaved toward violence and disorder. When read through the lens of 1920, and in light of Chesnutt's lobbying activity, this reference acts as a double critique both of the nation's tendency for imperial interference and of historical narratives that would downplay resistance to white supremacy and the nationalist sentiments it engenders.

Indeed, Chesnutt's description of this event indicates that he was bothered by just such existing accounts of the 1811 revolt. Certainly, as the novel unfolds, it places increasing pressure on this historical footnote. His knowledge of the insurrection would have come from his sources King and Cable, as well as the "more obscure records and chronicles from which they drew their information" (*Marchand*, 3). King's and Cable's well-documented literary relationship with Charles Gayarré helps place Gayarré as one of these more obscure records and directs the reader to his account of the 1811 insurrection.[16]

Gayarré's *History of Louisiana* records that two whites were killed in a slave uprising in the Parish of St. John the Baptist a little more than seven years after Louisiana was handed over to the United States. Sixty-six slaves died in battle, and another twelve (or so) were executed. Gayarré describes the revolt as easily subdued; when narrating the plight of one landowner, who held off the five hundred slaves with a single gun, he declares: "This . . . shows how little that population is to be dreaded, when confronted by the superior race to whose care Providence has entrusted their protection and gradual civilization" (267). He also notes that, to deter further insurrections, the heads of the dead rioters "were placed on high poles above and below the city, along the river, as far as the plantation on which the revolt began. The ghastly sight spread terror far and wide" (267–68). Gayarré's teleological and paternal account intends to prove the benefit of these events for all: the white race's superiority is made self-evident, and civilization can progress unchallenged. What is unnatural in Gayarré's historiography is insurrection, which occurs when "misguided negroes" are "deluded" into thinking they might gain "a position in society" (267). What is naturalized in this source picked up by local-color writers is white supremacy.

Chesnutt's representation of the 1811 insurrection does not include these details. In his version, the insurrection is not a success but a "costly failure." It represents not a return to the natural order but an unnatural suppression of the entire enslaved population: their failure costs them physically, as dismemberment and public display serve as terror tactics, and the severed body serves as a symbol to deter any communal (and thus resistant) inclinations. In fact, rather than engage with these gruesome details, Chesnutt follows his observation that the insurrection was costly with a passage about the Haitian Revolution: "Nevertheless, the awful example of San Domingo, where the land, for its sins, had been drenched in blood, was always before the eyes of those just across the Gulf of Mexico who still fostered the institution of slavery" (82). With this reference, Chesnutt directs attention away from the "ghastly sight" of the failed rioters and toward the "awful example" of Haiti. Here he identifies a glaring silence in Gayarré, since the earlier writer's account of the insurrection is devoid of this hemispheric context. To Chesnutt, Haiti is a significant analogue to the singular 1811 event, and his narrative accordingly maps within Gayarré's history a counterhistory. Here the singular insurrection may have been costly, but it is now also evidence of a potentially far greater opportunity that American slaves have seized. In other words, in Chesnutt's retelling, the "ghastly sight" is no longer the severed black body to spread terror "far and wide" but the *united* black body of independent Haiti. The new sight reminds readers that what has been severed is the *colonial* body across the Americas now that French rule is overthrown, a power shift that North American slaves have taken advantage of in an attempt to subvert their own debased position in the United States. Here, then, the Haitian Revolution is recharacterized as a successful model of the "deluded" gaining power, and its repercussions in the United States effectively destabilize the normative distinctions that Gayarré's record reinforces.

As Chesnutt draws his readers' attention to the Haitian Revolution, he recontextualizes Gayarré's history of slave revolt in New Orleans; the 1811 event is no longer an isolated and aberrational incident but a direct response to the successful insurrection in Haiti. In so doing, he inserts a different trajectory for narrativizing the history of slave rebellion in New Orleans history. When Chesnutt entreats us to keep Haiti "always before [our] eyes," he is reminding us that context profoundly manipulates knowledge. Because Gayarré's account forsakes Haiti, it offers a truncated record of the many events converging in the region that might unsettle the self-evident rule of white landowners. Through this revision, Chesnutt finds a way to emend that record. When the nonhistory of slave uprising takes center stage, Chesnutt's text opens up room to theorize how historical knowledge might be generated not through official (careful) record but through the what "might well have been," the possibility of action from a figure like Marchand or Zabet. As Chesnutt makes visible the processes by which History is produced, he suggests that it is not the only historical space available. Beyond its critique of History, then, Chesnutt's novel is significant because it begins to construct an alternative historical framework. The novel does so by developing a subplot about another New Orleans slave rebellion that functions as a reminder of these "missed opportunities."

Chesnutt's Counternarrative and the Historical Threshold

In one of the novel's earliest scenes, two paperless men of color, Jean Lebeau and Pedro Valdez, arrive in New Orleans. They are captured immediately and imprisoned; however, they go on to escape and stage a local insurrection that is informed by their knowledge of the Haitian slaves' success. Their presence is a significant revision to local-color histories, for their plot marks an additional slave insurrection, rendering the original claim by Gayarré of a single uprising after the Louisiana Purchase questionable. They thus represent the likelihood of localized revolts that have gone undocumented, just as they themselves are undocumented, paperless men.

Their homes are never identified, and they drift into the text by means of a shipwreck. Lebeau is a black man whose name signals French colonial space, while Valdez, a mulatto, has a name suggestive of a Spanish Creole or Spanish Main connection. Because the text never confirms their origins, it becomes relevant to note that they identify *only* with Haiti. Their fates intersect with Marchand's when he is jailed for committing a "serious breach of caste" (73). During his brief incarceration, he shares an adjoining cell with Lebeau and Valdez and overhears their plot to ransack a local plantation, Trois Pigeon. When Lebeau declares, "I hate them all, root and branch. I would kill the last one, even as our people did in San Domingo" (81), he establishes their connection to "our people" in Haiti. As the scene introduces a narrative trace whereby transnational communities are affirmed, it revises History's attempt to limit the effects of the revolution, and establishes Haiti's persistent influence in regional American spaces. In this new account of antislavery activity in the United States, Haiti is inserted back into the history of New Orleans not as an anomalous event but as a catalyst for collective action.

The potential of these Haitian associations unfolds in the climactic scene, when Marchand chases down the insurrecting men and thwarts the rebellion. Marchand's interference marks a turning point in the narrative.

As Paul Marchand, he hated all "these *sacré* whites" and would "have his revenge for the slights they have put upon me" (91). As Paul Beaurepas, though, he has a "substantial interest in the plantation" because the Beaurepas family holds the mortgage on Trois Pigeons (155). In the climactic scene, Marchand arrives just in time to end the insurrection by apprehending the fleeing Valdez. At the moment of their confrontation, Marchand, no "ordinary white man," pauses; he begins to see Valdez as something more than "a black brute" (159). His "quadroon training" allows him to identify with "the long night of crime which had produced [Valdez]"— a "steady process of imbrutement" which includes a barrage of transnational signifiers: "the midnight foray into the forest, the slave coffle, the middle passage" (159). Marchand sees in Valdez the myriad cultural experiences that collide to create the man before him. From battle in Africa, to capture and journey to the Americas, ending in enslavement and miscegenation, this man embodies the history of Africans in the Americas. For this, Marchand pities him. However, his pity is also "very nearly his undoing," as Lebeau, whom Marchand thought was dead, creeps up behind him (159). Lebeau, the man whose kinship claims link him to Haiti, is quickly dispatched by Marchand's sword. Thus ends the insurrection: Valdez runs off to be "the bane of the society which had produced him," and Lebeau lies dead under the bushes (160). Chesnutt's scene frames the severing of a Haitian connection as a necessary response, suggesting that empathy for the Haitian's violent inclinations is a dangerous weakness. In this moment we see Chesnutt struggling with what Haiti offers to his conceptualization of the future of African descendants in the United States. It is critical to note, then, that it lies dead. That Marchand identifies with the mulatto and kills the Haitian-identified man suggests that Chesnutt perceived racial life in the United States continuing without a successful enactment of the model of insurrection that Haiti represented.

However, this is not an entirely disillusioned reinstatement of History's suppression of revolutionary action because the transnational experiences that undergird racial identity in the Americas remain secreted inside Valdez and Marchand. Unspoken, hanging like a specter between them, this silence between draws readers' attention away from the failure of insurrection and toward the processes that instigate rebellion. What Chesnutt focuses on, then, are the repercussions of this meeting: the future before all these characters. Marchand's fleeting empathy is arguably what solidifies his decision to relinquish life in America as a white man, and his presence in the nation persists only as a what "might well have been." And Valdez's future is certain: he will become a haunting figure within the system that made him. With these details, Chesnutt's innovations take shape, for the scene draws readers into a different relationship to history; we are no longer looking backward but looking forward. Now the reader must approach the "careful" incidents in the text not from the standpoint of what (was said to have) happened but from the standpoint of what *could have* happened, and the haunting possibilities of what might well be.

Chesnutt thus offers a counterhistory in which he imagines how silences can unsettle History's self-evident progress. This is significant because he pushes the Haitian Revolution beyond its ingrained function as an awful specter to explore its possibilities as what Michel Foucault calls an epistemological threshold, a point where we must reevaluate how we come to know history. Indeed, *Marchand*'s revisions frame the revolution as such a threshold because the event exists in the text with the express purpose of displacing and transforming our conception of history. As Foucault writes, a threshold "suspend[s] the continuous accumulation of knowledge [and] force[s] it to enter a new time" (4). If we apply this theory to Chesnutt's revisions, we see that the suspended moment hanging between Marchand and Valdez functions in such a way: it suspends the accumulation of our historical knowledge. Marchand's recognition that the process of imbrutement *is* the process of Americanization, whereby one's race precludes one's historicity, allows us to recognize a similar process at work in the historiography of American regions. When Chesnutt encounters Gayarré, he sees the process by which the achievements of the insurrecting slaves are deformed, a process that sharpens the delineations between the ghastly and the noble, the deluded and the rational. Returning Haiti to the story of regional insurrection disturbs these delineations. Furthermore, it allows Chesnutt to theorize that future U.S. spaces will always be haunted by, not immune to, potential power shifts that the echoing revolution inspires. This formulation enables us to reframe the historical work that *Marchand* undertakes: the novel is a testament to ongoing, fleeting redistributions of power that have gone undocumented, and an impetus to view the nonhistory of the revolution no longer as what has been silenced but as what might still be seized.

The Ancestral Possibility

Sibylle Fischer argues that reading for historical "distortions" can reveal "the shadow of other futures" (23). The novel's conclusion offers us a glimpse of what shadows Chesnutt imagined in light of the distortions he encountered. As Chesnutt opens up space for other histories (like those of Zabet, Lebeau, and Valdez), he encounters the question of what future might be imagined if history is so altered as to think of Haiti differently. In his final speech, Paul Marchand implies that his identifications with the Caribbean characters have affected his vision of the United States. In fact, he cannot envision a U.S. future as distinct from that of Haiti: "I hope the change will not come, as it did in France or in the island across the Gulf, in a deluge of blood, but come it will, if not in our time, then in that of our children" (176). The moment when Marchand finally speaks of the revolution to warn against future bloodshed is also the moment when Chesnutt can no longer look to the past. With these cautionary words, *Marchand* departs from its 1820s landscape. The novel's conclusion moves quickly into the twentieth century, abandoning the characters who have invigorated its history: Zabet is forgotten, Lebeau is dead, Valdez is a haunt, and Marchand slips into narrative recesses once he moves to France.

Perhaps Chesnutt could not fully imagine these futures amid the violence toward the domestic and foreign black body in the 1920s. However, his narrative does propose that the nonhistory of the revolution is always already a crucial supplement to the U.S. nation's historical knowledge. In this sense, his retreat to, and revision of, local-color sources becomes a means for reclaiming what Hortense Spillers argues is the "calibanesque potential" of the transnational, which has been subjected to "the dreamful flattening out of textures of the historical" by nationalist discourses (5). The revolution is not simply a ghastly event but one with that calibanesque potential to alter the shape of American nationalisms in the future. As Chesnutt's novel reverses the flattening wrought by local color, he also suspends the haunting visage of insurgency before his 1920s audience, where the revolution no longer belongs to a stable past that reinforces the rightful progress of U.S. hegemony in the Americas. Rather, as a specter, it requires that one be open to the likelihood of its return in an unspecified future where, as Derrida theorizes, indetermination, not progression, "remains the ultimate mark" of a future yet to come (73). As Marchand concedes, he does not know the time or shape of this change; however, while it may not come "in our time," Marchand remains confident that "come it will."

The impact of *Marchand*'s ghostly historiography is felt most forcefully in the novel's concluding pages, since Chesnutt focuses not on Marchand's future but on the future before the "white" family that he rejects. Before he leaves for France, Marchand tells this family that one among them is not white: one "white" family member's ancestry can be traced to the insur-recting slaves in Haiti. However, the family chooses to remain ignorant to whoever among them is Haitian born; in the text's final line, the narrator "wonders if [they] ever learned of the ancestral possibility" (185). It is per-haps the very uncertainty raised by this "ancestral possibility" that deter-mines their future; they and their descendants go on to become national leaders in the struggle to keep racial lines distinct; they contribute to a hostile legal and social climate by assisting the Confederates in the Civil War, participating in the Ku Klux Klan, and seeking to nullify the Fifteenth Amendment. This vision in which the Haitian past so clearly affects pres-ent racial conditions in the United States becomes a powerful moment; we see that these familiar juridical and sociopolitical responses to racial anxiety in the United States not only further entrenched the color line but more importantly developed precisely to perpetuate a silencing of Haitian points of contact.

Chesnutt's novel may resist actualizing a vision of how Haiti's haunt-ing presence in the history of U.S. regions might overturn asymmetrical power relations across the Americas, but it does frame for us how Afri-can American writers were thinking through the revolution in complex if ambivalent representations, so that they might shift perception away from Haiti as a "ghastly sight" and toward Haiti as a space "always before [our] eyes." Chesnutt's reticence in the novel's concluding pages should be understood not simply as pessimism about the future or as an untimely retreat to a bygone era but as an openness to the ghost, to the indetermi-nate nature of, as Marchand acknowledges, its certain return.

Therefore I argue that Chesnutt is aware that the knowledge bound up in what has been manipulated postrevolution has the potential to be incendiary to the U.S. nation, but his reservations about the shape of this shadowy future become evident when his transnational characters depart from the narrative; what future they might have represented is deferred. Nonetheless the text performs a significant task: it imagines a future where the reader will not be able to see one nation without the other. To return to the critical conversation, then, the interpretative value we assign to *Marchand* will always speak to how scholars think of Haiti's place in Western historiography. *Marchand* scholarship has left unchallenged the deformation of Haiti's relationship to other American spaces. A transna-tional reading, though, makes visible the crucial revisions that transform a careful local history into a history of possibility, a speculative narrative of what America's history might have been, and provokes us to consider, had it been realized, how future national constructs might be different. The persistence of Chesnutt's entreaty that we keep Haiti before the eyes, then, should remind us that we are always in orbit with the ghost; indeed, a certain ghost-mindedness in our literary and cultural analyses can facilitate our efforts, as Glissant might say, to begin the work of repossessing those missed opportunities where ideologies about race are unsettled and to breach the blockade that has been erected around the story of revolution in the Americas.

NOTES

1. According to Chesnutt, he "kept in pretty close touch through the newspapers, principally the *Nation*, with conditions in Haiti" (*An Exemplary Citizen*, 159). Between 1920 and 1922, while Chesnutt was working on *Paul Marchand*, the *Nation* published more than thirty articles dealing with the occupation (Crisler, Leitz, and McElrath, 159).

2. Matthew Wilson argues that the "national extent of racism" would have "deeply shocked" the author and affected his composition of *Paul Marchand* (186).

3. Between 1906 and 1922, the literary world was remarkably bleak for African American writers. During the postbellum, pre-Harlem period, "no more than five African Americans had published significant works of fiction and verse" (Lewis, introduction, xv).

4. See Barbara McCaskill and Caroline Gebhard. Their text summarizes critical reaction to literature produced during this period, which some scholars refer to as the "Decades of Disappointment" (1–3).

5. See McCaskill and Gebhard for an overview of these readings. Their 2006 collection represents the most recent readings of "the nadir" and Chesnutt. The collection does not, however, treat *Paul Marchand*, nor does it address the effect that U.S.-Haitian relations might have had on national discourses of race.

6. See Lester D. Langley for further reading on the "anticlimactic" senatorial inquiry. Langley writes that despite the copious bad press about the marines and their "indiscriminate killings," the investigation concluded that the occupation was only a minor blunder that should not be terminated but rather reorganized (101–2).

7. See Langley. Between 1920 and 1922, press in the United States regarding the occupation was "tinged with a racist theme," and the articles largely represented the marines in Haiti as white southern men who "enjoyed torturing and even killing Haitians" (101).

8. Here I am thinking through Bryan Wagner. In his analysis of *The Marrow of Tradition*, Wagner argues that Chesnutt theorizes racial violence to be the "prerequisite for the very possibility of white identity" (332). My article builds on Wagner's interpretation by proposing that, with *Paul Marchand*, Chesnutt suggests that U.S.

nationalism is shaped through its participation in, and maintenance of, hemispheric racial asymmetries.

9. I adapt the phrase "quarrel with history" from Édouard Glissant. For further reading, see his *Caribbean Discourse*, 61–66.

10. According to John Cleman, "George Washington Cable is credited with 'discovering' New Orleans as a literary subject in the 1870s, and he is indeed largely responsible for shaping the image of the city and its inhabitants that appears in fiction through much of the twentieth century" (1). Cable's fiction may have been seminal in future representations of New Orleans, but it was his "habitual" reliance on research and his "historical tendencies" that distinguished his writing (Ladd, 43–44).

11. See Ladd and Kreyling for further reading on Cable's debt to Gayarré.

12. See Edward Larocque Tinker, who describes how Gayarré launched a "major assault" on Cable in 1885 by renting out a hall and delivering a lecture that combated Cable's assertions (219).

13. Gayarré made certain that his histories preserved the image of Creole purity by purging the term *Creole* from associations with the black race, which he feared were intimated in Cable's tales (Tinker, 215–20). Despite Gayarré's fears, Cable's work, according to Foote, does indeed "divorc[e] its black subjects from the domain of the term *Creole*" and thus, like Gayarré and King, contributes to the silencing of black subjects in New Orleans history (99).

14. Fetterley and Pryse observe that Chesnutt does more than make "free reference"; for example, he "paraphrases quite extensively" from King's local color history (387). They also discover that in *Marchand*'s "Quadroon Ball" chapter, Chesnutt is "paraphrasing so closely as almost to quote directly from Charles Gayarré as quoted in King" (397).

15. Fetterley and Pryse make note of this revision. They trace Zabet as a recurring character in nineteenth-century American regionalist literature. For example, Alice Dunbar-Nelson's "The Praline Woman" (1895) is one such representation. They also acknowledge that Grace King's seminal work on Zabet clearly influenced both Dunbar-Nelson and Chesnutt, providing them with "accurate" historical portraits of antebellum New Orleans (288–89). Their work makes clear a crucial thread of influence, moving from King to Dunbar-Nelson to Chesnutt, each of whom uses this historical figure to represent the complexity of race relations in the city.

16. According to Fetterley and Pryse, Grace King's *New Orleans* "draws heavily on the early nineteenth-century New Orleans historian Charles Gayarré" (387n18). In fact, their research suggests that much of the material that critics identify as Chesnutt borrowing from King is actually King borrowing from Gayarré; indeed, at times both King and Chesnutt are almost "quot[ing] directly" from Gayarré (396–97nn5–6). This trace renders Gayarré's presence in Chesnutt's text undeniable.

WORKS CITED

Baucom, Ian. *Specters of the Atlantic: Finance Capital, Slavery, and the Philosophy of History*. Durham, NC: Duke University Press, 2005.

Bryan, Violet Harrington. *The Myth of New Orleans in Literature: Dialogues of Race and Gender*. Knoxville: University of Tennessee Press, 1993.

Chesnutt, Charles. *An Exemplary Citizen: Letters of Charles W. Chesnutt, 1906–1932*. Ed. Jesse S. Crisler, Robert C. Leitz III, and Joseph R. McElrath Jr. Stanford, CA: Stanford University Press, 2002.

———. *Paul Marchand, F.M.C.* Ed. Dean McWilliams. Princeton, NJ: Princeton University Press, 1999.

Cleman, John. *George Washington Cable Revisited*. New York: Twayne, 1996.

Crisler, Jesse S., Robert C. Leitz III, and Joseph R. McElrath Jr., eds. *An Exemplary Citizen: Letters of Charles W. Chesnutt, 1906–1932*. Stanford, CA: Stanford University Press, 2002.

Derrida, Jacques. *Specters of Marx: The State of the Debt, the Work of Mourning, and the New International*. Trans. Peggy Kamuf. New York: Routledge, 1994.

Fetterley, Judith, and Marjorie Pryse. *Writing Out of Place: Regionalism, Women, and American Literary Culture*. Urbana: University of Illinois Press, 2003.

Fischer, Sibylle. *Modernity Disavowed: Haiti and the Cultures of Slavery in the Age of Revolution*. Durham, NC: Duke University Press, 2004.

Foote, Stephanie. *Regional Fictions: Culture and Identity in Nineteenth-Century American Literature*. Madison: University of Wisconsin Press, 2001.

Foucault, Michel. *The Archaeology of Knowledge and the Discourse on Language*. Trans. A. M. Sheridan Smith. New York: Pantheon Books, 1972.

Gayarré, Charles. *History of Louisiana*. Vol. 4. 3rd ed. 1885. New York: AMS Press, 1972.

Glissant, Édouard. *Caribbean Discourse: Selected Essays*. Trans. J. Michael Dash. Charlottesville: University of Virginia Press, 1989.

King, Grace. *New Orleans: The Place and the People*. 1895. New York: Negro University Press, 1968.

Kreyling, Michael. Introduction to *The Grandissimes: A Story of Creole Life*, by George Washington Cable, vii–xxii.. New York: Penguin, 1988.

Ladd, Barbara. *Nationalism and the Color Line in George W. Cable, Mark Twain, and William Faulkner*. Baton Rouge: Louisiana State University Press, 1996.

Langley, Lester D. *The United States and the Caribbean in the Twentieth Century*. Rev. ed. Athens: University of Georgia Press, 1980.

Lewis, David Levering. Introduction to *The Harlem Renaissance Reader*. New York: Penguin, 1994.

———. *When Harlem Was in Vogue*. New York: Penguin, 1997.

McCaskill, Barbara, and Caroline Gebhard, eds. *Post-bellum, Pre-Harlem: African American Literature and Culture, 1877–1919*. New York: New York University Press, 2006.

McCullough, Kate. *Regions of Identity: The Construction of America in Women's Fiction, 1885–1914*. Stanford, CA: Stanford University Press, 1999.

McWilliams, Dean. Introduction to *Paul Marchand, F.M.C*, by Charles Chesnutt, vii–xix. Princeton, NJ: Princeton University Press, 1999.

———. Notes to *Paul Marchand, F.M.C.*, by Charles Chesnutt, 187–90. Princeton, NJ: Princeton University Press, 1999.

Owada, Eiko. *Faulkner, Haiti, and Questions of Imperialism*. Tokyo: Sairyusha, 2002.

Rampersad, Arnold. "White Like Me." Review of *Paul Marchand, F.M.C.*, by Charles W. Chesnutt. *New York Times Book Review*, October 25, 1998.

Renda, Mary A. *Taking Haiti: Military Occupation and the Culture of U.S. Imperialism, 1915–1940*. Chapel Hill: University of North Carolina Press, 2001.

Spillers, Hortense J. "Introduction: Who Cuts the Border? Some Readings on 'America.'" In *Comparative American Identities: Race, Sex, and Nationality in the Modern Text*, 1–25. New York: Routledge, 1991.

Tinker, Edward Larocque. *Creole City: Its Past and Its People*. New York: Longmans, Green, 1953.

Trouillot, Michel-Rolph. *Silencing the Past: Power and the Production of History*. Boston: Beacon Press, 1995.

Wagner, Bryan. "Charles Chesnutt and the Epistemology of Racial Violence." *American Literature* 73, no. 2 (2001): 311–37.

Wilson, Matthew. *Whiteness in the Novels of Charles W. Chesnutt*. Jackson: University Press of Mississippi, 2004.

6

The Black Magic Island: The Artistic Journeys of Alexander King and Aaron Douglas from and to Haiti

—Lindsay Twa

"Blood-maddened, sex-maddened, god-maddened . . . danced their dark saturnalia" (fig. 1). Readers familiar with Haiti and its representation in U.S. culture will recognize this drawing by Alexander King from William Seabrook's 1929 best-selling pseudo-anthropological travelogue on Haiti, *The Magic Island*. We scholars of Haiti love to hate Seabrook's book and King's accompanying drawings, decrying how they are emblematic of European- and American-centric representations of Haiti at their most exoticizing, titillating, and racist extreme. Beyond the requisite excoriating remarks, however, few scholars have actually attempted a contextual artistic analysis of King's images.[1] This is perhaps because to engage with them would seem to dignify their representations, or perhaps because they seem so extreme and naked in their primitivism and racism that we assume any conclusions drawn must be tautological. But *The Magic Island* was not King's first or his last artistic engagement with Haiti. A longitudinal engagement with his visioning and revisioning of Haiti can reveal not only the cultural complexities of primitivism but also how such representations were shaped and helped to shape the idea of Haiti within the early twentieth-century U.S. imagination. Moreover, the Austrian American King's engagements with Haiti are surprisingly parallel to those of the famous African American painter Aaron Douglas. King's undercontextualized images have long stood as the paragon of white misrepresentations, while Aaron Douglas, as the quintessential artist of the Harlem (New Negro) Renaissance, has long been presumed to have represented black subject matter automatically with greater nuance and validity. A comparison of their artistic lockstep thus exposes how certain visions came to dominate and be accepted as "authentic" representations of Haiti. Moreover, their common trajectory maps how imaginative encounters with

Figure 1. Alexander King, " . . . blood-maddened, sex-maddened, god-maddened . . .
danced their dark saturnalia," ca. 1928. Drawing. Published in William Seabrook, *The
Magic Island* (New York: Literary Guild of America, 1929). Image used by permission of
Margie King Barab.

Haiti during the U.S. occupation (1915–34) gave way to greater aspirations
to document and ethnographically record firsthand experiences in Haiti
in the 1930s and 1940s. Such encounters, however, were still shaded by,
and in dialogue with, earlier primitivistic assumptions.

Alexander King's first artistic encounter with Haiti begins one year
before *The Magic Island*, with a series of illustrations for the 1928 Boni and
Liveright special edition of Eugene O'Neill's play *The Emperor Jones*. Many
literary scholars and historians have discussed the Haiti-inspired elements
that undergird this innovative play. I will not review their analysis here,

Figure 2. Francis Bruguiere, *Charles Sidney Gilpin as Emperor Brutus Jones*, (Provincetown Playhouse, 1920). Acetate negative. Photo by Vandamm Studio ©The New York Public Library for the Performing Arts.

Figure 3. Alexander King, *The Emperor Jones, Scene One*, ca. 1928. Drawing. Published in Eugene O'Neill, *The Emperor Jones* (New York: Boni and Liveright, 1928). Image used by permission of Margie King Barab.

but suffice it to say that O'Neill links the play to the U.S. occupation of Haiti by describing the play's setting as "an island in the West Indies as yet not self-determined by White Marines." Moreover, O'Neill acknowledged taking inspiration from biographical details of Haiti's King Christophe and President Sam (Gelb and Gelb, 438–39; Hanson, 23–43). And as the historian Mary Renda has shown, the play is a meditation on race, imperialism, primitivism, and national identity at the crossroads of Haiti-U.S. interactions (Renda, 196–212).

Inspired by the play's innovations, racial subject, and drama, many artists created their own interpretations of *The Emperor Jones*. They also capitalized on the play's popularity for publishing opportunities. Artistic renderings usually mirrored standard publicity photographs: well-known actors posed in the full military costume of the play's opening scene (fig. 2). Alexander King's illustrations for *The Emperor Jones* are unusual in that they do not portray a specific actor (fig. 3). King does, however, still borrow the publicity photographs' common visual vocabulary of tightly framed subject and dramatic lighting. Like the original photograph of Charles Gilpin, King's lounging enthroned emperor appears haughty, fearless, and without a neck. In the Gilpin photograph, this stems from the camera angle and the actor's slouched pose. King takes this neckless precedent and uses it to accentuate the brute nature of the emperor's column-like head with rough-hewn exaggerated features. King also gives the intelligent, cunning, and driven Brutus Jones an impossibly small cranium.

It is not shocking that King's circa 1928 drawing recycles long-standing racist caricature. That King ended up creating these illustrations, however, reveals what in the 1920s constituted credentials for producing "authentic" likenesses of the racial Other. The edition's book jacket justifies the selection of King as illustrator. It proclaims King as one of America's rising young artists (King was just twenty-eight at the time), then defensively adds:

> When he returned from a trip to Africa, with truly extraordinary drawings of negro types we felt that the long looked for illustrator of THE EMPEROR JONES had appeared. . . . Mr. O'Neill, on seeing the first sketches, expressed his admiration and his keen satisfaction with Mr. King's interpretations.

Though the book jacket assures us of the little-known illustrator's ordained authority, King's later memoir deconstructs the dust jacket's enthusiastic approval. A dejected aspiring painter, King had turned to book illustrating, a field that he noted accepted artists of lesser talent. Otto Kahn, an international banker and art patron, took pity on King and decided to send him to Paris for a year to develop in the traditional footsteps of the great modernists. King, however, quickly ditched Paris for the cheaper and more mysterious Tunis. There, however, he fell ill almost immediately, and it seems that he never traveled farther into the African continent. Nevertheless, upon his return, he was determined to illustrate *The Emperor Jones* and believed that his brief sketching excursion made him "peculiarly qualified" (King, *Mine Enemy Grows Older*, 223–24, 329).

King knew that Liveright planned to publish illustrated limited editions of O'Neill's plays and had yet to select an artist. Scheming that the author's approval would guarantee him the job, King developed an elaborate plan to meet O'Neill, eventually cornering him on March 14, 1927, at the Liveright offices. King introduced himself as an artist who had recently returned from Africa with "thousands and thousands of drawings of Negroes." King then escorted O'Neill to a nearby office, where three finished *Emperor Jones* oil paintings and around fifty drawings conveniently waited. King's autobiography proudly records O'Neill's response: "'I think they're very striking,' he said. 'And I'm glad to see that you understand that Negroes are not just white people with blackened up faces, that their humor, their dignity and their sorrows have all been conditioned by their present tragic status in this world of ours'" (King, *Mine Enemy Grows Older*, 332).

King's quotation of O'Neill alludes to both the artist's and the author's personal framing of the complex cultural term "primitivism." The international vogue of primitivism, which reached its popular height during the 1920s, combined pseudoscientific notions of race with a new positive valuing of, and expanded interest in, cultures deemed "primitive" in comparison to modern Western cultures. Primitivism also propelled the popularization and commodification of cultural blackness, which, among other aspects, was believed to offer a greater connection to emotions, spirituality, sexual potency, and the unconscious from which modern (white) society had lost touch owing to hyperindustrialization and civilization (Clifford, 901; Lemke, 25). The U.S. military occupation greatly elevated the visibility of Haiti to the American public and made the island a popular foil to the United States in primitivism's cultural binaries: white/black, rich/poor, civilized/uncivilized, rational/irrational and mysterious, and so on. This also allowed Haiti to serve as a convenient vehicle for wider conversations and concerns, from emerging discourses on the role and culture of U.S. imperialism to African American dreams of

Pan-African coalition and agitation for more civil rights within the United States (Renda; Thompson).

O'Neill embraced primitivism as a way to critique the modernist era. O'Neill's granting of a fuller range of emotions despite a "tragic status in this world" led to an embrace of greater racial equality. That O'Neill assigned *The Emperor Jones*'s star role to an African American actor was highly progressive for the time (Charles Gilpin broke the mainstream theater's color line for serious drama in his origination of the title role with the Provincetown Players in 1920) and opened up space for "dignity" and "sorrow" rather than just comedic roles for black actors. Additionally, as made manifest in *The Emperor Jones* and other plays, especially *The Hairy Ape*, O'Neill employed primitivism's stereotypes of African-derived cultures as a vehicle to address the sense of "pervasive alienation" and displacement that was the underside of fast-paced industrialized society (Eisen, 56). Furthermore, O'Neill used the black body as a vehicle to search for the primal unconscious to be found in all human beings in the face of what he described as "the impelling, inscrutable forces behind life" (cited in Eisen, 58).[2]

Alexander King's illustrations, however, show how primitivism's ability to critique could also devolve into base racist stereotypes. With O'Neill's professed approval, Liveright reluctantly acknowledged that King's "pretty extreme" artwork had "the right feeling for the play" and awarded the artist the commission (King, *Mine Enemy Grows Older*, 331–33). King's answer to the play's expressionistic qualities and psychological terror was a graphic style that compressed space and dissolved the setting into claustrophobic patterns to express the protagonist's visions and emotions. It is difficult, however, to get beyond King's "extreme types," a recycling of racist caricatures: distorted facial features, enormous lips, bulbous heads with diminished craniums, and apelike qualities. In offering "the right feeling " and not a vision of a famous actor, King's problematic images mirror many of the underlying racist and primitivizing aspects of the play itself. For example, instinct and emotion waylay Brutus Jones long before his subjects. Slipping easily into his racial past, Jones confirmed for his 1920s audience the easy atavism of a purportedly less-evolved race.

Surprisingly, African American cultural leaders like W. E. B. Du Bois and Alain Locke remained mostly silent about the problematic content of O'Neill's drama and its implications for African American representation. They held damning criticism of the play's racial and social implications at bay, at least for a time, in favor of championing the breakthrough of having an African American actor appear onstage in a serious lead role. Like the common publicity stills, their commentary focused predominantly on just the leading actor (Johnson, 4; Du Bois, 290).[3] Alain Locke used *The Emperor Jones* as a central example in his February 1926 *Theatre Arts Monthly* essay "The Negro and the American Stage." Locke highlighted the problems of the limited and stereotypical roles assigned to blacks by (mostly) white writers, propelled by popular taste for black minstrelsy. But in spite of this history, Locke then argued that it would be African American actors, rather than African American writers, who would first provide the transfusion of folk arts needed to create a thriving and serious national theater. Although Locke suggested that stereotypes of blacks as "natural born actors" are problematic, he still championed their naturalness over the mannerisms of "polite" (white) theater and noted that the gift of blacks to American drama is "the gift of a temperament" (112). Locke's main example for championing African American actors was the phenomenal success of Charles Gilpin, and later Paul Robeson, in *The Emperor Jones* (114).

Locke, however, then steered his racial uplift and nationalistic program away from the white-authored play and perhaps shocked his readers by suggesting that the greater possibilities for a national theater resided not in the serious dramatic talents of writers like O'Neill but in the current vogue for musical comedies with African American performers born out of the minstrel tradition and vaudeville. Locke also proposed that the flowering of serious dramatic American art could find its inspiration through African subject matter, finding in it "elemental beauty," "inherent color and emotionalism," "freedom from body-hampering dress," and "odd and tragic and mysterious overtones." Then, as proof that the U.S. theater would move in this direction, with all its dramatic possibilities, Locke again offered *The Emperor Jones* as evidence: "No recent playgoer with the spell of Brutus Jones in the forest underbrush still upon his imagination will need much persuasion about this" ("Negro and the American Stage," 119). Locke viewed the African American Brutus Jones lost in a West Indian forest as proof of the dramatic possibilities of African inspiration for building a mature national theater in the United States. Conflating and eliding the subtle play of imperialistic national identity and cultural difference within *The Emperor Jones*, Locke attempted to negotiate the play's complex primitivism to forward his aesthetic program that used the fine arts to call for (and attempt to bring about) a redefinition of national self, one that would recognize the important contributions of African Americans.

Figure 4. Aaron Douglas, untitled drawing, ca. 1926. Published in Alain Locke,
"The Negro and the American Stage," *Theatre Arts Monthly*, February 1926, 117.
© Heirs of Aaron Douglas/Licensed by VAGA, New York, NY.

Locke's ostensibly contradictory statements claim the language of primitivism but also attempt to reshape and expand its discourse. As the spokesman for the burgeoning New Negro movement, Alain Locke wielded the cultural tools that the era handed him: foremost was the era's fascination with primitivism and a self-conscious search to establish a U.S. culture that could compete with the elite cultural wealth of Europe and its developing modernism. Although primitivism reinforced several racial stereotypes, Locke used the era's popular interest in peoples of African descent both to build racial pride and to awaken the white mainstream to the long-standing and large contributions of African Americans to U.S. culture and society.

Locke and other New Negro cultural leaders also pushed *The Emperor Jones* as progressive black subject matter and an opportunity for young African American artists. Aaron Douglas, who would become the New Negro Renaissance's leading visual artist, received one of his early career breaks by creating two illustrations of *The Emperor Jones* for Locke's essay in *Theatre Arts Monthly*.[4] The first drawing presents a haughty enthroned emperor (fig. 4). Composed of silhouettes and dynamic patterns, this drawing exemplifies Douglas's early graphic style. Like Locke's writing, Douglas's drawing walks a fine line between an original modernist critique and a celebratory primitivism that reinscribes racial caricature. With his protruding white lips and indecorous positioning, Douglas's enthroned emperor appears to be a jigging blackface minstrel; the young artist seems to have imagined exactly what King said that O'Neill decried: a burned-corked comedic actor.[5] But as argued through Locke's text, such antecedents can be viewed as innovative sources for renewed artistry.

The *Theatre Arts Monthly*'s lengthy captions for Douglas's images, which are noted as "interpretive designs" rather than mere illustrations, belie an anxiousness to show that the hard-edged, simplified silhouettes are a deliberate and progressive modernist approach. The first caption, which accompanies the enthroned emperor, explains that the "young Negro artist" has used a technique of "arbitrary contrast of black masses and white spaces" and "clash of broken line" that is "highly expressive" and "recapture[s] the dynamic quality of that tragedy of terror." The second caption further explains that the illustrations show "an utter simplicity of means, yet with no sacrifice of psychological verisimilitude," and concludes that Douglas's "sharply defined sense of dramatic design" is a "power [that] is one often missing among men of greater technical skill but less vivid imagination" (Locke, "Negro and the American Stage," 117–18). Douglas's design elements challenge the viewer to look more closely at this seemingly simple drawing as he offers his own interpretation of the role of Brutus Jones rather than producing a more naturalistic rendering of a famous actor. The lengthy explanatory captions, however, reveal a fear that the periodical's mostly white readership would misinterpret Douglas's modernist visual strategies as the unskilled simplicity of a minority artist. Douglas himself had reservations about incorporating an African-inspired abstraction—modernist primitivism's early source of visual inspiration—into his own artwork. Both Locke and the German-born Winold Reiss, Douglas's Harlem art mentor, encouraged Douglas to look to his African heritage for inspiration. Reflecting on Reiss's enthusiasm for primitivism in a 1973 interview, Douglas noted, "He was interested in . . . getting me to translate this black thing that nobody had any notion about. . . . And I didn't either, as an artist. And, not only didn't have a notion, but wasn't really sympathetic toward it." Adding, "They [most likely referring also to Locke and Reiss] insisted so vehemently that I finally thought that maybe there is something to this thing. This primitive thing" (Shockley). For their part, Reiss and Locke understood that the artists of the European avant-garde at the turn of the century had made themselves into modernists in part through studying African sculpture (Lemke, 47; Flam). They wanted the young Douglas to reclaim modernism's inspiration and style as his own personal prerogative.[6] As an academically trained, college-educated artist, Douglas recognized that there were benefits but also pitfalls for the minority artist in adopting modernist primitivism as a visual strategy over a more traditional naturalism. Foremost was that his audience might mis-construe his intent and assume that he, as a minority artist, was atavis-tically regressing like Brutus Jones, rather than intentionally choosing a simplified abstraction as a modernist strategy.

To break into the art world, both King and Douglas had to engage with the vogue of primitivism and its shallow notions of blackness. *The Emperor Jones* was a highly popular vehicle for such engagement. Mary Renda has pointed out that *The Emperor Jones*'s complex national, racial, and cultural ambiguities created a modernist text that "helped to launch Haiti on a new phase of its career in U.S. American culture—for better and for worse" (200). Haiti's "new career" in U.S. culture during the late 1920s involved white travelers following Brutus Jones into the forest to experi-ence the throbbing drums and atavistic release of Vodou. Such travelers returned to tell their tales through sensational, illustrated travelogues. And here we find again the illustrations of Alexander King and Aaron Douglas, each taking another step closer to Haiti.

Illustrated travelogues were key in propagating images of Haiti to a wide audience. William Seabrook's *The Magic Island* (1929) led the way, becoming the era's most popular and best-selling example (Gregory, 169). More fictional accounts, such as the French diplomat-turned-travel-writer Paul Morand's *Black Magic* (1929), complemented Seabrook's standard. Morand arrived in Haiti during same period as Seabrook (winter 1927) and published his English translation just months after *The Magic Island*. Both authors use several strategies within their texts to present an authen-tic and authoritative account of Haiti, but both also deliberately blur the line between what is known and what is imagined. This is accomplished not only through literary constructions and conceits but also through the works' accompanying illustrations. King illustrated Seabrook's *The Magic Island*, and Douglas illustrated Morand's *Black Magic*.

Seabrook's ethnography is romantic and paternalistic, and he sexualizes and exoticizes Haitians. Manifestos to primitivism and dramatic flourishes aside, however, today's reader may find the text relatively mundane. Indeed, Seabrook does often achieve a solid ethnography. The noted anthropologist Harold Courlander deemed the work "a personal adventure story," but one that was "better researched than some of the books that came in its wake" (62). Rather, it is the book's illustrations that are its most contentious aspect. That the publisher assumed that King's memorable images would also help popularize the book seems clear. *The Magic Island* contains twenty drawings by Alexander King. Fourteen appear in the book's first two parts, which deal with Seabrook's investigations and observations of Vodou and additional outlying cult practices.[7] These are the sections most easily exploited by King's penchant for the extreme. In turn, all of Seabrook's own documentary photographs are pushed to the back appendix, allowing the reader to encounter King's imagined explorations before viewing Seabrook's visual documentation.

The style of the drawings, of course, is just as important as their distribution. In his autobiography, King proudly proclaimed, "Everyone concerned knew perfectly well that the blatant shock value of my drawings had had a decided influence on the [book's] quite phenomenal sales" (*Mine Enemy Grows Older*, 242).[8] Although impossible to quantify, the boast seems valid. King's deliberately enigmatic frontispiece draws the reader into Seabrook's adventure (fig. 5). Wearing a wide-brimmed hat and shapeless black frock, a hunched and leaning figure clutches a cross in his skeletal hands. Small black eyes peer from just below the hat's brim and are nearly lost in the vertical ridges King incorporates into most of his Africanized faces to give them the quality of a wood-carved mask. This discomforting figure is made all the more shocking by being shown riding on the back of a rolling-eyed goat, picking its way through a jumbled pile of bones. The cross clutched in the rider's hands makes the viewer wonder about the religious nature of the scene and encourages the reading of the swaying poses of the background figures gathered around a fire as gestures of ecstatic prayer in a religious ceremony. But what type of ceremony? Wrapped in a velvety blackness, King's drawings invoke a mysterious, if not sinister, explanation. The piled bones suggest a religion of ritualistic sacrifice, and their lack of differentiation or skulls leaves the possibility open for either animal or human remains.

Figure 5. Alexander King, "Here are deep matters, not easily to be dismissed by crying blasphemy," ca. 1928. Drawing. Published in William Seabrook, *The Magic Island* (New York: Literary Guild of America, 1929). Image used by permission of Margie King Barab.

This image plays on popular assumptions of the nature of Haiti: a nation of African descendants ruled by religious beliefs that have debased Christianity through an incorporation of spirit worship and blood sacrifice. The caption, "Here are deep matters, not easily to be dismissed by crying blasphemy," provides no explanation. Rather, it chides the viewer not to discount immediately either the image or the book until one has read a little deeper: what first appears to be profane could indeed be sacred. But it is the thrilling mystery, not understanding, that seems most lasting. King's shadowy figures reside in the memory long after the details of Seabrook's ethnographic explanations have faded.

The caption is a quote from page 20 of Seabrook's text, and the page number is notated under the image. In fact, most of the illustrations either are placed in direct relationship to the text from which their caption is derived, or cite a page number. This notational strategy makes it seem as if the image directly corresponds to the text, lending greater credence, if subconsciously, to King's imaginative drawings. Even if the viewer moves to check the corresponding text (in the case of the frontispiece, a passage about the deep but seemingly incongruent connections between Christianity and Vodou), the viewer may allow King symbolic license, believing that his art may still get at the heart of the text's meaning beyond what mere documentary realism could accomplish. This argument was put forth by the only contemporary reviewer to discuss the illustrations beyond just a passing remark, noting:

> Their mood and manner are strikingly congruent with the themes they
> depict, but a slight touch of unreal grotesqueness lends them "psychic
> distance" and keeps their ugliness from being painful. The objectification
> of any human emotion is a work of art. These drawings do not objectify joy,
> and hence they are not "beautiful," but they are very moving objectifications
> of horror. (Montague, 2)

The reviewer's cautious justification of King's extreme forms and stark style parallels the explanatory captions included with Douglas's illustrations for *The Emperor Jones*. Such validation, though, may give King too much credit for a conscious representative strategy, which he flippantly referred to as "blatant shock value." Most reviewers of the time simply labeled the illustrations "grotesque" or "inane and merely vulgar" or said nothing at all (Saxon, 713; Robbins, 70; Locke, "Review," 190).[9]

But beyond extreme figures, King does have a visual strategy: to visualize misunderstandings. King often illustrates passages of Seabrook's text where a deliberate rupture occurs, calling attention to the difference in impressions made by the participant-observer author and what an outsider might construe. The frontispiece instigates this tension, recognizing the reader as an outsider—a noninitiate, as it were—even as it invites the reader on a journey toward uncovering "great mysteries." This visual strategy is also what we find in the book's most infamous illustration, which opened this essay (see fig. 1). Its notorious caption is drawn from Seabrook's description of the inaccurate impressions made by a "literary-traditional white stranger" spying on a Vodou ceremony from the bushes.

In this passage, Seabrook relates that the hidden voyeur would have thought that he was witnessing "all the wildest tales of Voodoo fiction justified" (Seabrook, 42).[10] Excised from the context of Seabrook's prose and visualized through King's caricatures, the caption takes on a life of its own, making the mistaken impression more memorable than Seabrook's comparative explanation. King's strategy of visual misunderstandings, however, ultimately enforces a long-standing paradox in U.S. representations of Haiti: the more a work professes to explain the "truth" of Haiti, the more it seems to make the republic ineffable and unknowable.

In the wake of *The Magic Island*'s success, Seabrook gained entry into elite circles. The famous French travel writer Paul Morand became one of his newest acquaintances (and would later write the preface for the French translation of *The Magic Island*). Morand himself had just completed his own popular work of black primitivism, *Magie noire* (1928), a collection of eight fictional stories about various peoples of African descent. The illustrated translation, *Black Magic*, hit U.S. bookstores just months after *The Magic Island* became a sensation. Morand's work, in turn, provided Aaron Douglas the opportunity to illustrate a more directly Haiti-inspired narrative. Yet also like King, Douglas worked with a textual source that continued to represent Haiti through a popular primitivism.

Morand's vignette on Haiti, "The Black Tsar," traces the rise and fall of Occide, a mulatto Haitian intellectual who decries both the U.S. occupation and his apathetic countrymen. His gloomy anger and inferiority complex lead him to embrace socialism. When he is finally spurred into action, though, Occide singlehandedly battles the U.S. occupation by bombing the American Club. He then flees to the mountains, where he lives the life of a Haitian peasant. There he relishes hard manual labor propelled by work songs and finds among his adopted fellow peasants "the sum and substance of Africa implanted" (Morand, *Black Magic*, 89). But soon growing restless, Occide follows the sound of drumming to a voodoo ceremony one night, where, as a kneeling worshipper, he envisions his own decapitation. This experience inspires him to become trained in Haiti's folk religion. Morand's fast-moving yet highly detailed narrative concludes with a vision of a postoccupation Haiti where Occide has become the new dictator after the withdrawal of the U.S. Marines. Occide then becomes infected by communism, which compounds his frivolous despotism. Haiti falls into despair. The United States reinvades, and this time the Haitians welcome the Americans as liberators.

Douglas illustrates the most dramatic moment of Morand's narrative: Occide's transformative experience at the moonlit voodoo ceremony

Figure 6. Aaron Douglas, *The Black Tsar* (illustration for *Black Magic* by
Paul Morand), ca. 1928. Gouache and pencil on paper board, 14¼ x 9½ in.
Gift of Susie R. Powell and Franklin R. Anderson, North Carolina Museum
of Art. © Heirs of Aaron Douglas/Licensed by VAGA, New York, NY.

(fig. 6). The lightening tonal gradations highlight the heart of the action.
Occide crouches before the presiding priest and "executioner." A concentric circle highlights Occide's head, tonally severing it from his silhou-
etted body. Douglas transposes the severed head to the immediate left,
where it appears at the center of the brightest concentric circle held over
a ceremonial cauldron, an element *not* included in Morand's detailed
description. By centering the head over the pot, Douglas alludes to ritualistic cannibalism. Interestingly, while Morand includes cannibalism as
the climax to another vignette, Douglas obscures it in that story's illustration and displaces it onto "The Black Tsar." Douglas thus reinscribes this

common stereotype onto Haiti. Additionally, although Morand describes the event taking place within an "amphitheatre of rocks," Douglas centers his dramatically backlit ceremony within a diamond-framed silhouette of thickets and a canopy of foliage, invoking the trope of Haiti's impenetrable jungle. Douglas's illustration reveals that African Americans were just as susceptible as any other U.S. American to the ubiquitous stereotypes applied to Haiti.

In the end, King's and Douglas's travelogue illustrations accentuate the deep gulf between what Vodou actually is and what outsiders think they know about so-called voodoo. In "blood-maddened, sex-maddened, god-maddened," King's illustration of a voodoo ceremony places the viewer in direct confrontation with the imagined writhing adherents, who both invite and repel. The closed frame of Douglas's illustration, in comparison, holds the viewer at a great distance. Indeed, the viewer feels as if he or she is positioned observing from the bushes, literally becoming Seabrook's "literary-traditional white stranger."

The years of the U.S. occupation proved to be a watershed period for establishing in Americans an intense cultural fascination with Haiti, in particular the country's revolutionary history and religious practices, with the latter taking the form of a more generalized and sensationalistic understanding of voodoo. Both *The Magic Island* and "The Black Tsar" participated in the cultural commodification of Haiti and pushed primitivism to its end point.[11] More importantly, however, texts like Seabrook's and Morand's also provoked a host of academics and artists to go to Haiti to counterbalance these imaginative representations with direct experiences that highlighted the political, social, and economic realities of Haiti as a contemporary modern nation. And here, in the late 1930s, King and Douglas would arrive in Haiti with one more artistic parallel.

In late 1936, King found himself as an early associate for the new pictorial weekly *Life* magazine, hired because he understood the value of pictures and had displayed the audacity to criticize directly Henry Luce's initial test issues of the magazine (King, *Mine Enemy Grows Older*, 195). Growing restless after a year, King began searching for photographic news stories that would require him to make a "good long trip." In October 1937 he received private information about a "fierce but secret massacre" that had taken place on the border between Haiti and the Dominican Republic. The news was reported only in "skimpy accounts" in the press because, according to King, native correspondents on both sides of the border had been put under arrest, presumably to suppress the story. In what Haitians would come to know as *kout kout-a* (the stabbing), the dictator Rafael Trujillo ordered the murder of all ethnic Haitians living in the Dominican Republic's northwestern frontier. From October 2 to 8, Trujillo's troops, aided by some local leaders and civilian reserves, rounded up and slaughtered an estimated fifteen to twenty thousand ethnic Haitians (Turits, 590). King traveled to Haiti the following month with the photographer Rex Hardy Jr. and, in his memoir, describes smuggling out the film. The Haitian government tried to prevent any pictures and documentation of the massacre, fearing that it was Trujillo's provocation to war and a popular outcry would force Haiti to take the bait (King, *Mine Enemy Grows Older*, 195, 300–306).

In the face of those who had wanted to suppress the news, it was photographs, not just the oral testimonies of survivors and frontier witnesses, that could stand as proof that such an immense act of state violence had occurred. King and Hardy returned with images of the aftermath, which they published in a photo-essay titled "The U.S. Is Invited to Arbitrate a Massacre in Its Front Garden" in the December 6 issue of *Life*. The photo-essay appeared as part of the popular section "The Camera Overseas" and was sandwiched between "Stalin Shows His Daughter" and "King Leopold Crosses Channel," making it the most dramatic news event covered in that week's issue. The essay begins with a map of the island and a photograph of Haiti's iconic national palace, below which appeared a photograph of the U.S. minister Ferdinand Mayer meeting with Haitian president Sténio Vincent to negotiate Haiti's response. The facing page carries Hardy's most dramatic photographs: a long line of refugees receiving aid at Ouanaminthe, a young boy with distinct three-pronged knife scars striating his scalp, and another boy with his head and neck covered in bandages from fresh injuries sustained from a November 11 reprisal. King would later brag that the Dominican consulate cried libel concerning the massacre until *Life* published the boys' photographs (King, *Mine Enemy Grows Older*, 305).

In his work to call attention to the vast massacre of Haitian and Haitian-descended Dominicans, we could argue that King redresses in part some of his past extreme imaginings that did so much to shape U.S. perceptions of Haiti. He used visual evidence gathered onsite to influence a positive outcome for contemporary Haiti. Ensuring that the event came to the attention of the American public is certainly to his credit, and in this work he joined numerous anthropologists, social scientists, writers, and artists who arrived in Haiti in the 1930s and 1940s to document the nation and provide a counterbalance to more popular imaginings. It is in the text and the photo-essay's remaining two pages, however, where the restless and dramatizing hand of the King of old remains.

Life magazine was innovative in its minimization of text and privileging of large-scale and numerous photographs to relate stories. It split its focus between dramatic current events and society pages that preferred the pleasant and inoffensive. The two paragraphs and brief captions allotted to the Haitian massacre in "The U.S. Is Invited to Arbitrate a Massacre in Its Front Garden" reveal these split goals. For example, the closing three sentences of the refugee photograph's caption swing widely from drama to general interest and back: "News of the massacre is being suppressed in Haiti. The trees are flamboyants. Each of these peasants lost half a dozen kinsmen in the massacre by machete" (75). Similarly, while the article's opening two pages carry the "proof" of the massacre, upon turning the page, we encounter photographs of Port-au-Prince's glittering elite and a dramatic full-page portrait of a hougan, a Vodou priest.

As a follow-up, the next issue of *Life* features Haiti as the magazine's central photographic essay. It begins by invoking the massacre: a picturesque photograph of the Massacre River and a woman watering her horse, but with a caption that notes that earlier the east bank had run over with the blood of Haitians slaughtered by Dominican guards. This is enough to anchor the essay in current affairs, but the remainder focuses on "Black Haiti": a view of Haiti's architectural wonder the Citadel, a reprint of Zora Neale Hurston's first ever photographed zombie, and a series of fourteen photographs taking the viewer through various aspects of a Vodou ceremony ("Black Haiti," 26–31).

Certainly these two articles fail to treat the horrible massacre in a sustained and empathetic way. But though the photo-essay quickly moves to what must have been deemed more entertaining subject matter, we strangely do in the end come to a type of corrective for King's earlier representative excursions. The December 13 issue contains many images that have direct parallels to King's earlier illustrations. Compare, for example, King's *Magic Island* representation of a *mamaloi*, a female high priestess, to the later *Life* photograph. In the earlier illustration, "the *mamaloi* in a scarlet robe," King pushes his figure to the front of the picture plane, filling the entire right side of the composition with her lurking, glowing body (fig. 7). Stern and haunting with King's characteristically exaggerated features, the *mamaloi* grips an adorned staff tightly in her extended right hand. Her gesture challenges the viewer while also framing three

Figure 7. Alexander King, " . . . the *mamaloi* in a scarlet robe," ca. 1928. Drawing. Published in William Seabrook, *The Magic Island* (New York: Literary Guild of America, 1929). Image used by permission of Margie King Barab.

Figure 8. Rex Hardy Jr., "The *mambo* is a female priest who leads the singing. Once ritual is under way, she is more important than the *hungan*." Photograph published in "Black Haiti: Where Old Africa and the New World Meet," *Life* 3, no. 24 (December 13, 1937): 30.

male drummers, whom King stacks in the middle ground of the left side, allowing just two of the ritual drumheads to allude to their ceremonial role. In the *Life* magazine sequence, we also find a *mamaloi* placed right of center with a male drummer positioned on the far left of the composition (fig. 8). Hardy's photograph captures the priestess in a moment of relaxed motion as she turns in concentration without acknowledging the presence of the viewer. The caption explains her role within the ritualistic sequence of the full photographic essay: "The *mambo* is a female priest who leads the singing. Once ritual is under way, she is more important than the *hungan*" ("Black Haiti," 30). Rather than the mystery and drama of a secret ceremony that emerges from an inky backdrop, King's final excursion into Vodou presents a sequence of orchestrated images that actually help to introduce his audience to the dynamic elements of this profound New World religion.

Completing Douglas's artistic lockstep with King, the painter arrived in Haiti almost exactly one year later, with his own documentary goals and contradictory results. In 1937, Douglas received support from the Julius Rosenwald Fund to create a "contemporary portrait of the American Negro" through "racial types and characters" and "Negro environments." Douglas argued: "I am sure that a sympathetic, realistic portrayal would go far to raise the self esteem and self respect of our people . . . [and] help to awaken the creative urge of Negro youth" (Douglas, "Plan of Work"). After a year of painting landscapes and representative types in the U.S. South, Douglas applied for an extension to continue the project in Haiti and hold an exhibition there. Douglas proposed to "record on canvas . . . people of all classes with an eye to revealing racial, social and economic patterns; and pictures of scenes and landmarks, old and new" ("Plan of Work [renewal]").

Once in Haiti, Douglas seems to have abandoned his first goal of capturing a range of people and instead seems to have focused exclusively on his second goal of landscapes. The viewer swoops into Douglas's *Haitian Landscape (Haitian Cathedral Scene)* from an elevated position (fig. 9). The painting appears to be from the point of view of an upper balcony of an adjacent neighborhood, perhaps even from the Hotel Bellevue, where Douglas stayed while in Port-au-Prince. The canopies of the landscape's foreground trees act as visual stepping-stones to the buildings in the middle ground. Rather than serving as compositional devices, the trees actually obscure the structures, especially Port-au-Prince's 1915 Romanesque revival new cathedral. A figure seems to be placed underneath the shadow

Figure 9. Aaron Douglas, *Haitian Landscape (Haitian Cathedral Scene)*, 1938. Oil on canvas. Reproduced in Alain Locke, *The Negro in Art* (1940; New York: Hacker Art Books, 1968), 52. © Heirs of Aaron Douglas/ Licensed by VAGA, New York, NY.

Figure 10. Aaron Douglas, *Untitled Landscape (Waterfront Park)*, 1938. Oil on canvas, 20 x 24 in. © Heirs of Aaron Douglas/Licensed by VAGA, New York, NY. Image courtesy of ACA Galleries, New York.

of a tree in the lower left, and another tiny figure can be seen striding across the nearby green. While certainly Port-au-Prince in 1938 was not the overcrowded capital that it is today, Douglas presents a city emptied of its bustling life. In *Untitled (Landscape)*,[12] Douglas again produces an elevated view, reducing the waterfront park and wharf to a canopy of trees that compete with the yellow-roofed pavilion (fig. 10). Only a lone blue vehicle alludes to the presence of a people Douglas was fascinated by but seems to have refrained from representing after his arrival.

The main record of the body of work that Douglas produced while in Haiti comes from an exhibition in the following spring at the ACA Gallery in New York. The exhibition brochure lists ten *Scenes from Haiti*.[13] Of these Haitian works, I have located only three landscapes.[14] It is, of course, impossible to know the exact composition of the remaining paintings, though it seems likely that the majority were landscapes, as suggested by their grouping under the title *Scenes*. Additionally, Alain Locke reviewed the exhibition and also referred to the body of work as a "series of landscapes" (Locke, "Advance on the Art Front," 135). In contrast, Douglas's paintings of "racial types" are usually accompanied by titles suggestive of the specific sitters. The *New York Times* review of the exhibition does note "one or two portraits of Haitian types." From the exhibition list, however, these portrait types were probably the two works listed last, *The Street Urchin* and *Ex Slave*, which Douglas created the previous year during his Rosenwald fellowship in the U.S. South. Moreover, Douglas's correspondence with his wife Alta Sawyer Douglas also alludes to his abandonment of recording Haitian "people of all classes" closely. In one letter, Alta actually chided her husband for concentrating too much on landscapes and not working toward his other goal of capturing the Haitian people: "It would be a shame not to get a few of the outstanding Haitian types. The scenery, I'm sure will be most interesting, but it is also interesting to focus in what way particularly one group is different from another." Douglas resisted her pushing, however, and claimed in an article the following year that he had actually gone to Haiti specifically to paint landscapes, with no mention of the prior goal of documenting the people ("Color Shed").

It is impossible to know what Douglas experienced and felt, and why exactly he seems to have abandoned his project of documenting Haitian types. Parallels in his few extant paintings and oblique comments, however, offer a possible explanation. Douglas went to Haiti to embrace and document a contemporary culture, yet his resulting landscapes hold Haiti at a distance. This could be simply because he had problems negotiating subjects to sit for him, perhaps because of problems with the language, or even because of lack of time.¹⁵ Yet it could also be due to the artist's desire to smooth over difficult realities: not only the poverty, extreme class disparities, and decaying infrastructure that he would have observed, but also his experience of cultural differences that were perhaps a far cry from imagining Haiti's heroic past or expectations of an easy Pan-Africanist coalition. Alta had also written to encourage her husband to write thank-you notes to those who had provided his letters of introduction in Haiti. She recommended he include his "impressions of Haiti" but quickly added, "that is, the favorable ones," suggesting that Douglas's initial reports home were not completely positive (Douglas, October 5, 1938). Moreover, in a later interview, he noted, "There is room for much work and improvement in several respects in Haiti," but then added, "just as in other countries" ("Color Shed"). While it seems that he may have been privately critical of what he experienced, Douglas was nonetheless careful to avoid publicly giving a negative picture of Haiti.

His extant landscapes, which capture general topographic features but not intimate details, are a visual parallel. The Haitian landscapes are not blank wildernesses onto which notions of a primitive and Edenic space can be inscribed. Douglas makes sure to include the presence of modern structures to prove that the island is not a jungle paradise, redressing the reinscription in "The Black Tsar" of common stereotypes of Haiti. In fact, Douglas's distancing actually counters primitivism's close embrace of Haiti. Part of the most popularizing aspects of works like Seabrook's *The Magic Island* stemmed from the writer's claim to insert himself intimately inside the culture, usually to exoticizing and dramatic ends. In contrast to the intrusive detail of these earlier representations, Douglas's views maintain a discreet, impersonal distance.

For both King and Douglas, these projects would be their final public artistic interactions with Haiti.¹⁶ Each interaction had brought them closer to a contemporary reality. Each step along the way was also fraught with contradictions. But their ultimate arrival also exhibited a glimmer of redressing, if not redeeming, their past primitivizing extremes. If we return to King's photo-essay in the December 13 issue of *Life*, his text seems to be a direct rebuttal to our opening caption: "blood-maddened, sex-maddened, god-maddened . . ." He writes:

> Voodoo is not black magic. Neither is it, as most people suppose, a sense-less orgiastic cult accompanied by sex excesses and human sacrifice. It is a

religion with a precisely formulated ritual, with ancient chants and impressive symbolistic pageantry. It combines African paganism and Catholicism. It makes good sense to the Haitians, who practice it with humility and profound reverence. (28)

In the end, this examination is not meant to exonerate primitivism's more problematic aspects as reflected in King's and Douglas's early representations; these images did have significant repercussions on how Haiti came to be viewed within the U.S. social imagination. But rather than the silence or curt explanations these images have hitherto received, it is fruitful to examine and discuss their histories and representational strengths and failures. In examining the context and complexities of King's and Douglas's visioning and revisioning of Haiti longitudinally, it becomes possible to illuminate how individual artistic projects map themselves onto a wider public discourse entrenched in certain assumptions and habits of seeing. Moreover, each artist's return and re-presentation capture the era's evolving relationship with Haiti, from the titillating and extreme to more conscientious attempts to present positive documentation. In the decades following the U.S. military occupation of Haiti, although more direct and personal encounters attempted to expose some of the fissures and stereotypes found within primitivism's progressive modernist critique, these representations never quite fully escaped U.S. tastes for the more picturesque, exotic, and extreme aspects of Haitian culture. Although each artist clearly had his own artistic styles and strategies, the tight parallel of their careers exhibits a greater cultural dynamic of powerful presumptions about what the small Caribbean nation was and meant to U.S. cultural interests. Ultimately we learn as much, if not more, from such failures of vision as we do from successes.

NOTES

Initial research for this article was made possible through the support of the Henry Luce Foundation/American Council of Learned Societies' Doctoral Dissertation Fellowship in American Art, 2004–5. Research for its completion was supported in part by a grant from the Augustana Research and Artist Fund of Augustana College, Sioux Falls, South Dakota.

1. The anthropologist Steven Gregory and the historian Mary Renda have each provided the most in-depth scholarly engagement with Seabrook's work but offer only cursory comments on King's illustrations. See Gregory, 187; Renda, 252–53.

2. For a fuller discussion of O'Neill's primitivism, see Gagnon.

3. Du Bois opens by quoting harsh attacks on the play, thus suggesting the presence of strong public criticism by some African Americans, which would continue to grow. Surprisingly, the actor Paul Robeson's own writing is the period's closest engagement with (and defense of) the play's underlying racist primitivism. See Robeson, 368–70.

4. Recruited to Harlem during the previous summer by Charles S. Johnson, Douglas almost immediately became the signature visual artist of the New Negro Renaissance. In addition to illustrations for Johnson's National Urban League organ, *Opportunity*, Douglas also created illustrations for W. E. B. Du Bois's NAACP monthly, the *Crisis*. Locke took great interest in Douglas's career and used the young artist's drawings in many publications, including his famous anthology, and what would become the bible of the Harlem Renaissance, *The New Negro* (1925). For more on Douglas, see Earle; Kirschke.

5. A few scholars have noted how Douglas's enthroned emperor borrows heavily from the iconography of minstrelsy and a drawing by his Harlem teacher Winold Reiss, which appeared in the March 1925 issue of *Survey Graphic*. See Stewart, 60; Goeser, 224–25.

6. Locke most famously articulated the need for black American artists to look to Africa in his essay "Legacy of the Ancestral Arts," in his anthology *The New Negro*. Although Locke's and Reiss's pushing of African American artists to look to African art for inspiration was seemingly innovative, they were actually rather behind the times and were filtering their ideas of primitivism through European sources. By 1920, many of the European avant-garde viewed African art as old hat, "boring," and too "rational" and "naturalistic" (Flam, 12–14). Nevertheless Locke's ideas became (and in some respects remain) immensely influential. It is important to note, however, that not all African American artists accepted Locke's ideas. For example, Locke's Howard University colleague James Porter was passionately opposed to Locke's argument for claiming a cultural past in Africa.

7. Haitian Vodou is a complex amalgamation of many religious practices, both African derived, indigenous, and also influenced by Roman Catholicism. In English popular texts, the religion is commonly referred to as voodoo and is often reduced to a set of sensational superstitions. Throughout the chapter, I use the word "Vodou" to refer to Haiti's living and complex folk religion, and the word "voodoo" when I am referring to stereotypes of the religion.

8. King and Seabrook became friends after the success of the book, but King notes that their friendship always remained uneasy at best owing to Seabrook's jealousy of the role that King's illustrations played in achieving the book's fame and his fortune. King even recounts an incident where the vindictive Seabrook may have intentionally tried to drown him (242–44).

9. Given his concern for black representation, it is amazing that Locke's review omits any mention of the illustrations.

10. For further discussion of Seabrook's narrative voice and structural conceits, see Gregory, 186–87; Renda, 251–52.

11. On how occupied Haiti became a cultural commodity, see Renda, esp. 185–228.

12. Its original title may have been *Waterfront Park*, as recorded in "Exhibition of Haitian Paintings." See note 13.

13. "Exhibition of Haitian Paintings," April 2–15, 1939, ACA Gallery, 52 West Eighth Street, New York. Julius Rosenwald Fund Archives, Fisk University Franklin Library's Special Collections. The exhibition brochure lists ten *Scenes from Haiti*: (1) *Harbor Port au Prince*, (2) *Champs de Mars*, (3) *Kenskoff*, (4) *Going to Market*, (5) *Mango Tree*, (6) *Courtyard*, (7) *Shadowed Courtyard*, (8) *Haitian Cathedral Scene*, (9) *Mountains in Haiti*, (10) *Waterfront Park*. Two other paintings were also included in the exhibition: (11) *The Street Urchin* and (12) *Ex Slave*. These last two are "racial types" but were produced the year before while Douglas was painting on location in the United States. *Going to Market*, however, does suggests a canvas focused on racial types and most likely includes representations of the picturesque Haitian market woman, which had become an icon of artistic representation of Haiti by that time. Douglas's version may have formed the basis for his later *Haitian Mural* (see note 16).

14. In addition to the two landscapes that I discus here, a third, *Haitian Landscape* (1938), appeared in the 1966 exhibition "The Negro in American Art" at the Dickson Art Center, UCLA, and was auctioned by Swann Galleries, New York, on February 19, 2008, lot 21. The painting, a slightly elevated view, is dominated by two reaching palm trees that flank and tower over two small thatched huts. In the foreground, very small figures go about their daily business: a straw-hatted man bends, perhaps to tend to a garden plot, while a woman strides down a path to the right. At least one more woman is visible in front of the small hut on the right. See http://catalogue.swanngalleries.com/asp/fullCatalogue.asp?salelot=2136++++++21+&refno=++594999&saletype=.

15. Though Douglas had spent a year in France, it is unclear whether he felt comfortable communicating strictly in French. For the first part of his visit, however, he would have had the assistance of his good friend Arna Bontemps, who also held a Rosenwald grant for research in Haiti and was fluent in French. There may have been further difficulties, though, in communicating with the Kreyol-speaking majority, who were to be Douglas's subjects, though presumably contacts in Haiti could have assisted. Allowing time for painting, however, may have been the greater struggle. Douglas and Bontemps kept a full sightseeing and social schedule during their visit: they traveled to the citadel in the north and also to the Dominican Republic; they attended meetings and social gatherings with the cultural elite; and they gave presentations on African American art and culture. Such a schedule would have severely impacted his time to create finished paintings, as Douglas only remained in Haiti for about two months.

16. In what seems to have been the only time Douglas chose to revisit Haitian subject matter, he created *Haitian Mural* in 1942 for a home in Wilmington, Delaware (Earle, 42). In turn, King's fourth and final autobiography references a summer "during the mid-thirties" when he rented a home in a small mountain village just outside Port-au-Prince, where he composed a play about the Haitian Revolution, *The Color of Freedom*, which was never staged (King, *Is There a Life*, 308; Marjorie King Barab, personal e-mail correspondence, December 26, 2011).

WORKS CITED

"Black Haiti: Where Old Africa and the New World Meet." *Life* 3, no. 24 (December 13, 1937): 26–31.

Clifford, James. "Negrophilia." In *A New History of French Literature*, ed. Denis Hollier, 901–8. Cambridge: Harvard University Press, 1994.

"Color Shed When One Crosses into Mexico—Aaron Douglas." *The Call* (Kansas City), September 15, 1939. Fisk University Franklin Library's Special Collections. Aaron Douglas Collection. Box 8 clippings, folder 1, 1930–1949.

Courlander, Harold. "Recollections of Haiti in the 1930s and 40s." *African Arts* 23, no. 2 (April 1990): 60–70.

Douglas, Aaron. "Plan of Work." Fisk University Franklin Library's Special Collections. Julius Rosenwald Fund Archives. Box 408, folder 13, Aaron Douglas.

———. "Plan of Work" (renewal). March 1, 1938. Fisk University Franklin Library's Special Collections. Julius Rosenwald Fund Archives. Box 408, folder 13, Aaron Douglas.

Douglas, Alta. Letter to Aaron Douglas in Port-au-Prince, October 5, 1938. Schomburg Center for Research in Black Culture, New York Public Library. Aaron Douglas Papers.

———. Letter to Aaron Douglas in Port-au-Prince, October 25, 1938. Schomburg Center for Research in Black Culture, New York Public Library. Aaron Douglas Papers.

Du Bois, W. E. B. "Criteria of Negro Art." *Crisis* 32 (October 1926): 290.

Earle, Susan, ed. *Aaron Douglas: African American Modernist.* New Haven, CT: Yale University Press, 2007.

Eisen, Kurt. "Theatrical Ethnography and Modernist Primitivism in Eugene O'Neill and Zora Neale Hurston." *South Central Review* 25, no. 1 (Spring 2008): 56–73.

"Exhibition of Haitian Paintings." April 2–15, 1939. ACA Gallery. 52 West Eighth Street, New York, NY. Fisk University Franklin Library's Special Collections. Julius Rosenwald Fund Archives. Box 408, folder 13, Aaron Douglas.

Flam, Jack. Introduction to *Primitivism and Twentieth-Century Art*, ed. Jack Flam with Miriam Deutch, 1–22. Berkeley: University of California Press, 2003.

Gagnon, Donald. *Pipe Dreams and Primitivism: Eugene O'Neill and the Rhetoric of Ethnicity.* Ph.D. diss., University of South Florida, 2003. http://www.eoneill.com/library/pipedreams/contents.htm.

Gelb, Arthur, and Barbara Gelb. *O'Neill.* New York: Harper, 1962.

Goeser, Caroline. "'Not White Art Painted Black': African American Artists and the New Primitive Aesthetic, c. 1920–1935." Ph.D. diss., Rutgers, State University of New Jersey, 2000.

Gregory, Steven. "Voodoo, Ethnography, and the American Occupation of Haiti." In *Dialectical Anthropology*, vol. 2, ed. Christine Gailey, 169–207. Gainesville: University Press of Florida, 1992.

Hanson, Philip. "The Emperor Jones: Naturalistic Tragedy in Hemispheric Perspective." *American Drama* 5, no. 2 (1996): 23–43.

Johnson, James Weldon. "A Great Play and a Great Actor." *New York Age*, November 13, 1920, p. 4, col. 4.

King, Alexander. *Is There a Life after Birth?* New York: Simon and Schuster, 1963.

———. *Mine Enemy Grows Older*. New York: Simon and Schuster, 1958.

Kirschke, Amy. *Aaron Douglas: Art, Race, and the Harlem Renaissance.* Jackson: University Press of Mississippi, 1995.

Lemke, Sieglinde. *Primitivist Modernism: Black Culture and the Origins of Transatlantic Modernism*. Oxford: Oxford University Press, 1998.

Locke, Alain. "Advance on the Art Front." *Opportunity* 17 (May 1939): 135.

———. "The Negro and the American Stage." *Theatre Arts Monthly* (New York) 10, no. 2 (February 1926): 112–20.

———. *The New Negro*. New York: Albert and Charles Boni, 1925; Simon and Schuster, 1997.

———. "Review: 'The Magic Island.'" *Opportunity* 7 (June 1929): 190.

Montague, William Pepperell. "A Proud and Bloody Island: Review of *The Magic Island* by W. B. Seabrook." *New York Herald Tribune Books* 5, no. 16 (January 6, 1929): 1–2.

Morand, Paul. *Black Magic.* Trans. Hamish Miles. London: William Heinemann, 1929.

O'Neill, Eugene. *The Emperor Jones*. New York: Boni and Liveright, 1928.

Renda, Mary. *Taking Haiti: Military Occupation and the Culture of U.S. Imperialism, 1915–1940*. Chapel Hill: University of North Carolina Press, 2001.

Robbins, Frances Lamont. "Speaking of Books: A Week's Reading." *Outlook and Independent*, January 9, 1929, 70–71.

Robeson, Paul. "Reflections on O'Neill's Plays." *Opportunity* 2, no. 24 (December, 1924): 368–70.

Saxon, Lyle. "Voodoo in Haiti." *Bookman* 68, no. 6 (February 1929): 712–14.

Seabrook, William. *The Magic Island*. 1929. New York: Paragon House, 1989.

Shockley, Ann Allen. Interview with Aaron Douglas, November 19, 1973. Fisk University Franklin Library's Special Collections. Black Oral History Collection.

Stewart, Jeffrey. *To Color America: Portraits by Winold Reiss*. Washington, D.C.: Smithsonian Institution Press for the National Portrait Gallery, 1989.

"The U.S. Is Invited to Arbitrate a Massacre in Its Front Garden." *Life* 3, no. 23 (December 6, 1937): 75.

Thompson, Krista. "Preoccupied with Haiti: The Dream of Diaspora in African American Art, 1915–1942." *American Art* 21, no. 3 (Fall 2007): 74–97.

Turits, Richard Lee. "A World Destroyed, a Nation Imposed: The 1937 Haitian Massacre in the Dominican Republic." *Hispanic American Historical Review* 82, no. 3 (2002): 589–635.

7

Foreign Impulses in Annie Desroy's *Le Joug*

—Nadève Ménard

The Caribbean has long been recognized as a point of contact between several peoples. Over the years, this contact has taken various forms, ranging from violent conquest to peaceful cohabitation. The American occupation of Haiti, from 1915 to 1934, brought about brutal contact between two groups who had little previous experience with each other, Haitians and Americans. Many Haitian novels of the period reflect the societal turmoil caused by the occupation. The six novels that most directly represent the culture shocks of the time—Fernand Hibbert's *Les Simulacres* (1923), Léon Laleau's *Le Choc* (1932), Stéphen Alexis's *Le Nègre Masqué* (1933), Cléante Valcin's *La Blanche Négresse* (1934), Annie Desroy's *Le Joug* (1934), and Maurice Casséus' *Viejo* (1935)—all use romantic and sexual relationships as metaphors for the U.S. occupation of Haitian land.[1] Annie Desroy's *Le Joug*, published in Port-au-Prince in the final year of the U.S. occupation, presents certain particularities that distinguish it from other texts of the period; Desroy and her contemporary Cléante Valcin problematize gender and sexuality in more complex ways than their male counterparts. While examining Valcin remains outside the scope of this essay, looking at Desroy's novel shows how these female authors explore the ways in which nationalism is couched in gendered terms.[2] Furthermore, the narrative techniques deployed by Annie Desroy allow her to offer a nuanced portrayal of both Haitian and American characters.

Literary critics have often commented on the careful psychological development of foreign characters in *Le Joug*. An American, Colonel Harry Murray, is at the center of the plot, and Desroy even considered titling the novel *Murray l'indigénophile* (Desroy, 8). The American protagonist is known for his appreciation of natives and is presented in contrast to his predecessor, Colonel Kick, "réputé pour sa grossièreté et sa haine des noirs et qu'on accusait à tort ou à raison d'avoir provoqué la méfiance générale" (Desroy, 25). Murray is also presented in contrast to his wife Arabella, who is portrayed as a stereotypical racist. The other married couple in the novel is a Haitian one: Frédéric and Fernande Vernon, the Murrays' next-door neighbors. An analysis of the interactions between these two couples helps to elucidate the novel's racial and sexual politics. As Myriam Chancy explains in her article "Ayiti çé ter glissé: L'occupation américaine en Haïti et l'émergence de voix féminines en littérature haïtienne," "à travers deux couples, l'un américain et l'autre haïtien, Desroy examine la dynamique raciale, sexuelle et de classe pendant l'Occupation" (19). While I find Desroy's representation of class dynamics somewhat biased and superficial, I do agree that the ways in which she engages with issues of race, gender, and sexuality in the novel add depth to her portrayal of U.S.-Haitian relations. Relationships between members of the two groups as presented by Desroy—be they friendships or sexual liaisons—are clearly shown to be intricately embedded within the overarching political structure of the occupation, but also within the context of prevailing hierarchies of class, race, and gender.

Because the novel's focus is on group dynamics, not the development of an individual character, Desroy uses an omniscient narrator. This choice allows the reader access to the thoughts and actions of all the main characters. In illustrating the multilayered relationships that exist between Haitians and foreigners during the occupation, Desroy is one of very few authors to offer a sustained American perspective of the intervention. Yvette Tardieu Feldman explains that

> le propos implicite de l'auteur consistant à servir d'interprète entre Occupants et Occupés, la situation haïtienne est analysée selon l'optique d'un étranger, et la mentalité américaine est montrée en direct ainsi qu'à travers les réactions des observateurs haïtiens. Or ce point de vue de négociateur diplomatique place Annie Desroy en position minoritaire par rapport à ses confrères chez qui la haine de l'Occupant va de pair avec l'idéalisation de l'Occupé. (37)

Thus readers of *Le Joug* are able to view the Americans from a Haitian perspective and vice versa. Indeed, the American occupation is first evoked through Fernande Vernon's eyes. As she watches the Murray couple move into the house next door, Fernande thinks: "Seuls ces gens peuvent se payer les plus belles maisons du Pays. Et sa rancœur d'haïtienne non resignée monta en elle contre cette maudite Occupation qui s'imposait à son Pays, l'opprimant et l'appauvrissant" (Desroy, 17). The American occupation is thus immediately presented in unambiguously negative and oppositional terms, regardless of any subsequent sympathetic portrayal of individual Americans. In fact, my reading of *Le Joug* hinges on Fernande Vernon's perspective of her neighbors, Americans in general, and the occupation that has brought them to Haiti. In adopting this approach, I depart from traditional readings of the novel that insist on Colonel Murray's perspective and view him as a benevolent foreigner. In "Haitian Writers and the American Occupation: Literary Responses to a Political Crisis," Renée Larrier affirms that "what distinguishes *Le Joug* from other novels is its one sympathetic American character. In all the others, the Americans are all portrayed as evil, brutal, uncultured, and racist" (211–12). In "Images of the American in Haitian Literature during the Occupation, 1915–1934," Yvette Gindine goes even further, claiming:

> Annie Desroy's *Le Joug* (1934) uses an American as a positive hero and makes him at times the author's spokesman. Not only is this a complete reversal of the prevailing norm—emphasis on the Yankee as irreducible enemy and racist incarnate—but the American even assumes the attitude of a true Haitian patriot, concerned by his adopted country's future, a unique case in Haitian fiction where only two French professors ever received such privilege. (48–49)

Michael Dash shares this opinion, stating, "Possibly the most distinctive feature of this novel is that it is a rare instance of an outsider used as the author's 'porte-parole' in Haitian literature" (40). In *Images de la société dans le roman haïtien*, Marie-Denise Shelton refers to Murray as "guide" and "juge" of the Haitian characters (105). However, I contend that a careful reading of the sexual politics represented in the novel undermines these previous critical interpretations.

Although an indigenophile in many respects, Colonel Harry Murray does not view Haitians as his equals, let alone consider himself to be one of them. As Chancy states, "Murray, en fait, n'épouse pas les idéaux nationalistes d'Haïti, il adopte une attitude pseudo-libérale depuis son poste d'autorité, ce qui cache tout simplement une condescendance profondément enracinée envers la culture haïtienne" (23). The condescension that Chancy identifies in Colonel Murray's attitude toward Haiti and its inhabitants is in fact informed by the same racism espoused by his compatriots.

Murray is acknowledged by the U.S. Marine Corps as an indigenophile: "C'était un aimable et bon garçon estimé de ses soldats et tolérés par les gradés qui ne lui pardonnaient pas cette familiarité avec les indigènes philippins. C'est justement cette familiarité qui avait porté ses chefs hiérarchiques à l'envoyer aux Antilles" (Desroy, 22). In fact, Murray was transferred from the Philippines in part because of his affairs with Philippine women. Arabella Murray's attitude toward Haitians is the opposite of her husband's. She is not at all shy about voicing her concerns about having to deal with black people on an everyday basis. Several times she mentions a particular odor that she finds disturbing. Mrs. Murray claims, "Il me semble que cette chose détestable est partout, dans toute la maison, sur les meubles, sur moi, sur le colonel même" (Desroy, 53–54). Her friend Kitty Darking (another American character) responds with laughter, since everyone except Arabella knows about Murray's affairs with black women in Haiti.

Most critics of the novel see Colonel Murray's sexual conquests of Haitian women (and Philippine women before them) as evidence of his openness toward the natives. For example, Gindine states, "Not only is Murray exempt from color prejudice, but he is sexually stimulated by ethnic differences and engages liberally in interracial affairs" (49). However, racism has never prevented colonizers from having affairs with indigenous women, in Haiti or elsewhere, and the U.S. occupation was undoubtedly a form of colonization (albeit one where it is acknowledged by the parties involved that the occupation must eventually come to an end). Murray's affairs can thus be understood as a manifestation of his prejudice. Robert Young explains in *Colonial Desire*:

> The forms of sexual exchange brought about by colonialism were themselves both mirrors and consequences of the modes of economic exchange that constituted the basis of colonial relations; the extended exchange of property which began with small trading-posts and the visiting slave ships originated, indeed, as much as an exchange of bodies as of goods, or rather of bodies as goods: as in that paradigm of respectability, marriage, economic and sexual exchange were intimately bound up, coupled with each other, from the very first. (181–82)

In colonial Saint-Domingue, the French colonizer wielded economic power that enabled him or her to establish the terms of the sexual exchange. Similarly, in the case of the U.S. occupation of Haiti, Americans controlled the country's finances and dominated Haitians economically. Thus, within the historical context of *Le Joug*, initiating sexual relations constitutes a privilege and is further evidence of Murray's power as a colonel in the occupying military. It is not the Haitian women that seduce him but he who pursues them. The colonel is himself conscious of the power relations reflected in his sexual adventures: "Lui, concédait qu'il aimait la négresse. C'était son plaisir, son vice caché. Il préférait leurs caresses ardentes à celles de n'importe quelle blanche. Nulle comme elles ne possédait ce pouvoir, cette adresse d'exaspérer constamment les sens pour mieux les satisfaire" (Desroy, 175). Murray sees his conquests not as individuals but as a type. He evokes them fondly, but as one would speak of a favorite brand of cigarettes or rum. For Murray's affairs to truly indicate his exemption from color prejudice, he would at least have to be open to all interracial affairs (although even such acceptance would not mean that he had no color bias at all). Yet "Murray n'était pas arrivé au stade d'égalité avec le nègre malgré sa philanthropie. Et souvent il était secrètement choqué par la hardiesse des haïtiens qui dévisageaient les américaines" (Desroy, 174). Thus it is the American male's privilege to seduce Haitian women, a privilege that both stems from and reinforces his position of authority in a country that is not his own. The Haitian male, stripped of all power and authority in the occupied space, should not even consider seducing an American. Indeed, when the colonel discovers his wife's affair at the end of the novel, he is relieved that her lover is not black. He pities his colleague Darking (with whom Arabella has the affair) because his wife, Kitty, has had an affair with a black man. To Murray, Arabella "est une compagne plus digne que Kitty. La joie emplit son cœur à savoir que Darking avait un rival nègre" (Desroy, 220). This anecdote reveals Murray's hidden racist sentiments and makes it difficult to see how his affairs show that "he is exempt from color prejudice," as stated by Yvette Gindine.

Upon discovering her affair with Darking, Murray beats Arabella. (This scene does even more damage to his image as a sympathetic foreigner as interpreted by Gindine and Larrier). However, he regrets his aggressive behavior almost immediately because "ces petites créatures sont si fragiles. . . . Elles sont toutes les mêmes, elles ont un instinct animal" (Desroy, 219). It is clear that for Murray, both women and blacks are inferior to him and must be treated accordingly.

Contemplating his imminent departure from Haiti, Murray becomes nostalgic for the black women whom he will leave behind: "Il se rappela les larmes de ces pauvres femmes de son District qui lui baisaient la main et le suppliaient de rester. Elles l'aideraient à travailler, promettaient-elles, sur les propriétés qu'il achèterait" (Desroy, 217–18). Murray goes on to speculate that "c'était la reconnaissance de ces noirs que sa Race méprisait. Tandis que sa femme, pour le luxe qu'il lui donnait sans marchander, remerciait par l'adultère" (218). The combination of erotic and economic language present in this formulation persists throughout the scene. According to Murray, "les unes l'aimaient sans calcul, l'autre se vautrait dans le mensonge" (218). What he is looking for in a woman is blind adoration and servitude. Because of their inferior socioeconomic status, the indigenous women provide exactly that.

In fact, the poverty of Murray's Haitian conquests helps explain his supposed generosity. He does a lot of good for his district; among other things, he is instrumental in bringing a clinic and a school to the area (Desroy, 158). However, his philanthropy is not at all disinterested. Murray's district is not a wealthy one. Making improvements demonstrates his power and status. He makes weekly visits "dans les moindres coins du district. Dès qu'on annonçait sa venue, les jolies filles s'attiffaient, et souvent elles se crêpaient le chignon pour s'être l'une l'autre supplantée. Le Colonel s'amusait de cette rivalité qui lui amenait après la bataille des filles ardentes" (159). Young women of modest conditions are willing to have sex with him to gain access to the money and power that he flaunts. He is thus amply rewarded for his generosity.

Another explanation for Murray's inclination toward colored women, specifically those in foreign lands, is that they represent the unknown. He is fascinated with Fernande Vernon because she is part of the new and exciting scenery that he discovers in Haiti: "Le divan drapé de couleurs vives rehaussait l'éclat et la beauté de Fernande. Telle une fleur exotique, étrange et captivante, elle était étendue parmi la verdure des plantes où vacillait l'ombre tamisée du soleil" (Desroy, 178). Black women also represent danger and savageness in the stereotypes of his culture. However, the author reverses that paradigm:

> Madame Vernon qui arrivait s'étonna de la pression nerveuse de sa poignée de main. Elle était coquettement vêtue. Sa robe très décolletée et transparente découvrait une chair polie, attirante, fraiche, ambrée et qui répandait le parfum suave d'une récente ablution. Les manches courtes révèlaient les aisselles non épilées et si prometteuses que Murray s'angoissa, pris du *désir sauvage* d'étreindre dans ses bras puissants cette femme si séduisante, et dont le charme était doublé par l'attrait de *l'inconnu*. (Desroy, 109–10; italics mine)[3]

It is Murray's desire that is described as savage in this passage. He is the untamed one. Also, the mention of his powerful arms hints that he might (and does eventually) resort to force to satisfy his desires.

Nonetheless Murray's attitude cannot simply be reduced to sexism. American females can also use their sexuality as an expression of racism. Kitty Darking's attitude toward Haitians oscillates between the opposing manifestations of racism evidenced by the Murray couple. One literary critic describes Kitty thus:

> Relatively emancipated from the taboos of her own culture, mocking, elegant, coquettish, she drives her own car, smokes, tans herself daily and adores Haiti without knowing anything about it since at first she circulates only in closed American circles. Gradually she opens up to the surroundings, admires non-caucasian beauties, the splendors of tropical landscape and chooses a discreet Haitian lover who provides her with a radiant well-being. This venture is not paraded and belongs to the realm of private life, but is an exceptional sign of liberation even though Kitty lacks the frankness of Murray and uses only verbal irony or diplomatic silence to counter the racist declarations of her compatriots. (Gindine, 50)

Kitty's silence indicates that her liberation does not include facilitating that of others, and she is perfectly content to enjoy the spoils of belonging to the privileged group, the foreign occupiers. For example, when she says to Arabella Murray, "Ce Pays est charmant. On y mène une vie délicieuse, c'est une fête continuelle" (Desroy, 56), it is painfully obvious that this "on" refers to a minuscule group of people. Furthermore, the juxtaposition of terms referring to sex and merchandise in the description of Kitty's affair shows that her relationship with her lover is not at all equal. Indeed, simply being an American in Haiti during the U.S. occupation invests her with a power that she would not otherwise have as a woman. The mere existence of the occupation complicates gender dynamics for both Haitians and Americans. The description of Kitty's affair with the unnamed Haitian man illustrates this reversal of gender dynamics:

> Dès son arrivée en Haïti, elle s'était éprise d'un haïtien. Sous le fallacieux prétexte de choses exotiques à acheter—une pièce rare—elle sortait toute la journée. Son amant, fort beau mulâtre, polyglotte, était aussi passionné de jupes, d'affaires que d'objets d'art. Il l'avait brutalement prise un jour

qu'ils se trouvaient seuls. Il était venu lui offrir un bijou. Elle acheta sans souci du prix excessif, offrit de l'argent qu'il accepta. Quotidiennement elle lui téléphonait et, comme elle conduisait elle-même sa machine, passait le chercher. (Desroy, 161–62)

It does not take much imagination to read the metaphoric interpretation of the jewel that the nameless Haitian man is selling and that Kitty is willing to buy regardless of price. Some of Kitty's friends guess what she is up to "pour avoir connu elles-mêmes—par goût ou par curiosité—la volupté d'une étreinte indigène savante ou sauvage, inoubliable caresse!" (Desroy, 162). Thus desire for the black man is not unusual. Haitian men, too, are part of the spoils offered to the occupiers. Nowhere in *Le Joug* is there mention of a romantic relationship between a Haitian and an American, a relationship based on anything other than power and sexual satisfaction. As Feldman puts it, "Les américains relativement libérés décrits par Annie Desroy . . . se délectent à explorer la sensualité exotique et ne se lancent que dans des entreprises à capital affectif limité—délicieuse liaison provisoire ou rapides aventures. Pour eux la différence ethnique, loin d'être obstacle ou scandale, s'affirme comme stimulation, attrait de l'inconnu, promesse de découverte" (39). Sexual liaisons constitute another way of exploring the new and exotic land that Haiti represents for the Americans.

Just as Murray cannot accept a liaison between a Haitian man and an American woman, so American women in the novel are quite critical of Haitian women taking American men as lovers. At one point, a group of American women evoke an incident in which an American officer used his dog to attack a Haitian woman, supposedly a Caco spy. The American women are especially gleeful that the dog attacked the woman's sexual organs; one of them says, "On aurait du faire de même à toutes celles qui prennent des blancs pour amants" (Desroy, 168). The women go on to discuss the merits and disadvantages of interracial relationships. Apparently a relationship between a white woman and a black man is preferable because "celles-ci n'enfantent pas. Pour elles le partenaire c'est le plaisir. Il vient quand on l'appelle et part quand on la [*sic*] congédie, sans murmurer" (168). The American women feel threatened and perceive the Haitian women as purposely seducing American men. Haitian women and Haitian men are sexually threatening to their American counterparts because of the stereotypes attributed to them in U.S. culture. Blacks, and in the context of Desroy's novel, Haitians, due to their supposedly primitive nature, are believed by the Americans to be sexually superior to whites.[4]

Colonel Murray's wife Arabella does not indulge in interracial affairs. However, her profound aversion to black people is partly a way for her to curb any impulses she might have toward black men. Frightened by her own desires, Arabella proclaims her racism loudly and often. However, the text clearly shows her fascination with black men. She often fantasizes about them, seeing herself as the object of their desire. At the residence of the high commissioner, Arabella finds herself attracted to a black man who turns out to be the Haitian president. After meeting him and being unable to speak coherently in his presence, Arabella says, "Je me suis laissé dire tant d'horreurs sur tous ces nègres et surtout sur leur président que je ne pensais pas qu'il existât un seul comme celui-là. Il est élégant, charmant, séduisant. Je ne regrette pas de l'avoir rencontré. Je le reverrai même avec plaisir" (Desroy, 75). The president is not the only Haitian man Arabella is attracted to. She considers her neighbor Frédéric to be "un beau mâle . . . une brute," yet she asks herself "quelle devait être l'étreinte d'un être pareil. . . . Elle imagina la peau ambrée de Vernon contre sa chair mate, le sang afflua à ses joues . . . un frisson la parcourut" (63). She is simultaneously attracted to and repulsed by black men, and it is precisely their supposed animal quality that fascinates her. Arabella sees Frédéric as a male specimen, not a person; and a brute brings to mind a monster or an animal. (In contrast to her husband, Arabella's attractions are limited by socioeconomic status. She is not attracted to poor men and confides to Kitty that she does not detect any odor among Haitians of the upper classes [72–73].)

Like the French Gaude de Senneville in Stéphen Alexis's *Le Nègre Masqué* (1933), Arabella blames her sexual feelings and experiences in Haiti on the country itself: "Elle accusait maintenant le climat toujours tiède, le soleil toujours ardent, les nuits au ciel profond que la clarté des étoiles éclairait d'une lueur si poétiquement pâle. Elle accusait toutes ces forces créatrices de sensualité qui lentement lui avaient fait subir l'attirance des choses défendues" (Desroy, 221). This perception of Haiti as a site of overwhelming sensuality explains why the American women believe that Haitian women are the ones seducing American men. Foreigners cannot help but be seduced by the island and its inhabitants and are not to be held responsible for their actions.

Arabella's attraction to Frédéric is reciprocated and he would like to seduce her, but "celle-ci devinant le désir du voisin se plaisait malignement à l'aiguiser, plutôt méchamment; car, au fond, elle méprisait trop profondément la Race pour se donner à Vernon" (Desroy, 173). Arabella likes to tease Frédéric, wearing revealing clothing in the hopes that he will notice her. Her husband does not realize what she is doing, since "aucun américain blanc ne se serait imaginé que sa femme pût désirer plaire à un nègre" (174). Here the text again makes explicit the intersection of sex, race, and power in occupied Haiti and does not distinguish Murray from any other white American man. Therefore it is difficult to understand how Murray could be read as the author's spokesperson.

If any character were to fulfill that role, it would most likely be Fernande Vernon, for it is her analysis that helps the reader understand the various racial, political, and sexual dynamics at work within the context of the occupation. From the start, she is more astute when it comes to their American neighbors than her husband, Frédéric. He says to her, "On dit beaucoup de bien du colonel. Il parait que le préjugé de couleur ne l'atteint pas" (Desroy, 35), of which she is skeptical. She immediately evokes the tendency of American men to have affairs with Haitian women, thus recognizing the link between sex and power. Fernande is also aware of the symbolic positioning of the two couples' houses. The Murrays can look down on the Vernons from their house, which prompts Fernande to say to her husband: "Ne restons pas ici, cela me gêne. Ils nous dominent de chez eux" (47). Fernande refuses to be the object of the Americans' gaze. At the same time, her statement could also be read as referring to Haiti's geographic location in relation to the United States.

Indeed, spatial dynamics are crucial when analyzing a text that deals with the occupation of one country by another. After the initial invasion, occupiers attempt to exert control and dominion over a space that is not theirs while the native inhabitants struggle to maintain their grasp on that which belongs to them. Referring to the close proximity of Haiti and the United States, Frédéric Vernon uses an analogy to express his objections to the occupation of his country. He asks Colonel Murray, "Que diriez-vous, par exemple, Colonel, d'un grand propriétaire qui à côté de ses terres florissantes, voyant celles de son voisin péricliter, s'arrogerait le droit de se les approprier sous prétexte de les faire fructifier?" (Desroy, 151). Frédéric uses this metaphor to show that an occupation is not justified simply because one country is more developed than another. However, in contrast to his wife, Frédéric Vernon remains somewhat naive to the end of the text, in spite of periodic debates with his American superior. At a ceremony held in Murray's honor, "Vernon partageait la joie de son chef. Il était fier et supputait la transformation heureuse qu'aurait subie son Pays si tous les américains avaient la mentalité, la probité de Murray" (204).

Several scenes in the novel call such an assessment into question. One example takes place at a police station, where one Haitian man is given electric shocks to encourage him to denounce others. A woman is brutally kicked, causing her to miscarry. Murray is appalled by what he has witnessed, stating, "Je viens d'assister à une scène horrible. Ah! c'est ce qu'ils appellent coloniser" (Desroy, 90).[5] However, although Murray pleads with the officer in charge to stop hurting the Haitians, he takes no action to put an end to their torture, which makes it difficult to comprehend Michael Dash's statement that "Desroy, through her character, sees the true villain of the Haitian situation not as the American officer but as the Haitian elite" (Dash, 40).

No matter how insensitive members of the elite may be, they are not the ones shown to be beating poor Haitians to death or watching as it happens. In spite of Murray's outrage, his passivity at the scene aligns him with his fellow officers. In fact, Colonel Harry Murray of *Le Joug* corresponds almost perfectly to the image of the "colonisateur qui se refuse" as described by Albert Memmi in his *Portrait du colonisateur*. In spite of his good intentions (which are often questionable), Murray cannot fully integrate Haitian society. It is impossible for an American to do so during the occupation. As Memmi puts it, "Refuser la colonialisation est une chose, adopter le colonisé et s'en faire adopter en semblent d'autres, qui sont loin d'être liées" (61). Colonel Murray is unable to completely free himself from the stereotypes and arrogance of his culture and position in the occupying military, nor does he choose to fully conform to them. This ambiguity will cause his eventual expulsion from the Haitian territory.

The only Haitian character to truly grasp these conflicting aspects of Murray's personality is Fernande Vernon, as evidenced by the scene in which he makes sexual advances toward her. Murray is convinced that he will succeed in seducing Fernande but is worried that Frédéric might find them and is unsure of his reaction. However, Murray then decides that "il saurait bien gagner son silence en lui offrant sa voiture que celui-ci désirait acheter. Il la lui céderait à un prix dérisoire, ce serait encore une bonne affaire, la voiture étant abimée et sur le point d'être changée" (Desroy, 176–77). For Murray, Fernande is an object whose value is roughly equivalent to that of a used car, and he assumes that Frédéric will agree with this assessment. Before attempting to seduce Fernande, Murray drinks a heavy dose of rum "pour se donner du courage" (176). He then goes next door and begins to talk to her, all the while fascinated by the movement of her bare legs. He finally professes his supposed love, in reaction to which,

Fernande riait de bon cœur. Elle s'amusait de l'embarras de Murray, qui,
oubliant qu'elle parlait anglais, baragouinait un français baroque. Mais à
la vue de la bouche rougie s'ouvrant sur des dents menues, une vraie folie
s'empara de lui. Il se leva et toute sa masse se jeta sur la jeune femme. Les
mouvements de ce corps souple qui se débattait sous lui achevèrent de
l'affoler. Il fut brutal. Voyant sa proie lui échapper, il essaya de l'étreindre,
de la retenir. D'un brusque tour de rein, Fernande se trouva debout. Son
écart inattendu fit perdre l'équilibre à Murray qui s'affaissa de tout son
long. Il voulut se ressaisir, mais ne le put, alors il resta ainsi à quatre pattes.
(Desroy, 179)

Going back to Fernande's remarks on the positions of the two houses, we
can note the power reversal in this scene, with Murray sprawled on the
floor and Fernande standing over him.

Indeed, space appropriation and sex are often linked in the occupied
novels of various literary traditions. In his work on the American occupation of Japan and Okinawa, Michael Molasky asserts that "with remarkable
consistency, male writers from both mainland Japan and Okinawa have
articulated their humiliating experience of the defeat and occupation in
terms of the sexual violation of women" (11–12). Sexual relationships, violent or otherwise, become symbolic of political conflicts. Sexual violation
represents political violation.[6] Indeed, toward the end of *Le Joug*, Murray's
true sentiments vis-à-vis Haitians become more obvious. Through various
devices, the text reveals him to be quite an unsympathetic character. That
he is "brutal" toward Fernande is one such example. So is his linguistic
handicap. The image of the American officer unable to speak French is
a recurrent one in Haitian fiction of the time and is a strategy allowing
Haitian authors to assert a certain superiority over the occupiers. In this
scene, Colonel Murray proves himself to be both ridiculous and power-
less. Fernande is forced to call on a servant to escort Murray to his house,
since he cannot move on his own owing to his drunken state. The American is unable to return to his own space.

Certain literary critics see Fernande Vernon as an insipid character
with no real role in the text. For example, Yvette Tardieu Feldman declares:

Dans la galerie des jeunes mulâtresses haïtiennes, Fernande occupe une
position spéciale: ni jeune fille à marier, ni mère de famille, ni partenaire
ambitieuse d'un conjoint apathique ou complaisant, elle figure une vari-
ante de la femme-objet, passive, conformiste, oisive, tuant le temps par des

ouvrages d'aiguille, 'se morfondant' en l'absence de son époux-raison d'être, qu'elle adore et vouvoie. Toujours sédentaire elle paraît le plus souvent en position d'attente, au poste d'observation, cachée derrière des jalousies, épiant les voisins ou comme stimulant de désir—galbe et aisselle-gouffre s'offrant à Murray avec une inconsciente provocation. (50)

This passage is misleading on several counts. First, the Vernon couple "tutoie" each other. Second, Fernande does not "offer" herself to Murray, subconsciously or otherwise. On the contrary, she refuses his advances. Last, it is true that Fernande often plays the role of observer in the text, but such a role in no way implies that she is a passive character. Her considerations about the Americans are much more probing than her husband's, even though he has more opportunities to interact with the invaders than she does. Fernande's thoughts are crucial to the reader, as they offset those of the principal American character. In reference to both Desroy and Cléante Valcin, author of *La Blanche Négresse* (1934), Myriam Chancy claims, "Les deux auteurs cherchent à redéfinir la société haïtienne d'un point de vue féminin, en même temps qu'elles se trouvent incapables de présenter des personnages féminins forts" (18). Yet I would contend that Fernande Vernon *is* a strong female character because she refuses to place the occupier's desires above her own.

Feldman again misreads Desroy's intentions when she laments that the author "a beau excuser de son mieux l'agresseur intempestif en multipliant les circonstances atténuantes, il n'en reste pas moins que l'érotisme maladroit du gaffeur à demi saoûl révèle une sérieuse erreur de jugement de sa part et réduit la stature de l'"indigénophile' à celle d'un faune vieillissant et ridiculisé" (44–45). Revealing Murray as a typical occupier in spite of his many claims to the contrary is the whole point of this scene. If "Japanese male writers—journalists as well as novelists—were especially quick to link individual instances of rape and prostitution to the fate of the entire nation under foreign rule" (Molasky, 11), in *Le Joug*, a Haitian female author chooses to make the correlation between sexual violation and political exploitation. In so doing, she subverts the usual power relations between occupier and occupied female subject, since the heroine is able to escape from the foreigner. In his analysis of Gobineau's racist theories, Robert Young finds that "in the relation of hierarchical power, the white male's response to the allure of exotic black sexuality is identified with mastery and domination, no doubt fuelled by the resistance of the black female. This sadistic imperative, increased by the repugnance felt by the black for the white, is inevitably accompanied by the requirement of a masochistic submission by the subordinated, objectified woman" (108). Fernande Vernon refuses to be relegated to the role of the colonel's "subordinated, objectified woman," maintaining the integrity of her body and of her will. A woman who does not engage in extramarital affairs, Fernande Vernon's portrayal stands in stark contrast to the stereotype of the lascivious black female espoused by the novel's white characters.

In her analysis of *Le Joug*, Feldman states that "qu'elle évoque avec Murray l'exemple du mâle étranger grand amateur de 'brunes filles' qui multiplie les rencontres faciles, ou avec Kitty le cas moins recevable de la rieuse Américaine qui s'en tient à un seul amant discret, Desroy s'abstient de commentaire, approbation ou censure" (40), conceding only that Murray "conserve des attitudes qui trahissent un reste de préjugé" (44). However, Desroy does comment on the sexual preferences of her foreign protagonists, both in the construction of the text and through her narrative choices. Arabella is attracted to black men precisely because of the stereotypes associated with them; Kitty is willing to lavish money, but not affection, on her Haitian lover; and the colonel's numerous affairs demonstrate his power over poverty-stricken Haitian women. Consequently I agree with Myriam Chancy's determination that "à la fin, l'érotisme lascif qui est attribué d'une manière accablante à la femme haïtienne pendant l'Occupation se révèle comme la caractéristique qui définit les occupants" (32). This is true of each of the main American characters: Colonel Harry Murray, his wife Arabella, and her friend Kitty Darking.

Harry Murray's professed love for black women and Arabella Murray's aversion to black men are both put to the test during their year in Haiti. In the end, their impulses converge. They both continue to entertain racist stereotypes about Haitians while attempting to assert power over them. Nonetheless Harry Murray's attitude is perhaps more dangerous than Arabella's because of its subversive quality. Even more dangerous is the fact that some contemporary literary critics continue to view him as a benevolent foreigner, for by insisting on reading the relationships in *Le Joug* from the perspective of the character most invested with the power that stems from his position in an occupying army, literary critics run the risk of perpetuating the very erasure of Haitian women that Annie Desroy contests in her novel.

NOTES

An earlier version of this chapter was presented at the conference "Contextualizing the Caribbean" at the University of Miami, September 2001.

1. See Nadève Ménard, "Private Occupations."

2. See Anne McClintock, "No longer in future heaven," for a discussion of the ways in which gender has traditionally been omitted from national narratives.

3. I have left the accents as they appear in Desroy's text throughout.

4. For discussions of representations of black sexuality, see Fanon, *Peau noire, masques blancs*; and Hoch, *White Hero, Black Beast*.

5. Note that this quote presents colonization and occupation as identical political situations.

6. I have analyzed these issues within the context of Haiti's occupied novels in "Private Occupations" and more extensively in *The Occupied Novel*.

WORKS CITED

Alexis, Stéphen. *Le nègre masqué, tranche de vie haïtienne.* Port-au-Prince: L'Imprimerie de l'État, 1933.

Chancy, Myriam. "Ayiti çé ter glissé: L'occupation américaine en Haïti et l'émergence de voix féminines en littérature haïtienne." In *Elles écrivent des Antilles (Haïti, Guadeloupe, Martinique),* ed. Suzanne Rinne and Joëlle Vitiello, 17–36. Paris: L'Harmattan, 1997.

Dash, J. Michael. *Haiti and the United States: National Stereotypes and the Literary Imagination.* 1988. New York: St. Martin's Press, 1997.

Desroy, Annie. *Le Joug.* Port-au-Prince: Imprimerie Modèle, 1934.

Fanon, Frantz. *Peau noire, masques blancs.* 1952. Paris: Seuil, 1995.

Feldman, Yvette Tardieu. "Une romancière méconnue, Annie Desroy (1893–1948)." *Conjonction* 124 (1974): 35–51.

Gindine, Yvette. "Images of the American in Haitian Literature during the Occupation, 1915–1934." *Caribbean Studies* 4, no. 3 (1974): 37–52.

Hoch, Paul. *White Hero, Black Beast: Racism, Sexism, and the Mask of Masculinity.* London: Pluto Press, 1979.

Larrier, Renée. "Haitian Writers and the American Occupation: Literary Responses to a Political Crisis." *CLA Journal* 33, no. 2 (1989): 203–12.

McClintock, Anne. "'No longer in future heaven': Gender, Race, and Nationalism." In *Dangerous Liaisons: Gender, Nation, and Postcolonial Perspectives*, ed. Anne McClintock, Aamir Mufti, and Ella Shohat, 89–112. Minneapolis: University of Minnesota Press, 1997.

Memmi, Albert. *Portrait du colonisé*, preceded by *Portrait du colonisateur*. 1957. Utrecht: L'Imprimerie Bosch, 1966.

Ménard, Nadève. *The Occupied Novel: The Representation of Foreigners in Haitian Novels Written during the U.S. Occupation, 1915–1934*. Ph.D. diss., University of Pennsylvania, 2002.

———. "Private Occupations: Interracial Love Triangles in Haitian Novels." *Contemporary French and Francophone Studies* 15, no. 1 (2011): 57–65.

Molasky, Michael. *The American Occupation of Japan and Okinawa: Literature and Memory*. London: Routledge, 1999.

Shelton, Marie-Denise. *Image de la société dans le roman haïtien*. Paris: L'Harmattan, 1993.

Young, Robert. *Colonial Desire: Hybridity in Theory, Culture, and Race*. London: Routledge, 1995.

IV

GLOBALIZATION
AND CRISIS

8

The Rhetoric of Crisis and Foreclosing the Future of Haiti in *Ghosts of Cité Soleil*

—Christopher Garland

Nothing that has ever happened should be regarded as lost for history.
—Walter Benjamin, "Theses on the Philosophy of History"

Notre passé nous crie: Ayez l'âme aguerrie!
[Our past cries out to us: Have a strong soul!]
—From *La Dessalinienne*, the national anthem of Haiti

I

Asger Leth's documentary film *Ghosts of Cité Soleil* (2006) follows the lives of two gang leaders in the largest slum in Haiti during the months leading up to the fall of President Jean-Bertrand Aristide's government in 2004.[1] Two centuries after the revolutionary leader Jean-Jacques Dessalines declared independence for the former French slave colony—creating what Hardt and Negri call a "specter [that] circulated throughout the Americas in the early nineteenth century just as the specter of the October Revolution haunted European Capitalism over a century later" (123)—Aristide, a former Catholic priest who became the country's first democratically elected leader since Haiti's independence, had seen his presidency ended by a range of external and internal pressures. On February 28, 2004, Aristide was forced from office, leaving the leadership of the country in the hands of soldiers from the Haitian army that Aristide had earlier personally disbanded. As Paul Farmer notes, Aristide immediately "claimed he'd been kidnapped and didn't know where he was being taken until, at the end of a twenty-hour flight, he was told that he and his wife would be landing 'in a French military base in the middle of Africa.'" However, the main critics of Aristide and his leftist social and economic policies, including members of Haiti's wealthy elite and the U.S. NGOs in Washington (for instance, the International Republican Institute) that had actively sought the toppling of Aristide's government, contend that the president fled from office.

The film's subheading claims that Cité Soleil is "the most dangerous place on earth," a description bestowed on the area by the United Nations in 2004. Located on the waterfront of Port-au-Prince, Cité Soleil, which is the largest slum in the Western Hemisphere, has come to represent in mainstream Western media all that is wrong with Haiti today: the ineffectiveness of local police, the so-called necessity of foreign military intervention, and the incessant cycle of poverty and violence. While Cité Soleil might be emblematic of stereotypes about Haiti's abject state, it also produced many of Aristide's most fervent supporters in Port-au-Prince. By recognizing the huge gulf between Haiti's elite and the rest of the country's population, and harnessing popular support through the Fanmi Lavalas political movement, Aristide had risen to power with the support of many of the country's poorest citizens. Among these supporters were gangs of youths known as *chimères*, a Kreyol term that translates to "ghosts." When Aristide's leadership came under threat, some of these groups used violent means to demonstrate their support for Aristide and to intimidate political opponents. The film's primary subjects are two of the *chimères'* leaders: the aspiring rapper Winson "2Pac" Jean and 2Pac's younger brother, James "Bily" Petit Frere, a sometime rival to 2Pac and fierce supporter of Aristide.

As one academic who has shown the documentary in a number of undergraduate classes at a North American university points out, *Ghosts of Cité Soleil* is an "extremely seductive" documentary, particularly for a non-Haitian audience or an audience unfamiliar with Haiti's history.[2] Whether through the slick montages—where shots of Aristide and audio clips of him speaking are rapidly and repeatedly intercut with images that include a decomposing corpse being eaten by a wild pig, surging mobs, a room filled with dead bodies, and another body lying in a pool of blood— or by way of the sound track, composed by one of Haiti's most famous public figures, Wyclef Jean (who is also one of the film's producers), the mise-en-scène is clearly influenced by the visual and aural elements of the contemporary hip-hop music video.[3] Moreover, *Ghosts* is closer, in terms of both the visual style and the presentation of the "gangster with a heart of gold," to fictional feature films like *City of God* (2002), located in the favelas of Rio de Janeiro, and *Tsotsi* (2005), set in the shantytowns of Johannesburg, than the approach of a journalistic documentary about this moment in Haiti's history.[4] At the expense of providing background about Aristide's predicament, and by consciously reinforcing stereotypes of Haiti as an inherently failed state via the film's visual language, *Ghosts* values the style of a tour into the ghetto over the substance of political and historical contextualization.

As in the aforementioned fictional feature films, the primary narrative strategy of *Ghosts* is an attempt to be "economically successful internationally" by mimicking what Barbara Mennel identifies as "the American urban ghetto film that exploits the representation of poverty" (169). Alongside the exploitative representation of a ghetto in the global South, the commodification of gangs, gangsters, and poverty has a specific transnational political meaning in *Ghosts*, *City of God*, and *Tsotsi*: no matter the national locale, young black men from the ghetto are frightening subjects who are seemingly incapable of avoiding involvement in criminal activity, whether as a willing participant or being reluctantly "drawn in" owing to friendship or familial connections. Thus, at the same time as audiences in the global North are granted access to various exotic global South ghettos via these films' settings, the similarities with the North American ghetto film through the filmic subjects are overt. These foreign films are concerned with what Mennel sees as central to films of the foundational American hood genre, which tell "stories of violence among urban Blacks associated with drugs and gang warfare and are set in decaying urban locales made to represent such problems as policing, drugs, gentrification; lack of jobs, resources, and education; incarceration and gang warfare" (156).[5] This is certainly the case in *Ghosts*, where the extremely impoverished setting of Cité Soleil amplifies these social ills, setting the standard as the abject überslum.

Keeping in mind the characteristics of the urban ghetto film, my interest in *Ghosts* is the problem with it as a documentary: first, in the close resemblance between its narrative strategy and those of the aforementioned fictional ghetto films; second, in how the employment of ghetto film conventions serves the film's alignment with critics of Aristide (both in Haiti and abroad) who opposed Aristide's presidency and wished to justify the toppling of his government. To contest this historical narrative, it is necessary to explore how *Ghosts* is a Trojan horse of conservative ideology fitted out with the form and style of the ghetto film; moreover, to contest the film's representation of this historical moment, one must both acknowledge and address how the film both trades in and appeals to the stereotypes and decontextualization that accompany the visual rhetoric of contemporary Haiti. And while *Ghosts* is admittedly not a documentary that explicitly claims to interrogate Haiti's history, the omissions and denials that have marked historical reflections about Haiti are manifest in the film's telling of this recent moment. From the outset of *Ghosts*, questions about the way documentary film represents history—crucial questions of inclusion and omission, perspective and bias—are put to the forefront. The opening sequence, which works as an epilogue for the film's main action, is a series of five shots (four live action and one still image). The first four shots attempt to tell a short history of Haiti by way of matching visual images with superimposed text, and the last shot is a lead-in for the human subjects of the documentary.

The sequence begins with what appears to be an artist's representation of the untouched precolonial landscape; the center of the frame, in plain white text, features the following words: "On Christmas Eve of 1492 Christopher Columbus discovered the 'Earthly Paradise' now called Haiti." The following long shot is of steep cliffs sloping down into the evening sea, accompanied by text: "In 1804, African slaves successfully revolted and Haiti became the world's first black republic." The cut between these shots calls to mind issues raised by Michel-Rolph Trouillot in *Silencing the Past* (1996), a work that considers how "the production of historical narratives involves the uneven contribution of competing groups and individuals who have unequal access to the means of such production" (xix). The silencing that Trouillot details—silences that are both inherent and "active, dialectical counterparts of which history is the synthesis" (48)—is discernible in the opening sequence of *Ghosts*. In the omission and thus silencing of the residual effect of centuries of French colonialism, we are reminded how history is "created . . . [by] mentions or silences of various kinds or degrees" (48). When no mention is made, for example, of the ninety million gold francs paid in restitution to France by numerous postindependence Haitian governments (restitutions of which Aristide demanded a refund of $21 billion), or of the U.S. military occupation from 1915 to 1934 (not to mention the United States' ongoing economic and political interests in Haiti), the centrality of inclusion and exclusion to the construction of this historical narrative is made clear. Like the fictional hood film, which, for example, shows the "drug game" without providing context about how and why crack cocaine proliferated in numerous American cities, the residual effects of the restitution and occupation are glossed over in favor of character-oriented storytelling.

Moreover, as opposed to the marginalization of peripheral details due to the multitude of established facts, a process that Trouillot refers to in his theorization of different types of silencing in historical narratives (49), the documentary's opening sequence is marked by a paucity of information. A long shot of a beach with waves rolling in toward the wreck of a ship is accompanied by the following text: "A string of dictators and foreign trade embargoes have since left Haiti in a state of desperate poverty and political turmoil." Here the context of Aristide's election—as well as what David Nicholls notes as "the continuance [in Haiti] of a relationship of economic dependence on the former metropolitan power and later on other large powers" (247)—is ignored in favor of a vague reference to the brutal and exploitative Duvalier dictatorships. An extreme long shot of downtown Port-au-Prince is the final shot in this brief history sequence, accompanied by the following text: "In 2004, with demonstrations in the street and rebels closing in, President Aristide and his *Lavalas* party enlisted the support of armed gangs from the slum of Cité Soleil. These gangs are known as Chimeres." Whereas the opening sequence locates the narrative in time and place, the final shot introduces the reader to the film's thesis: the relationship between the *chimères* and Aristide is simply that of a despot and his thugs.

The connection drawn between Aristide and the Duvalier dictatorships is particularly damning for Aristide because of the legacy of the Duvalier regime's Tonton Macoutes, the infamous network of informers, intimidators, and violent enforcers. The opening sequence of *Ghosts* implies that Haiti's latest bogeymen are Aristide's *chimères*, a claim that frames Aristide as a despot by categorizing him alongside the Duvaliers. Simply put, the history of Aristide's leadership—including the coup attempts against his administrations and the 1996 formation of the popular, social reform-focused Fanmi Lavalas—is silenced at the same time as Aristide is posited as merely the latest in the "string of dictators" referred to in the preceding shot. In *Modernity Disavowed* (2004), Sibylle Fischer argues that the silences in historical discourses about Haiti emerge from a "fear" of the precedent set by the establishment of the world's first independent black nation-state and result in "denial of [its] transcendence"; yet despite their powerful effect on narrative, "silence and fear are not beyond interrogation" (ix). Taking a lead from both Trouillot and Fischer, if silences have been a way of defining Haiti and its history as what Fischer recently called the "cliché of the nightmare, the basket case," to interrogate and critique historical narratives is a way to disrupt the silences.[6]

II

The main protagonist of *Ghosts* is 2Pac, a *chimères* leader whose relatively fluent English, love of American hip-hop culture, and desire to use music to escape the ghetto provides Western audiences of the film with a sympathetic protagonist. The content and narrative design of *Ghosts* evoke a number of specific hood films including *Boyz n the Hood* (1991), *South Central* (1992), *Menace II Society* (1993), and *Clockers* (1995), where the death of an angry young black man from the ghetto is instrumental to the climax of the narrative.[7] The film also aligns Haitian 2Pac with his deceased American counterpart, Tupac (2Pac) Amaru Shakur. A proponent of gangsta rap, which celebrates the power of the loaded gun and the trials and spoils of the "drug game," Tupac starred in two prominent hood films, *Juice* (1992) and *Poetic Justice* (1992). Tupac also occasionally espoused lyrics referring to the necessity for respect for women in African American communities ("Brenda's Got a Baby") and to address the prevalence of gun violence and the high rate of incarceration among young black men across America ("Changes"). In *Ghosts*, Haitian 2Pac, in an act of mimesis rather than mimicry, preserves Haiti's politics and his own experience in a Haitian prison as a context for the Tupac-influenced rap that he composes. Even with this mimesis, 2Pac is clearly the most American subject in the documentary (particularly in contrast to both Aristide and 2Pac's brother Bily) due to his language, which draws on African American Vernacular English, and his Tupac-esque persona as a socially and politically conscious gangster rapper.

While the uncanny presence of American Tupac as evoked by Haitian 2Pac's speech and rap references is central to the main human subject, the documentary's form also draws on another American hip-hop cultural product. The gun toting and drug use of 2Pac and the other *chimères* are presented in the manner of a gangsta rap music video. The popularity of gangsta rap, which first gained the attention of mainstream audiences through the controversial Los Angeles–based group NWA (Niggaz with Attitude) in the late 1980s, reached its apex in the mid- to late 1990s with the American East Coast–West Coast rivalry.[8] The celebration of guns, gangs, and criminal activity—now a staple subject matter of many rap artists—became visual motifs in the music videos produced to market the rappers' album and single releases.[9] A scene in *Ghosts* where the influence of the American gangsta rap music video comes to the fore is during the wake for 2Pac's "soldier" Gabriel, who 2Pac claims was "killed by the cops" when the young man ventured out of Cité Soleil to downtown Port-au-Prince. For the course of this scene, documentary verisimilitude takes a backseat to high stylization. A bass-heavy hip-hop beat plays while the *chimères* smoke marijuana, raise guns in the air, and dance. Shot in night vision, with the nondiegetic music sound track drowning out the diegetic sound, the form of the documentary morphs into a full-blown rap video.[10]

This sequence reinforces just how deeply the form and content of *Ghosts* draw on both the hood film and another hip-hop cultural product, the rap video. But the filmmakers' appropriation of the generic conventions of the hood film is not merely an aesthetic choice: it clearly shapes the film's implicit political rhetoric about this time (the events leading up to and directly following Aristide's removal from office) and place (the much-maligned ghetto Cité Soleil). As Murray Forman argues, through hip-hop culture the spaces of "the ghetto, 'hood, street, and corner all surface as representations of a particular image inscribing an ideal of authenticity or 'hardcore' urban reality" (5). The key terms in this assertion are, of course, "authenticity" and "reality"; hip-hop is a discourse layered with narratives purporting to tell how it "really is" in the streets. But as with the (often) fictional tales of guns, drugs, and criminality that are staple themes of rappers' first-person narratives both in the United States and around the globe, or the stories conveyed through the American hood film and its international counterparts, *Ghosts*' presentation of the "hardcore" reality of Cité Soleil (and by extension this moment in Haitian political history) must not be consumed as an uncontestable, "true" story.

Additionally, the Cité Soleil of *Ghosts* is not just another "hood" but is, as mentioned earlier, presented as the hyperghetto. This notion is reinforced by the seeming verisimilitude proposed by the documentary form: the audience is granted access to the so-called "most dangerous place on earth," a space occupied by both Aristide's gangsters and the film's hero, 2Pac. Accompanying 2Pac and the other *chimères* as they drive through the narrow lanes of Cité Soleil, the handheld camera captures a number of close-ups, including young men wearing bandanas and baseball caps, drinking and waving their guns at the camera, with the cuts between each shot accelerating to a frenetic, MTV-style pace. This sequence includes a staple of the contemporary hip-hop video: the attractive woman (or women) who is often positioned as both the rapper's admirer and his object. Here a white French aid worker, Eleonore "Lele" Senlis, provides the feminine figure to the sequence's hypermasculine content. The final shot of the wake scene features Lele resting her head against 2Pac.

Shortly after, Lele and 2Pac are shown in bed together. "It's no lie / This is 2Pac's dream," he raps. "Corrupt and greedy thief. President." After kissing Lele, 2Pac says, "Black and white, nigga, we love each other for real." His union with Lele and his denial of Aristide are both analogous to the film's overarching message: the "dream" of Haiti's future rests not with the homegrown, democratically elected president but with the foreign body's presence and intervention.

The construction of 2Pac's persona as gangster rapper–cum–politically conscious figure is also present in the marketing of the film. At the beginning of the most widely viewed theatrical trailer for *Ghosts* on You-Tube, a sequence that includes a close-up shot of a handgun being loaded and pointed directly at the camera is followed shortly by a head-and-shoulders shot of 2Pac with an accompanying voice-over ("I'm a thugster, gangster") and a rapid montage of close-up shots of hands holding guns and money: omnipresent visual signs from the hood film. Yet by the end of the trailer, 2Pac, as the film's primary subject, moves from gangster rapper to a voice for the people of Cité Soleil: "What we need, we need peace. We don't want to fight each other. We don't want people to die in Cité Soleil— we die of hunger already, what, we're going die by arms now?"

The link between Haitian 2Pac and Tupac is made further explicit when Haitian 2Pac raps along to "Never B Peace," a track included on the posthumously released album *Better Dayz* (2002). Turning to the camera, Haitian 2Pac enthusiastically raps the following lyrics: "I know there'll never be peace / That's why I keep my pistol when I walk the streets / 'cause there can never be peace." The significance of these lyrics in the film's diegesis is unnerving: the last stand by the *chimères* will lead to more bloodshed and violence, with 2Pac's death allegedly coming months later at the hands of fellow *chimères* leader Thomas "Labanye" Robinson. Like the American Tupac's murder on a street in Las Vegas, the tragedy of Haitian 2Pac's life and death enables pathos for the "gangster with a heart of gold." By including the rough details of Haitian 2Pac's death in the film's epilogue, the hood film narrative cinema elements of *Ghosts* become even more pronounced. Therefore, when we consider the visual rhetoric and filmic narrative strategy that I have highlighted thus far, *Ghosts* is not about the investigation of a complicated moment in Haiti's history.

Instead, like a number of mass-distributed films from the global South that imitate the American hood film, *Ghosts* relegates to a distant background the political and socioeconomic conditions that give rise to slums, favelas, shantytowns, and barrios. But this might not be the most insidious element of the global South hood film. Barbara Mennel argues that these films also "fetishize the violence of the ghetto at the cost of low-budget films that more subtly address issues of urban poverty. [This fetishization] not only creates a misconception about the urban poor in specific Third World countries, but also lends itself to seeing entire Third World countries as ghettos" (169).

The fetishization of violence and seeing "entire Third World countries as ghettos" are especially explicit elements of *Ghosts'* visual rhetoric; Cité Soleil, with its history and residents glossed over in favor of the story of gun-toting gangsters, becomes a substitute for Haiti as a whole. Because of this narrow focus and lack of context, the entire country, not just Cité Soleil, becomes the "most dangerous place on earth." The lack of distinction between Cité Soleil and the rest of Haiti is not merely a subtext made apparent by a close reading of the film but an overt part of the film's marketing. On the back cover of the DVD version, there is a short synopsis of the film, the second line of which states that the "reality of life today in *Haiti* unfolds before us as we get to know two brothers and their stories intimately"; the last line of the synopsis claims that "speaking the language of violence and knowing that staying alive in *Haiti* is a very day-to-day proposition" (italics mine). In the film's title and the generalizations about Haiti made on the DVD's back cover, Cité Soleil and its reputation—a set of stereotypes perpetuated by proclamations such as the one emblazoned on the DVD's front cover ("the most dangerous place on earth")—become representative of Haiti as a whole.

While endorsing the naming of Cité Soleil as "the most dangerous place on earth" is a marketing attempt to appeal to audiences who are interested in taking part in a poverty tour tinged with extreme violence from the comfort of a cinema or living room, to critique this choice is to consider how naming plays into the discourse of contemporary Haiti. In *Edgework* (2005) Wendy Brown calls for a "local criticism" that seeks specificity rather than attempting to overhaul an imagined social totality: for example, the neoliberal economic policies and practices that continue Western imperialism in the global South. Brown asserts that "naming practices" are "among the objects of local criticism; interrogation, challenge, discernment, and displacement are among its actions" (viii). In a parody titled "How to Write about Haiti," the journalist Ansel Herz aims his own "local" critique at the naming practices employed by the foreign media in Haiti:

> Today, Cité Soleil is the most dangerous slum in the world. There is no need
> to back up this claim with evidence. It is "sprawling." Again, there's no time
> for the thesaurus. Talk about ruthless gangs, bullet holes, pigs and trash.
> Filth everywhere. Desperate people are eating cookies made of dirt and
> mud! That always grabs the reader's attention.

Although Herz is addressing the print and television media coverage in post-earthquake Port-au-Prince, the repeated journalistic tropes that he mentions could be used to describe the visual rhetoric repeatedly employed in setting the scene of *Ghosts* as "the most dangerous place on earth." The repeated use of visual imagery of spectacular poverty, particularly presented as it is in high-speed montages, evokes the stylized sequences of the immensely internationally popular *Slumdog Millionaire* and *City of God*: adrenaline-inducing filmmaking that would not be out of place in the mainstream action film genre. But rather than the visceral thrill coming via a rapidly edited car chase or bank heist shoot-out, in *Ghosts* the audience gets a thrill ride through an exotic ghetto via stylized documentary footage, where Vodou practitioners blow smoke, children play in the dirt and rubble, and shirtless young black men brandish high-powered M16 rifles. The fundamental visual and aural elements of the U.S. hood film—guns, drug use and dealing, rap music, American slang—feature prominently in the story of an archetypal protagonist: the young black man unable to escape a sordid urban environment. In *Ghosts* the comparison with the American hood film is especially pronounced because of Haitian 2Pac's simulation of the rapper and hood film star Tupac Shakur. Again, like the hood film, which can be read as a left-wing critique of social inequality in the North American city in the wake of Reaganomics and associated social policies, these details are used to indict a political leader; inversely, in *Ghosts* they are used to mount a conservative critique of a left-wing president.

Moreover, as with narrative cinema that uses a ghetto in a major city as a primary location, including films like *City of God* and *Slumdog Millionaire* (as well as the American hood films), the Cité Soleil of *Ghosts* is a space marked by the superlative: like the slums of these narrative cinema films, Cité Soleil is the poorest, the most violent, the most overcrowded. The slum is, in a word, the worst, a space worthy of both pity for its abjectness and derision for its criminality.[11] The presentation of the slum as an exceptional space is taken to the extreme with this "most dangerous place on earth," where audiences are shown images that reemphasize the idea of

Haiti as "basket case": alongside shots depicting the impoverishment and lack of basic resources, *Ghosts* contains a series of shots depicting bodies covered by blankets, fires blazing in the streets, armed and balaclava-wearing young men, and raucous, violent mobs. The pointless violence depicted in the American hood film is taken to its absurd extreme in *Ghosts*, where the *chimères* attempt a futile stand for an already deposed leader, Aristide.

Emphasizing the impoverishment and violence that mark the slum of narrative cinema, the film exposes the viewer to the plight of infants and children. In *City of God* the teenage gangsters force a very young boy to shoot his friend; in another non-U.S. ghetto film, *Tsotsi*, the infant who has inadvertently been kidnapped by a young black South African gangster during a carjacking intensifies the division between the middle-class suburbs and the shantytowns. Likewise, in one brief scene in *Ghosts*, where 2Pac is explaining how he has come to have a car and a *laissez-passer* (permit) that allows him to drive throughout the city, two young boys sit in the backseat holding large, high-powered rifles. In another shot, we see a newborn child, who has not yet had his umbilical cord tied, being carried upside down by his feet by a nurse. Along with many of the images in the film, there is little explication. Who are the children? Are they 2Pac's youngest soldiers? His relatives? Is the newborn dying? However, what these singular images do is contribute to the visual rhetoric of the intrinsically chaotic Haiti, a mess of a state that cannot protect or care for its most vulnerable citizens. One might argue that in these images, the director Asger Leth is showing us "how it really is" (a view repeatedly expressed in the comments section below the streamed version of *Ghosts* that is available on YouTube). A number of these online comments praise the risk and effort involved in an "outsider" visiting Cité Soleil and documenting the *chimères*. Certainly the outsider can provide a valuable lens. In his praise of an outsider's depiction of Palestinian life, Edward Said draws attention to the value of intrepid journalism:

> Like Joseph Conrad's Marlow he is tugged at by the forgotten places and people of the world, those who don't make it on to our television screens, or if they do, are regularly portrayed as marginal, unimportant, perhaps even negligible were it not for their nuisance value which . . . seems impossible to get rid of. (iv)

I quote from Said at length because what he later determines as central to an outsider's representation—the ability to "unostentatiously transmit a great deal of information, the human context and historical events that have reduced [people] to their present state" (iv)—is precisely what *Ghosts* lacks. The film's narrative strategy deals in an uncontextualized visual language: the shots of the anonymous black faces; the bird's-eye view of the "sprawling" expanse of Cité Soleil; the soldiers searching the corrugated-iron-lined alleyways; the conversation between the gang leader and the American-based Haitian music superstar; the corrupt police officer handing the wanted gang leader travel documents; the *chimères'* food distribution conducted at gunpoint. Additionally, the audience is informed that Haiti is a two-hour flight from Florida, yet little of the relationship between these neighboring nations is explored. Concluding his appraisal of *Ghosts*, Charles Hinton claims that "the United States is the real ghost in this film—it simply does not exist." And while the Haitian Revolution, which, as Susan Buck-Morss argues, "lies at the crossroads of multiple discourses as a defining moment in world history" (13) and led to the "phenomenon called Haiti" (12), the filmmakers peddle a narrative that both denies Haiti's place in universal history and marginalizes the country as a "basket case."

The film's visual rhetoric is constructed through images that reify Haiti as not only a mad but also a diseased (and dying) nation-state. Through the montages that repeatedly show the dead bodies that are literally piling up under the rule of Aristide, the narrative also makes explicit a common trope in Western representations of Haiti: the images that J. Michael Dash identifies as "the rebellious body, the repulsive body, the seductive body and the sick body," which "constitute a consistent discourse that has fixed Haiti in the Western imagination: the 'Haitianizing' of Haiti as unredeemably deviant" (137). To demonstrate how this film uses the notion of the "deviant" and "seductive" body, I turn to an early scene in the documentary. 2Pac speaks on the phone in Kreyol with his younger brother; in the following shot, 2Pac, framed by a handheld medium close-up, is interviewed in the dark: a setting used for 2Pac's *piece de camera* confessionals throughout the film. Directly addressing the camera in English, 2Pac, shirtless and smoking marijuana, laughs at his younger brother's political aspirations. "Bily wants to be the president, you know, of Haiti," 2Pac says. There is a jump cut to a shot of Bily, sitting on the side of the road, before returning to 2Pac's *piece de camera*. "Fuck Haiti, man," 2Pac continues. "But my brother, I respect him. I respect him anyway." The juxtaposition of 2Pac—who by stating "Fuck Haiti" is made clearly identifiable as a critic of both Aristide and Haiti as a whole—and the pro-Lavalas Bily is particularly striking here. The film's protagonist dismisses Haiti, while the representative of Lavalas becomes the political Other: secondary, unrealistic, and idealistic.

Cutting to another handheld shot, the camera follows Bily as he walks into one of the makeshift shanties that provide the vast majority of housing in Cité Soleil. Approaching a young woman, Bily puts his finger, with the rest of his hand fashioned to resemble a gun, to her temple, while telling her, "You steal something, pow, you die!" Shortly after, a head-and-shoulders shot shows Bily talking as he drives on the outskirts of Cité Soleil. "If you are a rich man, you are supposed to help the poor people," Bily says. "If you see the life of people here—no house to sleep in, no job, no water, nothing to eat, no money to pay school for the children—but they have a gun. What do you think they can do? People of Cité Soleil have nobody to speak for them. There is only Aristide." In professing crude socialist ideals backed by the threat of menace and violence, Bily not only is depicted as a direct representative for Aristide but in fact is positioned as the stand-in for the president throughout the film. 2Pac, on the other hand, with his disdain for Aristide (despite his seemingly contradictory leadership of pro-Aristide *chimères*) and his desire to leave the ghetto (not to mention Haiti), is positioned as the film's heroic and tragic figure.

Furthermore, there is value in reading how 2Pac, Bily, and the Haitianized body—"rebellious," "deviant," and "seductive"—are presented on the cover of the DVD. Due to the film's relatively limited theatrical release, the DVD cover is the primary textual element that a large portion of the film's audience would have encountered before seeing the film. The cover is a paratext: the "zone," as Gérard Genette argues, "between text and off-text, a zone not only of transition but also of transaction: a privileged place of pragmatics and a strategy, of an influence on the public" (2).[12] The images on the *Ghosts* cover are indexical of both the film's appeal to Western audiences as poverty pornography and its conservative attack on Aristide and the leftist Fanmi Lavalas movement. The cover's central image is of a shirtless 2Pac, gripping the large semiautomatic rifle that he totes in a number of the scenes in the documentary. Eight smaller images surround the image of 2Pac, mostly from the film: Bily pointing a gun at a group of people (this comes from a sequence that depicts the distribution of aid in Cité Soleil); one of Wyclef Jean talking on the phone; a partial shot, focused on the breasts, of a young woman in a low-cut dress; and a still of 2Pac, sitting on a bed, his arm draped across Lele, the French aid worker.

In keeping with the thematic conventions of the hood film, the visual rhetoric of the cover conveys violence, sex, and danger—2Pac's black body, the muscles of his torso cartoonlike in their definition, grips the gun low, around his midsection, the barrel evoking a phallus—while immortalizing 2Pac, the film's anti-Aristide hero. Together these seductive bodies are employed to reify the notion of a deviant Haiti where sex and violence are intertwined and where representatives of Lavalas (the *chimères*) are shown to engage in criminal activity. A close reading of a paratextual element like the film's DVD cover allows one to consider audience reception as it might occur in the doorway to the film text proper: in the matching together on the back cover of an image of a shirtless young black man carrying an M16 rifle and the accompanying text that describes the film—"the reality of life today in Haiti"—the cover is where the film's (potential) audience is first exposed to the claims made through the documentary's visual language.

III

The filmic rhetoric of *Ghosts*—expressed through the arrangement of cutting and editing—presents Aristide as a corrupt president who abandoned his people. Director Asger Leth's weltanschauung is made particularly apparent in a number of sequences in the film (not all of which I have the opportunity to reference within this essay) that include the uncritical use of the voice-over of an American newsreader pronouncing that Aristide "resigned" and "fled into exile," two assertions that were put into doubt long before the documentary's postproduction. Another sequence, which was also used for the film's theatrical trailer, shows a medium close-up shot of Aristide speaking to a number of assembled journalists. Aristide says that "today, in Haiti, we have terrorists, drug dealers, [and] criminals acting and killing innocent people." Because the shot is used later in the documentary, after the case against Aristide is developed through the narrative's repeated suggestion that the *chimères* and their violent activities are under the direct command of Aristide, one takes its inclusion as demonstrating the embattled president's hypocrisy and dishonesty. Continuing the film's depiction of a maniacal Aristide, this shot is followed by a long shot of an unidentified body lying in a pool of blood, bringing to mind Dash's use of the "sick body" as a metaphor for the Haitianized subject.

But it is not just the editing of the narrative, where images of Aristide are regularly intercut with random images of horrific violence, which makes perceptible the film's position on Aristide and his aborted presidency. As its primary witness against the president, the filmmakers employ the testimony of André "Andy" Apaid. One of Haiti's largest employers, Apaid had criticized Aristide's doubling of the minimum wage in 1991 during Aristide's first presidential term, a tenure that ended with a coup orchestrated by the disgruntled military and elites and backed by the United States. Due to the conditions in the apparel factories that Apaid owns and runs, he has been described as the "biggest sweat-shop operator in Haiti" (Sanders, 42). At the time of his appearance in *Ghosts*, Apaid's factory workers were "reportedly paid only a paltry, slave-wage salary of 68 cents a day" (42). During his appearance as one of the film's few talking heads, Apaid tells an unsubstantiated anecdote about a female public official who, according to Apaid, was murdered because she refused to shake the hand (at Aristide's request) of a gang leader. If the filmmakers' bias was not already reinforced through decisions regarding the editing and scope of the documentary, the inclusion of Apaid as *the* expert on the Aristide situation will, in an audience familiar with Aristide's removal from office, elicit feelings of "anger and frustration" in the viewer, especially when *Ghosts* turns to a practitioner of domestic exploitation in Haiti today as its key expert.[13]

Despite the film's overt glamorization of violence and its omission of views countering those of the anti-Aristide "experts," a number of critics in the mainstream press, echoing the aforementioned views expressed in the comments section of YouTube, praised the film. In his enthusiastic endorsement of *Ghosts*, David Adams of the *Saint Petersburg Times*, in perhaps the most egregious display of uncritical engagement with the film, reifies degrading and dehumanizing stereotypes about Haiti and Haitians by stating that Cité Soleil is a "rabbit warren" that symbolizes "everything that is wrong" with Haiti. In the same review, the director Asger Leth claims that he wrote a "storyline [that was] pretty clear" on the day that he met Lele and Bily, an admission that shows the confluence of narrative cinema and documentary film at work in *Ghosts*. Although Duncan Campbell, a writer for the *Guardian*, acknowledges that there are problems with the film's contextualization, he proceeds to conflate one part of Port-au-Prince and the city as a whole by stating that *Ghosts* "communicates much of the baleful nature of life in this corner of the country." But this is not the most disquieting element of Campbell's review. Quoting from an interview with Leth, who claims that in making the film he "didn't want to get swallowed up by the news," Campbell concludes his piece by asserting that *Ghosts* "could be a start of the recollection" of Haiti's history. (The notion that *Ghosts* could be a point of origin for understanding

Haiti's history is a deeply troubling one.) In contrast, Peter Bradshaw, also writing in the *Guardian*, directly addresses the film's political subtext. Bradshaw argues that *Ghosts* is both "politically and morally illiterate" and accuses the director of being "utterly incurious about the context of the *Chimères*, and the people that created them."[14]

By extension of the blinkered directorial vision articulated by Bradshaw, *Ghosts* is also an attempt to show another crisis in Haiti where foreign intervention is deemed simply necessary. Throughout the twentieth century, Haiti has been described repeatedly and consistently as a state in crisis. In contemporary usage, the term "crisis" has expanded to include a plethora of locales and contexts: psychological distress is described as a "personal crisis"; the recent failure of parts of the capitalist market, both in the United States and internationally, is deemed an "economic crisis"; impoverished communities in countries around the world are referred to as "humanitarian crises." The notion of crisis demanding immediate and drastic intervention is part of the word's etymology. The term is derived from the Greek *krisis*, which has its roots as a medical term for the period when critical decisions need to be made, by mandating, for example, medical intervention on the injured or diseased body (Nadal, 3).[15] Aristide's critics could argue that the appropriate intervention for the Haitian body politic took place in February 2004. Aristide, they might claim, was an ineffectual leader willing to subvert the rule of law to stay in power, and the militia provided a critical correction by promulgating the conditions for his departure from office. However, to persuasively argue this position, one would have to not only consider (in detail) the historical context of Aristide as a leader who came to power in the particularly politically unstable post–Duvalier/Tonton Macoutes era but also interrogate the motivation of Aristide's opponents and detractors. *Ghosts* fails to address these two issues. Rather, the film's visual rhetoric reifies preconceived notions of Haiti, makes generalizations about the country's history, and silences important contextualization about this "moment of crisis."

As mentioned earlier, crises in Haiti have been used to justify both foreign and domestic-driven intervention, whether with the U.S. military's occupation or through Haiti's own brutal dictators, who lined their pockets at the expense of the Haitian people. While the narrative that *Ghosts* presents about this moment concerns 2Pac and his *chimères*, the silenced historical discourse concerns how the combined effort of Haiti's elite and a militia trained outside Haiti succeeded in removing a president who had repeatedly threatened the elite through economic reforms designed to help the country's poor majority. Rather than contextualizing the history of U.S. intervention in Haiti's political sphere, the film simplistically portrays the 2004 coup d'état as a conflict between Aristide, the leader from the slum with untenable socialist beliefs who has been corrupted by power, and the conservative members of the Haitian elite and the leaders of the anti-Aristide militia as those, along with the elite, who have Haiti's "best interests" at heart. Furthermore, when the film glorifies 2Pac as a ghetto gangster caught up in a larger political struggle, the audience is left to reflect on the ethics of Aristide, whom the film posits as the manipulator of the thugs: a leader from the slums who gave rise to gang violence that spilled out of the slums into the schools, businesses, and downtown streets of Port-au-Prince.

By linking the notions of crisis and intervention in the context of *Ghosts*, to critique the film is to stage no less than an intervention on the past as it is written in a text, pick it apart, and challenge the film's representation of recent history, demonstrating that Haiti's future need not be foreclosed by the way its recent past is represented at a critical historical moment. By staging a critical intervention on the presentation of Haiti in *Ghosts of Cité Soleil* as a nation-state paralyzed by violence propagated by Aristide for political ends, one can show how the future can be transformed by what we do in the present about historical representations of the past.[16] Moreover, by critically engaging with *Ghosts*, a text that not only peddles simplistic explanations about this historical moment but also panders to stereotypes about Haiti and Haitians, my intent is to show that this kind of visual rhetoric should not go uncontested.

NOTES

1. This essay developed out of papers delivered at the University of Texas, Austin's "Postcolonial Actualities: Past and Present" conference in October 2009, the University of Florida's English Graduate Organization's 2010 conference, and the "Haiti and the Americas: Histories, Cultures, Imaginations" conference, October 21–22, 2010, at Florida Atlantic University, Boca Raton.

2. Conversation with Dr. Amy Abugo Ongiri, faculty member in the Department of English and Film and Media Studies at the University of Florida.

3. It is worth reflecting on Wyclef Jean's involvement with a film with such a clearly anti-Aristide agenda in light of his aborted run for the Haitian presidency in 2010.

4. See *Poto Mitan: Haitian Women, Pillars of the Global Economy* (dir. Renée Bergan and Mark Schuller, 2009) for a documentary that explores and contextualizes

economic conditions in Haiti. Also, *Haiti: Democracy Undone* (dir. Peter Bull, 2006) explores how American NGOs were complicit in Aristide's removal from office.

5. As Mennel rightly points out, the American fictional feature films can be read as responses to discourses on urbanity in the United States in the late 1980s: taking into consideration the socioeconomic conditions, national and local politics, ethnic demographics, and urban geography. This, too, is true of *Tsotsi* and *City of God*, both of which evoke questions of the stark disparity of wealth and resources in the megalopolises of the global South.

6. Comments made at the "Haiti and the Americas: Histories, Cultures, Imaginations" conference.

7. See Forman for a detailed critical analysis of the "hood film" genre.

8. This rivalry became more charged after Tupac's inflammatory lyrics about the renowned New York City rapper Notorious B.I.G.

9. See the video for NWA's single "Straight Outta Compton" for an archetypal example of the gangster rap video.

10. Gabriel's wake begins with a search for a generator, which, like an earlier argument between the *chimères* over the lack of guns, shows that Cité Soleil's scarcity of resources also applies to its gangsters.

11. I explore this idea of the slum as a space marked by the superlative in "Urban, Rural, or Someplace Else?"

12. In "Urban, Rural, or Someplace Else?" I also apply Genette's theory of the paratext to a different kind of "slum" cinema, Neill Blomkamp's *District 9* (2009).

13. From a conversation with J. Michael Dash.

14. I am constrained by space to limit my analysis of the many reviews of *Ghosts* available on the Internet. While some of the reviews do touch on the more problematic issue of this supposed documentary, many reviewers appear to be enamored with the access the filmmakers had to the gangs and the slum, which leads them to pay less attention to the lack of contextualization in the framing of Aristide as a corrupt politician.

15. In addition to its origin as a medical term, the word "crisis" shares an etymological basis with "critique" through the Greek *krisis*; while the word "critique" evokes the notion of separating and "picking apart," it also means "'to choose,' 'to judge,' and 'to decide'" (Nadal, 3).

16. The most recent "authoritative" account of Haiti's history, Laurent Dubois's *Haiti: The Aftershocks of History* (2012), omits a meaningful consideration of Aristide and his deposition.

WORKS CITED

Adams, David. "Rough Cut." *Saint Petersburg Times*, April 29, 2007.
Benjamin, Walter. *Illuminations*. Ed. Hannah Arendt. New York: Schocken Books, 1969.

Bradshaw, Peter. "Ghosts of Cité Soleil." *Guardian*, July 20, 2007.

Brown, Wendy. *Edgework: Critical Essays on Knowledge and Politics*. Princeton, NJ: Princeton University Press, 2005.

Buck-Morss, Susan. *Hegel, Haiti and Universal History*. Pittsburgh: University of Pittsburgh Press, 2009.

Campbell, Duncan. "Rude Recollection of Port-au-Prince." *Guardian*, July 12, 2007.

Dash, J. M. *Haiti and the United States: National Stereotypes and the Literary Imagination*. New York: St. Martin's Press, 1988.

Farmer, Paul. "Who Removed Aristide?" *London Review of Books*, April 15, 2004.

Fischer, Sibylle. *Modernity Disavowed: Haiti and the Cultures of Slavery in the Age of Revolution*. Durham, NC: Duke University Press, 2004.

Forman, Murray. *The Hood Comes First: Race, Space, and Place in Rap and Hip-Hop*. Middletown, CT: Wesleyan University Press, 2002.

French, Philip. "Ghosts of Cité Soleil." *Guardian*, July 22, 2007.

Garland, Christopher. "Urban, Rural, or Someplace Else? The Slums of the Global South in Contemporary Film." *Many Cinemas* 1, no. 1 (2011): n.p. http://www .manycinemas.org/mc01garland/articles/christopher_garland.html.

Genette, Gérard. *Paratexts: Thresholds of Interpretation*. Cambridge: Cambridge University Press, 1997.

Hardt, Michael, and Antonio Negri. *Empire*. Cambridge: Harvard University Press, 2000.

Herz, Ansel. "How to Write about Haiti." *Haiti Rewired*, July 23, 2010. http:// haitirewired.wired.com/profiles/blogs/how-to-write-about-haiti.

Hinton, Charles. "*Ghosts of Cité Soleil*—Don't Believe the Hype." *Haitian Action Committee*. http://www.haitisolidarity.net/article.php?id=182 (accessed February 21, 2011).

Hood, Gavin. *Tsotsi*. New York: Miramax Home Entertainment, 2006.

Leth, Asger, Milo Loncarevic, Wyclef Jean, and Jerry Duplessis. *Ghosts of Cité Soleil*. New York: Thinkfilm, 2007.

Mennel, Barbara C. *Cities and Cinema*. London: Routledge, 2008.

Nadal, Paul. "Infrastructural Futures: The Philippine Neocolonial State in Developmental Frame." Invited lecture hosted by College of Mass Communication, University of the Philippines, July 7, 2010.

Nicholls, David. *From Dessalines to Duvalier: Race, Colour, and National Independence in Haiti*. New Brunswick, NJ: Rutgers University Press, 1996.

Nichols, Bill. *Representing Reality: Issues and Concepts in Documentary*. Bloomington: Indiana University Press, 1991.

Sanders, Richard. "The G184's Powerbrokers—Apaid and Boulos: Owners of the Fourth Estate; Leaders of the Fifth Column." *Press for Conversion!*, no. 61 (September 1, 2007). http://coat.ncf.ca/our_magazine/links/61/42-43.pdf.

Said, Edward. Introduction to *Palestine*, by Joe Sacco. Seattle, WA: Fantagraphics Books, 2001.

Salles, Walter, and Fernando Meirelles. *Cidade de Deus: City of God*. São Paulo, Brazil: O2 Filmes, 2003.

Trouillot, Michel-Rolph. *Silencing the Past: Power and the Production of History*. Boston, MA: Beacon Press, 1995.

9

A Marshall Plan for a Haiti at Peace: To Continue or End the Legacy of the Revolution

—Myriam J. A. Chancy

In the weeks following the grand earthquake of January 12, 2010, what some Haitians have termed "goudou, goudou" to describe the shattering seismic shifts taking place beneath the earth's surface that resulted in the devastation of Haiti's capital and neighboring cities and villages in its southwest from Léogane to Jacmel, calls to reconstruct Haiti through an equally massive "Marshall Plan" were invoked by a variety of voices including political commentators and economists such as William Blum and Paul Collier, the International Monetary Fund's managing director Dominique Strauss-Kahn, large NGOs such as World Vision, and the activist physician Paul Farmer. Of them all, Farmer's call seemed the most shrill, the most persistent; indeed, Farmer had called for a Haiti Marshall Plan two years earlier in the aftermath of four hurricanes that descended on Haiti and wreaked then-unthinkable devastation—unthinkable until, that is, the earthquake of January 2010. Farmer, in a piece originally published on October 6, 2008, in the *Nation* under the title "Haiti's Unnatural Disaster," compellingly argued for global responsibility in the rebuilding of Haiti. He summarized Haiti's two-hundred-year history since the Haitian Revolution succinctly:

> That Haiti is a veritable graveyard of development projects has less to do
> with Haitian culture and more to do with the nation's place in the world.
> The history that turned the world's wealthiest slave colony into the hemi-
> sphere's poorest country has been tough, in part because of a lack of respect
> for democracy both among Haiti's small elite and in successive French and
> U.S. governments. During the first half of the nineteenth century, the U.S.
> simply refused to acknowledge Haiti's existence. In the latter half, gunboats
> pre-empted diplomacy. And in 1915 U.S. Marines began a twenty-year mili-
> tary occupation and formed the modern Haitian army (whose only target

has been the Haitian people). After the fall of Duvalier in 1986, Washington continued to support unelected, mainly military, governments. Indeed, it was not until after 1990, when Haiti had its first democratic elections, that assistance to the government was cut back and finally cut off. The decay of the public sector—through aid cut-offs and neoliberal policies—is one of the chief reasons Haiti, unlike neighboring Cuba, is unable to respond to hurricanes with effective relief.

Farmer thus concludes: "Haiti needs and deserves a modern Marshall Plan that rebuilds public institutions and creates jobs outside of the worn-down agricultural sector. Without one, it will have a hard time surviving the hurricane season. And next year will be worse." Though 2009 came and went quietly, 2010 saw the worst possible ravages to a country already mired in poverty, lack of infrastructural development, and the cumulative effects of one natural disaster after another from which the country had never adequately recovered. It was perhaps no surprise, then, that in the days and weeks following the earthquake, when interviewed, Farmer restated his call for a Marshall Plan for Haiti, though in his remarks to Congress in the spring of 2010, he discarded such language from his recommendations.

Meanwhile, in a blog post on January 22, 2010, the IMF's former managing director Dominique Strauss-Kahn suggested that the former "Pearl of the Antilles" could be "rebuilt as a prosperous nation" through a "type of Marshall Plan—an international effort to support the Haitian authorities in rebuilding the country and back its democracy, much as the United States helped rebuild Europe after the destruction of World War II" (1). He concluded, "If we seize this chance, we can help the people of Haiti escape their cycle of poverty and deprivation fueled by merciless natural disasters that plague the Caribbean nation. The international community owes it to them" (2). Though laudable in intent, Strauss-Kahn's remarks suggest that *only* natural disasters have had a hand in producing Haiti's cyclical poverty and also that the international community's response is one bound up in a response to what cannot be helped, that is, an act of God. Given the religious rhetoric that enveloped Haiti in the aftermath of the earthquake, from Pat Robertson's infamous remark equating Haiti to a cradle of evil, to various representations of Haiti and of Haitians as the wretched of the earth for whom the gates of heaven will one day open through the largesse of Western benefactors, I have to wonder why the international community's response is steeped in neoreligious ideals of pity or mercy rather than in a redressing of political wrongs.

While some NGOs like World Vision have expressed interest in having a stake in a long-term Marshall-like recovery plan by posting on their Web sites the needs of their constituents (in this case, the need to "prioritize children's best interests as a central focus in rebuilding the country" as they warn that "a failure to prioritize children in comprehensive plans now means a missed opportunity to improve Haiti's future development") (Wolff, 1), others, like the journalist William Blum, clearly believe that any U.S. involvement is doomed to failure given U.S. foreign policy toward its southern neighbor for the last hundred or so years. Blum opines that the U.S. military presence after the earthquake is seen by some as more of "an occupation than a relief mission," as the army blocked aid missions from entry into Haiti (an accusation in turn being leveled a year after the earthquake at the Haitian government as it levies import taxes on nonregistered NGOs), but he concludes that the U.S. control over Haiti serves two overarching logistical aims: to prevent Haitian refugees from reaching U.S. shores and to prevent a return of deposed leaders or their followers to power. Blum makes an even more astute point, which is that the two men appointed to head earthquake relief efforts by the current administration were Bill Clinton and George W. Bush, who in their own time prevented the democratic evolution of the country. Without entering into a debate over the pros and cons of Aristide's government, it is clear also to everyone that his deposition in 2004 by the United States violated any known convention of international law. Washington's interference in Haitian affairs has thus been relentless and never in favor of democracy in Haiti but in favor of U.S. corporate and national interests (although, in the case of Haiti, in the twenty-first century, these appear to be one and the same). Like Blum, Robert Creamer (whose wife, Jan Schakowsky, sits in Congress) argues that it is "our moral responsibility to help Haiti" ("we" here meaning Americans); Creamer believes that fostering Haiti's economic growth will ensure economic growth for Americans and the world. Using the kind of arguments used to draw attention to the losses of human ingenuity in the death tolls of the Holocaust, he writes, for instance: "Every kid in Haiti who grows up to be a surgeon or an engineer instead of a stoop laborer contributes to the common store of our wealth. If a girl is sentenced, by accident of birth, to spend hours each day washing clothes in a Haitian stream instead of going to school, all of us miss out on the possibility that she might contribute to finding a cure for cancer. Millions of minds indeed are a terrible thing to waste" (2). Paul Collier and Jean-Louis Warnholz also focus on development for Haiti's future through its youth and invoke a "Marshall-type" plan that would necessitate "several billion dollars": "Haiti deserves genuine rebuilding, applied not just to bricks and mortar but to its fragile social and economic fabric" (1). So far, however, whether on humanitarian, religious, geopolitical, or economic grounds, no Marshall Plan for Haiti has been advanced. What, then, would a Marshall Plan on an international scale, headed by the United States, look like in the case of Haiti? And why is it that for the leading economists, journalists, and activists who are interested in a better future for Haiti, the Marshall Plan has best come to mind as a solution?

In this essay, I explore what Farmer and others mean by invoking the need for a Marshall Plan for Haiti and whether what they envisage, if plausible, is feasible. I also explore whether or not such a plan would necessitate an ideological shift in the ways in which Haiti's place in history might be reconceived so that such a plan might actually create results that, to date, have escaped the engagement of the international community. In this sense, I question how Haiti's successful revolution but besieged sovereignty could be reread and negotiated under the auspices of a Marshall Plan devised to reconstruct not only Haiti's physical and economic infrastructures but also its ability to operate independently in the global arena.

Haiti: A War Zone?

That Haiti's problems could be solved by a Marshall Plan suggests that the country is in a state of war or that the natural disaster that has beset the island has left it in a state like that of a war-torn country. Michaëlle Jean, Canada's former (and Haitian) governor general, suggested in the days after the earthquake that Port-au-Prince looked as though it had been bombed or suffered a nuclear holocaust. Collier and Warnholz described the capital of Haiti as "in ruins. Most landmark buildings have collapsed. Thousands of people are feared dead" (1). Sean Penn, in an interview with Charlie Rose (summer 2010), declared that the ongoing struggle for foodstuffs and medicine in the camps, as well as the lack of security within them, amounted to a state of anarchy that could best be described as a "state of war" necessitating the deployment of further troops to Haiti as the number of U.S. personnel who had enabled his camp management to function was reduced from thousands to a mere few hundred. In the days and weeks after the earthquake itself, aid to Haiti functioned as if the country was in a state of war, even down to the form of medicine practiced by relief workers.

French doctors reported being appalled by what they termed the performance of "war medicine" on the part of American physicians. Only two weeks after the earthquake, Annick Cojean, a journalist for *Le Monde*, reported that amputations were taking place in the thousands in the Haitian capital, often without the administration of analgesics or painkillers. Reasons for these amputations ranged from lifesaving procedures (for example, freeing someone from rubble that could not be moved) to others performed under the rationale that fractures would become gangrenous, that hospital spaces needed to be liberated as soon as possible, and that no postoperative care would be available in a country without an organized health care system. One physician who refused to have his name cited for fear of French-American conflicts or reprisals declared to the journalist: "L'amputation est un geste de sauvetage et de dernier recours, quand un membre est broyé ou quand menace la septicémie. Mais les Américains l'ont rendue presque systématique, sans prendre le temps d'imaginer une autre solution, fiers de cet abattage leur permettant de se prévaloir de chiffres impressionants de patients" (cited in Cojean). François-Xavier Verdot, an orthopedic surgeon working under the auspices of the Humanitarian Firefighters of France, comes to a similar conclusion, referring to the American expression "guillotine amputations" by which limbs are severed as if by cigar cutter. He expresses dismay at the procedure, which carries a high level of risk of infection for the patient, as he explains, "car l'os est à découvert, et l'on n'a pas prévu une chirurgie secondaire pour modeler un moignon sur lequel pourrait être fixée une prothèse" (cited in Cojean). Secondary amputations that further reduce the length of limbs are then required, but whether any of these necessary surgeries can be scheduled or performed under present conditions is fairly uncertain, indeed, unlikely. According to one surgeon interviewed by Cojean, some U.S. doctors had a far more narrow understanding of why amputations were necessary. Said one: "Il me parlait d'une sous-population! D'un people trop peu évolué pour mériter la médecine des Occidentaux" (He spoke to me of a subhuman population! Of a people too backward to deserve Western medicine) (cited in Cojean; translation mine). Ironically, the lifesaving emergency procedure chosen mainly by U.S. doctors requires *more* aftercare and follow-up than other, less-invasive procedures that could have been considered but were not performed for specious reasons. All the related news stories coming from French and Canadian sources, as well as a few sources appearing in the *New York Daily News* and San Francisco Gate. com, repeat the refrain that "for those who have had an amputation, the first priority is to make sure the bottom of the residual limb heals cleanly and in a shape that makes it fit comfortably in the socket of a prosthetic arm or leg" (Ubelacker; Trapasso, 1). Most hurried amputations in the first weeks of rescue work, performed without the future of the human being in mind, did not take into consideration life with a prosthetic, meaning that if such patients have survived, they will either have to live with insurmountable disabilities that cannot be assisted with prosthetics or will have to undergo further invasive surgical procedures to do so. The result is that the humanity of Haitian patients continues to be denied. In the *Wall Street Journal*, Ianthe Dugan reports that experts estimate the number of people who underwent amputations to be around forty thousand, but the figure could be considerably higher given the numbers of crush victims who are yet to be identified. Of those who have been amputated, especially under the circumstances already described, where doctors do not believe in the humanity of their patients, patients do not return for postcare; indeed, they may be unaware that such care can and should be available. Few, if any, reports focus on what appear to be cases of renegade physicians who are providing services in Haiti for reasons that are difficult to comprehend and certainly have little to do with what we might commonly define as aid of a humanitarian nature. Martin Luther King Jr. once stated that "of all the forms of inequality, injustice in health is the most shocking and inhumane"; the ongoing inequity in health, though bettered in the last months with the presence of numerous NGOs in Haiti, gives credence to these words.

Aside from access to humane health care, security in the camps is also a continuing problem. Women's groups report that rape is a daily occurrence in all IDP camps, where no security has been provided for women and children despite the ongoing presence of UN personnel (indeed, two years after the earthquake, most camp dwellers have had to devise their own security measures privately, organizing volunteer watches). The protection of vulnerable citizens does not appear to be part of the UN mandate of keeping the peace; one wonders what is. Despite lack of coverage in the United States since the infamous case of religiously motivated child kidnapping took place earlier in the seismic year, in May 2010, in a brief story that few other sources carried, the *Winnipeg Free Press* reported that "safe houses" containing Haitian children had been found and closed in the Dominican Republic;[1] these were, of course, not "safe" spaces in the usual sense of the word but houses in which Haitian children had been smuggled out of Haiti by child predators posing as relief workers using their NGO credentials to do so without being detected. Because some of those arrested had Canadian citizenship, reports found their way into the Canadian press but were not carried elsewhere, giving the impression that child trafficking is not a current problem in the aftermath of the earthquake when in fact the opposite is true: some of those arrested were repeat offenders (which was one of the means by which they were apprehended). Gang and black market activity is also thriving. Haiti is in a *state of siege*, but do these conditions manifest a *state of war* with international implications for neighboring countries that would warrant a multilateral global aid effort?

The original Marshall Plan was designed to stabilize global trade between Europe and the United States after World War II; since the Soviet Union refused to be included in the plan,[2] it benefited the rebuilding of Western Europe, especially Britain and Germany. Though some remember the Marshall Plan as a humanitarian gesture, the foreign policy scholars Derek Chollet and James M. Goldgeier argue that "the policy was not about being magnanimous to former enemies and war-torn allies; as Truman and his team saw it, nothing less than the American way of life was at stake" (9). That "American way of life" was seen to be threatened by communist expansion if Eastern Europe became involved in the rebuilding of the West. The Marshall Plan thus set about to consolidate Western European markets to stabilize the U.S. dollar in global trade and to make the United States a central partner in global trade. The Marshall Plan was passed by the U.S. Congress in April 1948. NATO was formed exactly a year later. According to Chollet and Goldgeier, NATO provided a "protective zone" by which "the European nations could rebuild without worrying about the need to confront the Soviet Union on their own. . . . They could focus on economic integration without worrying about each other, particularly France and West Germany" (12). As administrator of the U.S. Agency for International Development (USAID), Andrew Natsios argued that the agency had its "roots" in the Marshall Plan (cited in Chollet and Goldgeier). According to its Web site, USAID was formed as the Marshall Plan was dissolved in 1961, replacing the short-term yet massive assistance provided by the Marshall Plan with a long-term, permanent program of foreign aid.[3] What proponents of the Marshall Plan index in its invocation are what they perceive as its results, that is, what the historian Dianne Kunz says "transformed its beneficiaries from poverty cases into partners" (162). It is this idea of shifting a foreign entity from being a burden to being self-reliant that seems to fuel the idea that a "Marshall Plan" might be the solution to foreign aid in a variety of circumstances from Afghanistan to Haiti, what former secretary of state Condoleezza Rice viewed as a "transformational diplomacy" as the Bush administration proclaimed its efforts to bring democracy to the Middle East (Chollet and Goldgeier, 12). As Kunz explains, however, the original Marshall Plan was an investment in national security, diverting the hungry masses in Europe from turning to perceived ideological and economic enemies through the U.S.-based foreign aid program. She writes: "Investing to protect prosperity at home generated peace and prosperity abroad, which in turn led to still greater prosperity for the donor. When the vital interest of the United States seem to be at stake, the expenditure of American dollars for foreign aid can be amply justified. That was true at the time of the Marshall Plan, and it is still true today" (162).

Writing in the early years of the twenty-first century, Kunz, as many others, believes that the Marshall Plan offers a blueprint for the political deployment of foreign aid. However, most Marshall Plan scholars and historians see no relationship between the end of the Marshall Plan and the growth of a corporate model of humanitarian aid (like USAID) that places the growth of U.S. interests before those of the nation (usually a developing country) it ostensibly seeks to assist. Chollet and Goldgeier, however, are clear that the Marshall Plan cannot easily be transposed into new circumstances. They argue, "Before there was a plan, there was a vision" (8); there is no coherent vision today for the Haiti of tomorrow. They state further that "the details of the Marshall Plan followed the economist practices of the day, developed from the lessons that came out of the U.S. experience with the Great Depression and the New Deal" (9), economic principles that have largely been forgotten. They also argue that the Marshall Plan was developed with and for European partners at a time when the United States enjoyed widespread popularity abroad, a popularity it no longer enjoys; and finally they argue that the security NATO provided in the years after World War II and the institution of the plan does not extend to developing or Middle Eastern countries to which pundits and politicians would now like to extend Marshall Plan–like operations. Finally, each of the countries assisted under the Marshall Plan had preexisting economic infrastructures and a largely educated population, two prerequisites that do not exist in Haiti.

Conditions in Haiti today, as I have briefly described them, perhaps could seem to resemble those of a country ravaged by war; but what would compel the international community and the United States in particular to reconstruct Haiti? Haiti is not the Germany of the U.S. basin, even though the United States occupied Haiti from 1915 to 1934 due to Germany's investment interests in the country. Although as a result of the U.S. occupation, Haitian intellectuals, like their European/French counterparts, became more widely invested in socialist and communist beliefs, Haiti was in no danger of becoming another Cuba, as the United States assumed control over its governance even after the almost thirty years of its occupation. In short, it would seem that Haiti poses no threat to U.S. security even though, as Edwidge Danticat's eloquent recounting of her uncle's incarceration in a Homeland Security detention center in Florida and his subsequent death there in her memoir *Brother, I'm Dying* shows, Haitian refugees were classified under the Bush administration as national security risks under Homeland Security laws. They were deemed so even though Haitians have no ties to the Middle Eastern terrorist plots or organizations that gave birth to homeland security post 9/11, making of Haitians the singular ethnicity to be so singled out. If a Marshall Plan were to be created for Haiti, not only would it have to be tailored to provide the small, devastated country with an influx of cash, but it would have to start with a vision, a vision that would reconsider the relationship of the United States and of the global community to Haiti from the historical constitution of the nation as a result of the Haitian Revolution. In short, what is needed is an ideological basis for a new vision for Haiti that would transform its infrastructures while also transfiguring the hegemonic relationships maintained since the revolution between Haiti, the United States, Canada, France, and the rest of the Caribbean.

Producing an Ideological Vision for Haiti's Future

The descendants of the enslaved Africans who founded Haiti have been paying for their temerity and bravery ever since Haiti was declared a nation-state and flew its flag on January 1, 1804, disrupting what had then been a lucrative colony for the French. Research shows that until the formation of its independence, at least 20 to 25 percent of the French citizenry made a living directly or indirectly from this French colony alone. With the revolution, France lost not only its most wealthy colony but the Louisiana Purchase, a huge swath of land stretching from Louisiana to the Rockies in the West, a loss that, ironically, consolidated the modern-day United States. In the subsequent decades, the United States refused to recognize Haiti as a nation-state, and President Boyer paid France 150 million francs "as restitution for property lost by its colonists during the Haitian Revolution" (Wucker, 39) so that Haiti could enter into global trade, an amount that in today's currency would be in the several-double-digit billions. Haiti was thus, in the late 1820s, quickly on its way to the poverty from which it cannot now recover. Despite lack of official recognition, the United States quickly and firmly established itself as Haiti's "chief trading partner," notes Paul Farmer. He elaborates: "By 1821, almost 45 percent of imports to Haiti came from the United States: 30 percent were of British origin, and 21 percent were French" (*The Uses of Haiti*, 78). Thus Haiti's future, even after independence, hung in the balance as U.S. market interests both took hold in the new nation and used other sources of cheap exports from Cuba, the Dominican Republic, and other Caribbean colonies to satisfy its own economic growth. In his 1988 article "Blood, Sweat, and Baseballs: Haiti in the West Atlantic System," Farmer noted, "Haiti is the world's largest producer of baseballs, and ranks among the top three in the assembly of such diverse products as stuffed toys, dolls and apparel, especially brassieres" (95), perhaps explaining the continued and overwhelming interest in holding Haitian labor captive for multinationals. Haiti was displaced from the top three only after the fall of the Duvalier regime and into the mid-1990s as other markets provided better tax incentives (e.g., Costa Rica for baseballs) or cheaper labor (e.g., China); Haiti still remained a highly exploitable labor force, as can be judged by the UN plan for Haiti's economic development just before the earthquake, a plan resting on the continued creation of factory-based jobs. The production of baseballs in Haiti, a lucrative business largely forgotten today, stands as a case in point.

Allan Ebert, in his article "Un-sporting Multinationals: Baseball Manufacturers Taking a Walk on Workers' Rights" of 1985, stated that "3,500 Haitian women [were] employed by five U.S. sporting goods companies to make 90 percent of the world's baseballs, including every baseball used in the major leagues" (1). In 1975, at the height of the manufacturing of baseballs in Haiti, Bill Brubaker, a reporter for the *Miami News*, reported on Major League Baseball's contract with Rawlings for its baseballs, which were then produced entirely in Haiti, where "a Haitian woman can earn anywhere from 40 cents to one dollar for every dozen baseballs she stitches. It can take from five to 25 minutes to sew the two covers of a baseball together" (cited in Damu, 2). Jean Damu, who wrote a damning editorial about the fact that MLB contributed only $1 million to Haiti earthquake relief efforts, adds: "Each baseball has 108 double or 216 single stitches." Damu's indignation at MLB's extremely low contribution to earthquake relief efforts stems from the fact that for about twelve years, MLB extracted a great deal of wealth from Haitian women factory workers who worked for as little as $1.30 a day putting in eight-hour days to produce about twenty baseballs a day for sale at US$2.50 to $4.50 (Damu, 2; Ebert, 1). Ironically, these women made more than the poor peasantry, who in 1985 made little more than US$320 per year,[4] while rural farmers barely made $160. Ebert noted: "The women who stand all day hand-stitching cowhide baseballs earn more than that. They make $3.10 per day, swinging their arms like butterflies to make 108 stitches per ball, 3 dozen balls per day, nearly 10,000 a year" (1).[5] Haitian women employed in this manner may have made more money relative to others, but theirs was an abject marginality of dividends; they also suffered for their relative "wealth" through indecent labor practices that disallowed them bathroom breaks, resulting in bladder and urinary tract problems, while the speed with which they were forced to execute their stitching for hours at a time without protective goggles and other safety measures also meant that many put out their eyes with their needles, among other accidental hazards of their employment.[6] Today one of the "solutions" that has been advanced for Haiti's reconstruction is to reposition it as a world producer of baseballs, rice, and local pigs, without any consideration of how those who would have to produce such products and crops have historically been cut out of the profit margins. Aside from a humanitarian impulse, the same impulse that drove individuals worldwide to donate multiple millions to Haiti relief funds, very few of which have disbursed those funds for aid and reconstruction (Doctors without Borders and Partners in Health stand as notable exceptions), there is no compelling reason for the United States, at the helm of Haiti's reconstruction commission (headed by Clinton and closed in October 2011), to invest in a Marshall-like plan which would assist Haiti and Haitians in becoming fully independent partners instead of dependents. The only incentive that remains is a moral one, one tied up not so much with the humanitarian impulse that should lead such an effort but with a desire to right a wrong of history that, today, the machinery of humanitarian aid only serves to perpetuate.

As scholars of humanitarian aid have been pointing out for some years, especially in the aftermath of the Rwandan genocide, humanitarianism, as a field in a transnational age, has been emptied of its *humane* purpose. Elaborating on her analysis of Western news reports of the

Rwandan genocide, Heike Härting states of her own inquiry that "the term
humanitarianist refers primarily to the cultural and narrative production
of *affect* as a form of global capital" (62; second italics mine). She argues
that "humanitarianist modes of perception develop through a process of
expropriating and appropriating representations of extreme violence and
strife," which is, of course, hegemonic (63), and "cultural responses to the
genocide take the West as their primary critical reference rather than the
genocide's political dimension or its dominant modes of representation"
(64). Härting convincingly argues that humanitarian narratives participate
in what Patricia Hill Collins has called "the new racism," which "refers to
those ideologies and practices that erase or disavow their own racialized
constitution," but also, more importantly, that "they heavily invest in plot-
ting a violent narrative of African abjection" (Hill Collins, 54–55). They do
so, states Härting, by "rely[ing] on and produc[ing] what might be called
necropoeia [as opposed to *prosopopoeia* . . . giving life to a character], that
is, an infusion of social, political, or physical death to negate rather than
construct the African subject" (64). The point of this process is to, paraphrasing Härting, rehabilitate the West (71), but this rehabilitation is produced through recourse to a colonial history that has not been effaced
between those who give aid and those who receive it. "On a global plane,"
writes Härting, "the making and narrating of the spectacular African body
in pain presupposes its prior symbolic animalization and petrifies African
subjectivity in a state of political and social death" (71). (Härting comes by
her analysis in large part by way of Achille Mbembe, who demonstrates
that the conviviality lived between colonial/colonized subjects/objects
carries with it a venality that reduces such relationships to that of master and animal.) Humanitarian aid in Haiti has taken similar dimensions,
placing Haitians and the Haitian state in a continued state of abjection
or infantilization to circumvent the will of the people and undermine the
sovereignty of the state. This is not to say that some humanitarian activities in Haiti are not well founded and doing good work, but, to go back
to Farmer's summary of Haiti's history vis-à-vis foreign interests, such
efforts, and more so since the earthquake, have resulted in a "graveyard
of development projects." Plans to develop the country via factories rather
than through education and economic infrastructures that lead away from
dependence to full sovereignty are consistent with the neocolonial plans
for Haiti's citizens for the last century; as noted earlier, a Marshall-like
plan for Haiti rests on these neocolonial foundations and, given USAID's
shift from European partners to developing-world dependents, makes the

claims of international humanitarian aid from nation-states increasingly suspect. Western needs are the base from which decisions are made from health to development with no regard for the future of those such decisions will directly effect. Finally, the treatment of victims at the height of the crisis shortly after the quake, as I have outlined earlier, signals the continuation of ideological positions steeped in colonial perspectives.

Ironically, in the Haitian context, political death is already part and parcel of the social fabric of the nation on the global stage, but the social death currently being experienced by new amputees and common Haitians is symbolically and perversely situated in the phantom limbs that permeate the lives of those who have survived the interventions of "guerrilla medicine" in a time of despair but also of ostensible peace. As a number of news reports note, also absent in the current situation is therapy for such patients to work through the very real psychological process of physical alteration, but also of the presence of the phantom limb, which recalls the former body and floats within the present. Epistemic amputations performed as part of a historical imposition in the presence of what some like Michel-Rolph Trouillot, Susan Buck-Morss, and Sibylle Fischer in particular have termed the "disavowal" of the philosophical and historical implications of Haiti's successful revolution, a revolution by which Haitian's humanity, and by extension that of African diasporic subjects, should have been affirmed, have resulted in compounding Haitian's invisibility in the process of their corporeal constitution. In her discussion of the phantom limb, Elizabeth Grosz suggests that "not only is there a displacement of sensory experience from the limb (now missing) and the phantom, there is also a denial that the amputation has taken place— or, rather than an unambiguous denial, there seems to be a process of disavowal" (72). In the current crisis, the phantom limbs are stand-ins both for the wholeness of the physical bodies that are now missing their extremities and also for the violated body politic. That, as Dugan reports, "Haiti's wounded [are] in worse condition than those in other countries hit by quakes, such as Pakistan and China . . . because Haiti's medical infrastructure was destroyed" is compounded by the fact that such infrastructures were fragile to begin with, undermined as they were by traditional aid practices in Haiti previously. Such practices are designed, says Härting, to position the postcolonial nation-state, "to oblige World Bank dictates and protect the economic interests of its former colonial rulers" (68). One could well ask what purpose might be served by further subjugating the populations of what are, in the end, rather small nations of the global South (Haiti and Rwanda have roughly the same population, each hovering at about eight million).

The point is that such subjugation maintains an ideological stronghold that perpetuates hegemonic relationships between the global North and South and, most pertinently for the United States, the subjugation of the only symbolic "African" nation in its hemisphere. Haitians stand in for the abject colonial, the African, whose descendants remain a part of the fabric of America; by virtue of having exteriorized the black other on the Haitian landscape, the United States is able to maintain a less visible, though no less troubling, hegemony with its raced others within the confines of its own nation. The continuous defeat of Haiti's sovereignty serves to defeat the hopes of inclusion in the nation-state for black others within the United States, even today as the nation is led by its first biracial president, just as the disavowal of the Haitian Revolution itself served to put down and interdict slave rebellions throughout the slave-owning Southern states. Just as when the Haitian Revolution stood as the exception to Hegelian thought, to the idea of an Enlightenment subject who could not be African, so Haiti's "failed" state today serves to legitimize the two hundred years of disavowal that scholars such as Fischer, Buck-Morss, and Trouillot have only lately brought to light. The activist Randall Robinson summarizes the situation adroitly when he asserts that postrevolution, globally engineered "interference" is Haiti's "punishment for creating the first free republic in the Americas" (20). Furthermore, he opines clearly on the racial dynamics of U.S.-Haiti relations: "From Thomas Jefferson onward, race largely explains the conspicuous historic, if unconscious, American affinity for rigidly anti-democratic forces in Haiti. . . . Lastly, there is America's peculiarly intense and age-old animus toward black Haitians—a compulsive contorting undertow of prejudice whose ruinous power measures inversely to the pride Haitians take in having been the only black military force in world history to rout and humiliate the best of Europe's armies" (25). In short, Haiti has served as the example par excellence of what will occur if a nation deemed "subaltern" displaces that categorization and upends a political and social order that has been naturalized by force. The disavowal of the Haitian Revolution's success ideologically serves to cement the United States as a sovereign power in a post–Cold War age but also makes clear that the global and transnational age is not free of imperial hegemonies. It is a disavowal that continues despite gestures toward respecting, finally, the sovereignty of the current Haitian government; left and right, heads of NGOs repeat the mantra that nothing should be done without consulting the Haitian government. Secretary of State Hillary Clinton declared early on that the United States was a "'friend, partner and supporter,' and will work with President Preval's government to provide humanitarian assistance."⁷ When reporters asked Préval in late January if "foreign troops threatened sovereignty" (according to the *Guardian*), he reportedly responded: "We are talking about people suffering and you are talking about ideology" (Carroll and Phillips, 2). What is especially troubling is that today's neoimperialist hegemony is being maintained primarily through global humanitarian avenues (the UN, U.S. military, USAID, etc.) that should endeavor to focus on the physical and psychic survival of human beings whatever their citizenship, ethnicity, or perceived race. Préval was right to say that human suffering trumps politics, but since it is clear that suffering has not been alleviated to a great degree for those still in camps, for those who have lost loved ones and homes, then we must ask ourselves what role ideology plays in all of this. Almost two years on, international eyes have turned to other natural disasters, and Haitians struggle on toward an undefined future, a future without a uniform vision.

When the United States partnered with Western Europe to institute the Marshall Plan, it did so because it needed to restore its economic trade partners to viability and to blockade against communism. Scholars of the Marshall Plan, whether they agree or disagree about its humanitarian aspect, agree that if it is not entirely responsible for the multilateralism later achieved by the French Schuman Plan that consolidated West Germany's participation in the new European economy, the Marshall Plan did, as Scott Newton writes, "further the cause of containment" (15). A Marshall Plan for Haiti, as being discussed today, would seek to contain a history of disenfranchisement rather than to alleviate it. In this sense, it continues Haiti's neocolonial relationship to outside forces in the same way that ill-guided efforts to assist Haitians after the earthquake have focused on quick fixes (amputations) through which the continued influx of ill-equipped NGOs and investors intent on "development" through factories and tourist trade operate, rather than the building of educational wealth for citizens and collaborative industries with the Haitian government.

In brief, no Marshall Plan is feasible in the Haitian context that does not shift the perception of Haitians as beggars into that of partners. Unlike their European counterparts, Haitians, like all subjects of African descent, are perceived as lesser constituents in global affairs; as such, they cannot be assisted into positions of sovereignty but must forever be subjugated.

For a Marshall-like plan to be instituted, two further shifts would have to take place: first, the success of the Haitian Revolution would have to be acknowledged against Enlightenment principles; and second, the subsequent two hundred years of subjugation by European and North American powers would have to be acknowledged and surrendered. Such a surrender would then permit U.S. stakeholders in Haiti to finally see Haitians as equals with choices rather than as expendable laborers for the making and purchase of American products. Haiti does not have the power to destabilize the continent, but the failure to restitute Haiti's nationhood may well destabilize any notion to moral superiority or world leadership to which the United States would want to continue to lay claim. If such shifts cannot take place, then those of us who cling to the beacon of light that the Haitian Revolution offered for once-enslaved Africans and their supporters must, in favor of those suffering still in camps and in everyday life as they remember the ravages of a broken and trembling earth, concede ideological defeat. If what Haitians have suffered these last hundreds of years, these last unspeakable months, is nothing else than the result of ideological warfare, then it may be wiser to reap the benefits of protectorate status, a status that seems to already be the unofficial present of the country, because nothing can erase the unique culture of defiance and ingenuity that such marginalization has given birth to. And future Haitians might still, at a later date, lay claim to their agency, knowing that their children sleep on clean sheets, that clear water runs in their taps and latrines, that health care is accessible to all, not just the richest of the rich, and that the right to an education is not just a dream but a social fact. If ideological death is all that is wanted, Haitians are willing to pay that price, as the graffiti that appeared in the streets of Port-au-Prince shortly after the quake, asking for an intercession from U.S. president Barack Obama, so clearly proclaimed. It might be the only way that the revolution itself might be recognized, once and for all, once the ultimate price is paid: it might be the only way that Haiti for Haitians can be saved.

NOTES

1. See "Safe Houses Set Up by Sexual Predators."

2. See Kunz.

3. The information about USAID's relationship to the Marshall Plan can be found at http://www.usaid.gov/who-we-are/usaid-history.

4. In 2008, according to UNICEF, this figure stood at US$660; for UNICEF'S Haiti Statistics table, see http://www.unicef.org/infobycountry/haiti_statistics.html.

5. Lily Cérat, codirector of Haitian Women for Haitian Refugees, recounts that many women working in the baseball factories needed to take home baseballs to make extra money or to make quota, either continuing to work themselves or employing others in their families or communities to lace baseballs, by hand, after hours (personal conversation June 27, 2010).

6. See Miriam Neptune's essay "In Search of a Name," in *The Butterfly's Way: Voices from the Haitian Dyaspora in the United States*, ed. Edwidge Danticat (New York: Soho Press, 2003).

7. See "Clinton: U.S. 'Friend, Partner' to Haiti."

WORKS CITED

Blum, William. "Haiti, Aristide and Ideology." Counterpunch.org, February 10, 2010. http://www.counterpunch.org/blum02102010.html.

Carroll, Rory, and Tom Phillips. "Haiti Earthquake: Sovereignty Takes Back Seat as U.S. Takes Command." *Guardian*, January 29, 2010. http://www.guardian.co.uk/world/2010/jan/29/haiti-us-aid-role.

Chollet, Derek, and James M. Goldgeier. "The Faulty Premises of the Next Marshall Plan." *Washington Quarterly* 29, no. 1 (Winter 2005–6): 7–19.

"Clinton: U.S. 'Friend, Partner' to Haiti." *CBS News*, January 16, 2010. http://www.cbsnews.com/stories/2010/01/16/world/main6104525.shtml.

Cojean, Annick. "En Haiti, les médecins face au dilemme de l'amputation." *Le Monde*, January 30, 2010.

Collier, Paul, and Jean-Louis Warnholz. "We Need a Marshall Plan for Haiti." *Globe and Mail*, January 12, 2010. http://www.theglobeandmail.com/news/opinions/we-need-a-marshall-plan-for-haiti/article1430309.

Collins, Patricia Hill. *Black Sexual Politics: African Americans, Gender, and the New Racism*. London: Routledge, 2005.

Cox, Michael, and Caroline Kennedy-Pipe. "The Tragedy of American Diplomacy? Rethinking the Marshall Plan." *Journal of Cold War Studies* 7, no. 1 (Winter 2005): 97–134.

Creamer, Robert. "It Is Our Moral Responsibility to Help Haiti—and It's in America's Interest." *Huffington Post*, January 13, 2010. http://www.huffingtonpost.com/robert creamer/it-is-our-moral-responsib_b_422104.html.

Damu, Jean. "Haiti: Blood, Sweat and Baseball." *San Francisco Bay View*, January 24, 2010. http://www.sfbayview.com/2010/haiti-blood-sweat-and-baseball.

Dayan, Colin. "'Civilizing' Haiti." *Boston Review*, January 20, 2010. http://www.bostonreview.net/BR35.1/dayan.php.

Dodds, Paisley. "No More Soccer, Rollerblading, Dancing: Haiti's Young Amputees Adjust to New Reality." *Minneapolis Star Tribune*, February 2010.

Dugan, Ianthe Jeanne. "For Haiti's Countless Amputees, a Hard Road Ahead." *Wall Street Journal*, February 8, 2010. http://online.wsj.com/article/SB100014240527487 04041504575045630456902538.html.

Ebert, Allan. "Un-sporting Multinationals: Baseball Manufacturers Taking a Walk on Workers' Rights." *Multinational Monitor* 6, no. 18 (1985): 1–4. http:// multinationalmonitor.org/hyper/issues/1985/12/ebert.html.

Farmer, Paul. "Blood, Sweat, and Baseballs: Haiti in the West Atlantic System." *Dialectical Anthropology* 13 (1988): 83–99.

———. "Haiti's Unnatural Disaster." *Nation*, September 17, 2008. http://www.thenation .com/article/haitis-unnatural-disaster.

———. *The Uses of Haiti*. Monroe, ME: Common Courage Press, 1994.

Fischer, Sibylle. *Modernity Disavowed: Haiti and the Cultures of Slavery in the Age of Revolution*. Durham, NC: Duke University Press, 2004.

Grosz, Elizabeth. *Volatile Bodies*. Bloomington: Indiana University Press, 1994.

Härting, Heike. "Global Humanitarianism, Race, and the Spectacle of the African Corpse in Current Western Representations of the Rwandan Genocide." *Comparative Studies of South Asia, Africa, and the Middle East* 28, no. 1 (2008): 61–77.

Hill Collins, Patricia. *Black Sexual Politics: African Americans, Gender, and the New Racism*. London: Routledge, 2005.

Kunz, Diane B. "The Marshall Plan Reconsidered: A Complex of Motives." *Foreign Affairs* 76, no. 3 (1997): 162–70.

Mbembe, Achille. *On the Postcolony*. Berkeley: University of California Press, 2001.

Newton, Scott. "How Successful Was the Marshall Plan?" *History Today* 33, no. 11 (November 1983): 11–15.

Robinson, Randall. *An Unbroken Agony: Haiti, from Revolution to the Kidnapping of a President*. New York: Perseus, 2007.

"Safe Houses in the DR Set Up by Sexual Predators." Institute for Research in Socioeconomic and Public Policy, May 28, 2010. http://irsp.org (accessed May 19, 2011).

Solnit, Rebecca. "When the Media Is the Disaster: Covering Haiti." *Huffington Post*, January 21, 2010. http://www.huffingtonpost.com/rebecca-solnit/when-the-media -is-the-dis_b_431617.html.

Strauss-Kahn, Dominique. "Why We Need a 'Marshall Plan' for Haiti." *Huffington Post*, January 22, 2010. http://www.huffingtonpost.com/dominique-strausskahn/why -we-need-a-marshall-pl_b_432919.html.

Trapasso, Clare. "Plea to Aid Haiti Amputees: Boro Doc Says Victims in Need of Rehab Center." *New York Daily News*, February 16, 2010. http://www.nydailynews.com/new-york/queens/ plea-aid-haiti-amputees-boro-doc-victims-rehab-center-article-1.198700.

Ubelacker, Sheryl. "Push On to Get Prosthetics, Rehab for Thousands of Haitian Amputees." *Moose Jaw Times*, March 6, 2010.

Varma, Monika Kalra, and Loune Viaud. "Give Haiti Control over Its Recovery." *Boston Globe*, March 8, 2010.

Wexler, Laura. "Seeing Sentiment: Photography, Race, and the Innocent Eye." In *Female Subjects in Black and White*, ed. Elizabeth Abel, Barbara Christian, and Helene Moglen, 159–86. Berkeley: University of California Press, 1997.

Wolff, Rachel. "World Vision: A 'Marshall Plan' for Haiti? To Succeed, It Must Deliver for Children." WorldVision.org, February 2, 2010. http://www.worldvision.org/content.nsf/about/20100202haiti-Marshall-plan (accessed September 2010).

Wucker, Michele. *Why the Cocks Fight: Dominicans, Haitians, and the Struggle for Hispaniola*. New York: Hill and Wang, 1999.

AFTERWORD

Neither France nor Senegal:
Bovarysme and Haiti's Hemispheric Identity

—J. Michael Dash

Duvalierism without Duvalier

If the Haitian writer, diplomat, and politician Léon Laleau is remembered today, it is for his short poem "Betrayal," which first appeared in 1931. The poem too might well have been forgotten had Léopold Senghor not included it in his *Anthologie de la nouvelle poésie nègre et malgache* (1948), almost certainly because of the poem's last lines, which explicitly evoke the agony of cultural alienation in rhyming couplets.

> Do you feel this suffering
> And this unequalled despair
> In taming with words from France
> This heart that has come to me from Senegal?

The poem captures perhaps a little too neatly the dilemma of the tragic mulatto. How seriously the Francophile Laleau saw himself as a cultural exile is open to question. There is no evidence of him ever being associated with the *indigéniste* movement or the radical politics of the twenties. There is, on the contrary, every reason to see this stylized "suffering" not as personal anguish but as Laleau's clever manipulation of the rhetoric of the time. Indeed, it seems as much a mannered as an abject confession to being afflicted by the pathological psychological state that the Haitian writer Jean Price-Mars a few years earlier had criticized as the collective *bovarysme* of the elite.

Over time, we have tended to lose sight of the influence of Price-Mars and his ideas. However, in post-Duvalier Haiti, Price-Mars remains arguably important today although it is now some eighty years since *Ainsi parla l'oncle* was published in 1928. It was as much a founding text of Haitian *indigénisme* as it was of Parisian Négritude. Indeed, Senghor baptized Price-Mars the "father of Négritude." Price-Mars's relative absence from contemporary discussions of Négritude is in part due to the appropriation of this text and its author by the Duvalier dictatorship in Haiti. Price-Mars's essay was a product of the ethnological movement that was an integral part of the nationalism produced by the U.S. occupation of Haiti between 1915 and 1934. What was sought in the 1920s was a clear definition of Haiti's national identity and cultural difference. Price-Mars took exception to talk of the "Latin mentality" of the Haitian people, which he saw as a betrayal of their true nature. This idea was promoted by a small Francophile minority in Haitian society: the Haitian elite. Price-Mars argued that there was an authentic, rural Afro-Haitian self that the urban, assimilated elite preferred to ignore or repress. Much of *Ainsi parla l'oncle* was devoted to studying popular religion in particular and the way in which Vodou not only retained elements of Haiti's African past but held the key to understanding a Haitian mentality. Price-Mars's concepts of Haiti's "collective self" and its "spiritual unity" soon became the rallying cry of militant nationalists in Haiti and spread to black nationalists of the Négritude movement. It is precisely Price-Mars's argument for black authenticity that François Duvalier would use to confer legitimacy on his dictatorship and to attack the mulatto elite as traitors to the Haitian nation.

Central to Price-Mars's promotion of the ideal of cultural authenticity and his reaction against the aggressive modernizing and colonizing presence of the United States is Jules de Gaultier's term *bovarysme*, which is cited in the preface to *Ainsi parla l'oncle*. If nothing else was retained from this work, it was Price-Mars's use of *bovarysme* to criticize the cultural alienation of Haiti's elite, who, like tropical Emmas bedazzled by the bright lights of European civilization, were condemned to a blind and sterile imitation of European modernity. In Price-Mars's account of Haiti's postindependence history,

> Haiti's black community donned the cast-off garments of Western civilization in the aftermath of 1804. Since then, with an unflinching consistency undeterred by failure, sarcasm, or setback, they sought to accomplish what they believed to be their superior destiny by shaping their thought and sentiments in order to draw closer to the former metropole, to look like it, to identify with it. (44)

This came about because, for Price-Mars, postindependence Haiti suffered fatally from *bovarysme collectif*, a "society's capacity to see itself other than it is" (44). The elite's inability to lead was caused by the fatal flaw of a servile imitativeness for which the nation paid the price of foreign occupation. For Price-Mars, Haitian identity was fixed, inherent, and unchanging. He saw *bovarysme* as the ultimate form of self-denial. The scorn poured on the *bovarystes* of the elite was palpable:

> All that is authentically indigenous—language, customs, sentiments, beliefs—has the stigma of bad taste in the eyes of the elite smitten with nostalgia for the lost mother country. Furthermore, the word "Negro," formerly a generic term, has acquired a pejorative connotation. As for the term "African," it has always been and continues to be the most humiliating way to offend a Haitian. Strictly speaking, the most distinguished man in this country would prefer that one sees him as having some resemblance to an Eskimo, a Samoyed, or a Tungusian rather be reminded of his Guinean or Sudanese ancestry. (45)

His use of Jules de Gaultier's term *bovarysme* to signify racial and cultural alienation helps explain the rapprochement in the 1930s between Price-Mars and the American ethnographer Melville J. Herskovits. Herskovits's theory of "socialized ambivalence" was used to explain the psychic disequilibrium resulting from the clash between fundamental African values and assimilated European culture in the African American psyche. What Laleau dramatizes in his short poem is the embattled psychological state of Haiti's Eurocentric elite, which he saw as an arena where Cartesian ego and Senegalese id were apparently locked in a never-ending, ultimately debilitating struggle.

In contrast to the urban elite's troubled state, Price-Mars envisaged an ideal Haiti in terms of a rustic idyll of milkmaids and shepherds in a tropical Arcadia. At the end of *Ainsi parla l'oncle*, he describes the village of Kenscoff as if it were a microcosm of Haiti's pastoral serenity, a Haitian Eden with no hint of *bovaryste* alienation: "Because of the altitude and the fertility of the soil it is a pleasure to see how the vegetables and the fruit trees native to temperate countries grow so exuberantly.... On the whole here rural life takes on an aspect of ease that is quite remarkable" (273). Léon Laleau shared this view of Haiti as paradisiacal garden when he wrote in 1937 that in Haiti "life is simple, amusing, smiling. There the foreigner experiences the feeling that it is perhaps one of the few civilized countries where economic problems and the struggle to survive do not have the same carnivorous intensity that marks certain parts of the world with a terrible jungle-like quality" (cited in Roumain, "La tragédie haitienne," 4). Laleau's condescending view of Haiti is surprising not only because it was written at a time when the U.S. occupation had left in its wake a dispersed peasantry but also because it was published in the very year that thousands of Haiti's migrant workers were massacred on the Dominican border by Trujillo's army. It would probably have gone unnoticed had Jacques Roumain not taken issue with Laleau's misleading reinscription of Haiti as a secluded rustic haven. In his response, Roumain's article cites Laleau's comments in the epigraph as he shifts the focus from Laleau's Parnassus in Pétionville to Haiti's frontier with the Dominican Republic. Roumain puts the emphasis on Haiti's place in the hemisphere. The migrant worker, Dominican genocide, and U.S. imperialism are his concerns, not Laleau's pastoral fiction.

> What separates Ouanaminthe from the Dominican village of Dajabon is a thin flow of water: the Massacre River, a name atrociously prophetic. . . . It is doubtful that racial difference can suffice to explain the explosion of hate that made of the Dajabon-Montecristi region the site where a bloody orgy was enacted. I prefer to think that this people, driven to hostility by the distressing condition inflicted on them by the Trujillo dictatorship, obeyed the same obscure impulses that [in] the South of the United States drive a mob of "poor whites" to lynch a black man. . . . The ruling classes and dictatorships are in accord in fostering and instigating these feelings which direct away from them, as a lightning rod does, the fury of the downtrodden. (5)

It mattered little to Roumain whether Haiti was African or European, and he objected strongly to Laleau's view of Haiti as an oasis of calm in the modern world. He found Laleau's celebration of Haitian exceptionalism offensive and reactionary. For Roumain, Haitian society was increasingly fragmented and irreversibly cosmopolitan. He said as much when he collaborated with the *indigéniste* movement. The experience of the mass of the population should not be camouflaged and marginalized in terms of either an ancestral past or a quaint premodernity. Indeed, by the end of the U.S. occupation, Haitian peasants were increasingly becoming liminal citizens in a hemisphere transformed by U.S. imperialism. As Roumain demonstrated in *Masters of the Dew*, it was not their isolation in the

Haitian interior but their participation in a hemispheric proletariat that could lead to a revolutionary consciousness.

In this regard, Roumain's hemispheric geopolitics hark back to an idea that predates Haitian independence. In Saint-Domingue, American identity was used to designate a revolutionary Creole consciousness that characterized Haitians not as African or European but as American. As John Garrigus points out in *Before Haiti*, "Some of the most important roots of Haitian revolutionary consciousness lay in the South Province, [where] inter-Caribbean commerce and a long history of mixed European, African, and native American families created a powerful sense of local, American identity" (312). The impact of this hemispheric consciousness later manifested itself in the refusal to reach back to ethnic origins in naming the new nation. In using the Taino name for the island, Haiti's revolutionaries wished to associate independence with the desire to avenge the original people who were wiped out because of the brutal colonial past. In staking their claim as New World Africans, they saw the new nation as a profoundly hemispheric project. This dimension of Haitian identity would be almost completely lost in the three decades of Duvalierism that made Haiti a hermit state in Americas.

With the election of François Duvalier in 1957, the "Authentiques" or "Marsistes" came to power and set about ridding Haiti of all symptoms of cultural *bovarysme*. This cultural and racial cleansing of the body politic became the cornerstone of an inward-turning, isolationist dictatorship that lasted twenty-nine years. After the departure of Baby Doc in February 1986, the desire for change manifested itself in jubilant and angry crowds who tried to physically erase the Duvalier dictatorship from the face of Haiti. Uprooting the physical traces of Duvalierism does not, however, guarantee the end of the politics of the regime, which divided Haitians into patriots and *apatrides*, authentic and *bovaryiste*. As Dany Laferrière writes in *Le cri des oiseaux fous*, "With Papa Doc in power, it is dangerous to maintain contact with someone in exile. The exile is Duvalier's personal enemy. And Duvalier is the state. He even identifies himself with the national flag" (45–46). The brutal excesses of the regime were the culmination of the racial politics of *Marsiste bovarysme*. Laferrière believes that the real tragedy of the sixties was Haiti's inability to move beyond an old idea of pastoral seclusion epitomized by the tattered copy of *Ainsi parla l'oncle* with the faded photo of Price-Mars in the office of the newspaper *Le Petit Samedi Soir*, where he worked in the 1970s.

I worked in Port-au-Prince in the mid-seventies with a weekly politico-cultural newspaper called *Le Petit Samedi Soir*, which pulled together a group of twenty-year-olds who were dynamic, courageous, curious. The image of Haiti that we had at the time was rather blurred and a bit out-of-date. We still had that old photo of Price Mars (1876–1969) with the canonical work *Ainsi parla l'oncle* (1928). Because it had been passed from hand to hand, it had lost its power. (Laferrière, *Les années 80*, 10)

To borrow the image used by Laferrière, the romantic vision of the now-aging uncle Price-Mars had become "trop tripoté" in 1980s Haiti by opportunist poets and the weapon of choice of fascist politicians. No longer an unchanging world of pastoral retreat and smiling milkmaids, Laferrière's Haiti was associated with mobility, speed, and fleeting moments. His was an aesthetic *dechoukaj* (uprooting) that would privilege quintessentially American artifacts like the Polaroid camera, the Remington typewriter, and his 1980s Ford.

Books of Emma

In his essay "Traveling Theory," Edward Said identified four stages in the way an idea travels. After the first and second stages, which represent the origin and journey of the idea, Said described the third stage as a set of local "conditions of acceptance" that allow the idea to be introduced. The fourth stage is reached when the newly accommodated idea is "transformed by its new uses, its new position in a new time and place" (227). If we apply this model to the adoption of the term *bovarysme* in Haiti, we see that in Said's last two stages, "accommodation" leads to distortion, and ultimately "transformation" leads to ideological dogma. We need, perhaps, to add a fifth stage to Said's mapping of how ideas travel. What if the idea is reintroduced and its original meaning restored to a new set of conditions of acceptance (or resistance)? Oddly enough, it was Victor Segalen, who was not very interested in the Caribbean, and even less in Haiti, who made it possible for the idea of *bovarysme* to be recirculated, but this time in a positive light. The application of Segalenian *bovarysme* to the Caribbean was made possible by Édouard Glissant, who in the 1950s, influenced by the work of Segalen, conceived of an ideal of diversity and multiplicity in a world threatened by closed ideological and political systems. Glissant's concern with the transcendent hegemony of the West, what he called the reductive force of the Same, echoed Segalen's obsession with the fear that the world's diversity would inevitably succumb to the forces of entropy. In his *Essay on Exoticism*, Segalen writes:

> There is dreadful expression, I no longer know where it comes from: "*The Entropy of the Universe tends toward a maximum*." This notion has weighed upon me—in my youth, my adolescence, my awakening. Entropy: it is the sum of all internal, non differentiated forces, all static forces, all the lowly forces of energy. . . . I imagine Entropy as a yet more terrifying monster than Nothingness. (48)

Whereas Segalen was horrified at the probability of global entropy, Glissant went on to elaborate a theory in which diversity would continue to evolve because of the unpredictable transformations that would be produced from global creolization.

Writing at the peak of French colonial expansion, Segalen feared the loss of cultural specificity in the face of the relentless spread of Westernization or homogenization. Glissant, looking at French colonization from the perspective of the colonized, felt that cultures did not collapse as easily as Segalen feared. Because of the experience of departmentalization in the French West Indies, Glissant was, naturally, acutely aware of the threat of a totalizing sameness, but he felt entropy unlikely because of the capacity of cultures to create new orders of difference. Indeed, Glissant saw Caribbean culture as heterogeneous and unpredictable and radically different from Price-Mars's *bovaryste* ideal of cultural authenticity or fixed identity. Both Glissant and Segalen agreed on the importance of alterity or opacity in a world of global contact. The theorizing of the importance of otherness leads Segalen back to Jules de Gaultier's idea of *bovarysme* as the creative principle behind theorizing diversity. Segalen actually declares that "the master" of *bovarysme* "is he who allows me to think," and "everything that Jules de Gaultier says about Bovarysm can be applied word for word to diversity" (53). Hence de Gaultier's *bovarysme* is recuperated to explain that individuals do not have an immutable essence but are in a perpetual state of becoming other. So whereas *bovarysme* for Price-Mars was a form of self-denial and alienation, Glissant, following the lead of Segalen, felt that the detour of otherness and elsewhere was essential to understanding identity. Detached from its negative connotations, *bovarysme* became the essential principle to imagining cultures as composite and inexhaustible. As Glissant declares in his homage to Segalen, *Introduction à une poétique du divers*, "If today's world were seen from a panoramic perspective, a major question that arises is this: how to be oneself without shutting out the other, and how to open oneself to the other without losing oneself? That is the question that is posed and illustrated in the composite cultures of the Americas" (23). The redeployment of Segalenian thought in a New World context has given a strange and ironic afterlife to *bovarysme* in the Caribbean. For Glissant the real threat to composite cultures came from their atavistic turning inward, from their refusal of the other. He concluded his early essay on Segalen with the following declaration: "The other is in me because I am me. Similarly, the I from whom the Other is absent will perish" (*L'intention poétique*, 95).

Glissant, furthermore, saw this rethinking of otherness as at least as important as political and social activism. In *Introduction à une poétique du divers*, he accepts "the necessity of sustaining political and social struggles in those places where we are located," but more importantly "the need also exists to open each individual's imaginary to something else, which means that we will change nothing in the situation of the peoples of the world, if we do not change the belief that identity must be rooted, fixed, exclusive and unaccommodating" (66). Perhaps this is what Claude Moise and Emile Ollivier had in mind when in the conclusion to *Repenser Haiti*, they declare that for Haiti to move beyond Duvalierism, "it will take daring and imagination" (252). Modern Haitian literature may be crucial in this regard, as it can provide a site for experimentation with the question of identity. Indeed, Ollivier himself has illustrated this kind of failure of the imagination in the tragic figure of Normand Malavy in his novel *Passages*. As his name suggests, Malavy is doomed to failure because he cannot adapt to a new life and cannot fully detach himself from anti-Duvalier resistance. The subjective stability he craves is forever lost, and he is incapable of accepting a new, dynamic Haitian identity. In a sense, the novelist saves Normand by writing his story from different viewpoints, a perspective he was incapable of adopting. In this regard, Ollivier was following the lead of the almost forgotten Haitian writer Jean Claude Charles, who first attempted to make uprooting the very principle of his creativity by imagining the airport, the hotel lobby, and public transport as sites for the Haitian imaginary. As he confesses in the part reportage, part autobiographical work *De si jolies petites plages*, "I love public places: station platforms, ports, subway stops, taxi stands, bus stops. And airports" (24).

The ghosts of Duvalierist discourse haunt the present unending transition from the politics of Duvalierism. Today the use of the word

"Dyaspora" to designate Haitians who live outside Haiti has all the sting of Price-Mars's *bovarysme*. For instance, Edwidge Danticat speaks of her own personal experiences of being called "Dyaspora" when expressing an opposing political point of view in discussions with friends and family members living in Haiti, who knew that they could easily silence her by saying, "What do you know? You're a *Dyaspora*." (*The Butterfly's Way*, xv). As she confesses in her new book of essays *Create Dangerously*, the founding moment for her artistically was Duvalier's public execution of two members of Jeune Haiti in 1964.

> Marcel Muna and Louis Drouin were patriots who died so that other Haitians could live. They were also immigrants, like me. Yet they had abandoned comfortable lives in the United States and sacrificed themselves for their homeland. One of the first things the despot Duvalier tried to take away from them was the mythic element of their stories. In the propaganda that preceded their execution, he labeled them not Haitian, but foreign rebels, good-for-nothing *blans*. (7)

Otherness could be deployed in a deadly manner by the Duvalier state. Danticat goes on to say that the late agronomist turned journalist Jean Dominique was one of the few to defend those who were not seen as true Haitians. She quotes him as saying, "The Dyaspora are people who have their feet planted in both worlds" (*Create Dangerously*, 51). In an apparently unwitting response to Price Mars's use of *bovarysme*, Jean Dominique argued for the importance of recognizing multiple Haitian identities, for a kind of intellectual *dechoukaj*. Dominique's own experience of exile, return, and assignation makes him a latter-day Muna or Drouin. He therefore could, in Danticat's words, "commiserate with all of us exiles, émigrés, refugees, migrants, nomads, immigrants, naturalized citizens, half-generation, first-generation, American, Haitian, Haitian-American, men, women, and children who were living in the United States and elsewhere" in a post-Duvalier Haiti (51).

As unlikely as it may seem, rethinking *bovarysme* has become crucial to the poetics of modern Haitian writing. It is difficult to resist the temptation to see in Marie-Célie Agnant's *Le livre d'Emma* (The book of Emma) a sly reference to the theme of *bovarysme*. After all, the main character lives in a fantasy world where, as she confesses to the psychiatrist, "the intensity of the blue causes a kind of madness" (26). Emma Bratte, like her literary predecessor Emma Bovary, is haunted by a ubiquitous and ultimately deadly blue. Also, Lyonel Trouillot's world-weary intellectual in *Street of Lost Footsteps* describes the uptight upper-class woman he wishes to seduce as an "Emma Bovary sans lovers" (8). Dany Laferrière could be said to have defiantly embraced the poetics of *bovarysme* by exploring what he sees as the absolute need to be other than you are. This is particularly explicit in his recent novel, tellingly titled *Je suis un écrivain japonais* and dedicated "To all those who would like to be someone else." Diasporic space is crucial to his rethinking of the question of Haitian identity. His narrator admits to being baffled by the question of literary origins. "I am amazed to see the attention that is devoted to a writer's origins. For, as far as I was concerned, Mishima was my neighbor. I repatriated, without giving it the slightest thought, the writers I was reading at the time. All of them" (29–30). The first on the list that follows, not surprisingly, is Flaubert. His early novel *L'odeur du café* is not a typical novel of childhood, that is, a return to origins. It is set not in the place where he was born but in the place where his literary sensibility came alive. Petit Goave in 1963 is remembered not as a quaint provincial town but one that has all the features of a cosmopolitan, urban New World space. It is open on all sides to the surrounding towns. It is also a port whose meandering main street leads to the Caribbean Sea. In Laferrière's fiction, to quote Vargas Llosa, "almost nothing exists for itself alone, since almost everything is duplicated in something that confirms and denies it" (146). Petit Goave is not a point of origin but Montreal's double. The young narrator is called "vieux os" as if to suggest the precarious in-between persona of Legba, a recurrent narrative device in Laferrière's novels.

Irreverent and disruptive, Laferrière's later novels engage directly with the ghostly residue of a Duvalierist identitarian discourse. In *Pays sans chapeau*, his novel of a return to his "native land," he mocks the Haitian *noiriste* ethnographer J. B. Romain, a disciple of Price-Mars. In this satirical portrait of Professor Romain, the author visits him and enters a tiny office that is completely disconnected from the real world, as it is "cluttered with old papers, African sculpture, Pre-Columbian statuettes and marine charts dating back to the glorious time of the buccaneers" (134). Romain is so paralyzed by this anachronistic view of Haiti, which he calls "ce vieux pays," that he is no help to the narrator in understanding contemporary Haiti. When Romain speaks of honoring Haiti's roots, the exasperated narrator exclaims, "I must tell you Professor, that the word roots, no matter where it comes from, makes my hair stand on end. If we can do it, why can't the Germans do the same?" (220). In the paratext at the end of the novel, Laferrière directly addresses the reader and explains the origin of the entire book. The idea came from his neighbor, an illiterate artist called Baptiste. Baptiste always painted a world of fantasy that he had dreamed up instead of the mundane reality. When asked by a foreign reporter why he did not paint reality, he replied that there is no need to dream reality. Baptiste is no Normand Malavy; rather, he is a Haitian Emma Bovary who survives because of a rich imaginary life, a capacity to see himself other than he is.

The idea of a hemispheric dream identity is as old as the Haitian Revolution. Laferrière in his short essay "Je suis fatigué" returned to this question of Haiti's American identity when he wrote: "For the last few years I have got into the habit of believing that we are in America, I mean that we are part of the American continent. This allows me to resolve a few small technical problems on the question of identity. This means that living in America but outside of Haiti, I no longer consider myself an immigrant nor an exile. . . . I have become quite simply a man of the New World" (71). Laferrière claims as his birthright a New World imaginary. The "imaginative daring" that Moise and Ollivier felt was needed for true *dechoukaj* can be felt in the work of a real-life painter (not Laferrière's imagined neighbor Baptiste), Edouard Duval-Carrie, whose lavish paintings of the *ambaglo*, the submarine gods, set Haitian identity adrift on a sea of liquid indeterminacy. These marine pageants tell the tale of divine nomads whose seaborne culture is not about beginnings and endings, inside or outside, but the ever-multiplying middle passages of the Americas.

WORKS CITED

Agnant, Marie-Célie. *Le livre d'Emma.* Montreal: Editions du Remue-Ménage, 2001.

Charles, Jean-Claude. *De si jolies petites plages.* Paris: Stock, 1982.

Danticat, Edwidge. *The Butterfly's Way.* New York: Soho, 2001.

———. *Create Dangerously.* Princeton, NJ: Princeton University Press, 2010.

Garrigus, John. *Before Haiti.* New York: Palgrave, 2006.

Glissant, Édouard. *Introduction à une poétique du divers.* Paris: Gallimard, 1996.

———. *L'intention poétique.* Paris: Gallimard, 1997.

Laferrière, Dany. "Je suis fatigué." *Passerelles: Revue d'Études Interculturelles* 21 (Fall–Winter 2000): 71.

———. *Je suis un écrivain japonais.* Paris: Grasset, 2008.

———. *Le cri des oiseaux fous.* Quebec: Lanctot, 2000.

———. *Les années 80 dans ma vieille Ford.* Montreal: Mémoire d'Encrier, 2005.

———. *Pays sans chapeau.* Montreal: Lanctot, 1996.

Laleau, Léon. *Musique nègre.* Port-au-Prince: Imprimerie de l'Etat, 1931.

Moise, Claude, and Emile Ollivier. *Repenser Haiti, Montreal.* Montreal: CIDIHCA, 1992.

Ollivier, Emile. *Passages.* Montreal: L'Hexagone, 1991.

Price-Mars, Jean. *Ainsi parla l'oncle.* Quebec: Lemeac, 1973.

Roumain, Jacques. "La tragédie haitienne." *Regards* 18 (November 1937): 4–6.

———. *Masters of the Dew.* 1947. London: Heinemann, 1978.

Said, Edward. *The World, the Text, and the Critic.* Cambridge: Harvard University Press, 1983.

Segalen, Victor. *Essay on Exoticism.* Durham, NC: Duke University Press, 2002.

Senghor, Léopold, ed. *Anthologie de la nouvelle poésie nègre et malgache de langue française et malgache.* Paris: Presses Universitaires de France, 1948.

Trouillot, Lyonel. *Street of Lost Footsteps.* Lincoln: University of Nebraska Press, 2003.

Vargas Llosa, Mario. *The Perpetual Orgy.* London: Faber, 1986.

Contributors

Carla Calargé is assistant professor of French and Francophone studies in the Department of Languages, Linguistics, and Comparative Literature at Florida Atlantic University. She holds a Ph.D. from the University of Iowa (2006) and specializes in the Francophone novel of the Arab world. She is particularly interested in examining the various ways in which Francophone writers have expressed their opposition to the rise of religious radicalism in the Middle East and North Africa. She has published several articles on French and Francophone literature and cinema.

Matthew Casey is assistant professor of history at the University of Southern Mississippi. He is currently writing a social history of the individuals who circulated between their homes in rural Haiti and the eastern regions of Cuba during the first four decades of the twentieth century. In 2012 he was cowinner of the Andrés Ramos Mattei–Neville Hall prize, which was awarded by the Association of Caribbean Historians for best article in Caribbean history.

Myriam J. A. Chancy, Ph.D., is a Haitian-born writer and scholar. Her first novel, *Spirit of Haiti* (Mango, 2003), was a finalist in the Best First Book Category, Canada/Caribbean region, of the Commonwealth Prize 2004. She is also the author of *Framing Silence: Revolutionary Novels by Haitian Women* (Rutgers, 1997), *Searching for Safe Spaces: Afro-Caribbean Women Writers in Exile* (Temple, 1997; Choice OAB Award, 1998), a second novel, *The Scorpion's Claw* (Peepal Tree Press, 2005), and *The Loneliness of Angels* (Peepal Tree Press, 2010), winner of the 2011 Guyana Prize Caribbean Award for best fiction and shortlisted in the fiction category of the Bocas Prize for Caribbean Literature 2011. Her third academic work, *From Sugar to Revolution: Women's Visions from Haiti, Cuba, and the Dominican Republic*, has just been published by Wilfrid Laurier University Press (2012). Her work as editor of *Meridians* (2002–4) garnered the CELJ Phoenix Award for Editorial Achievement in 2004. She currently sits on the editorial advisory board of PMLA, serves as a humanities adviser for the Fetzer Foundation, and is professor of English at the University of Cincinnati.

Bethany Aery Clerico is a visiting assistant professor at the University at Albany, SUNY. Her research focuses on representations of the Caribbean in U.S. writing. She has an article forthcoming in the *Faulkner Journal*, which identifies in *Go Down, Moses* a Caribbeanist imagination that developed in response to national discourses about the Good Neighbor policies. She is currently completing her book *Caribbean Hauntings: Transnational Regionalism in Nineteenth- and Twentieth-Century American Literature*, which uncovers ghostly traces of a Caribbean presence in regional U.S. literature.

Raphael Dalleo is associate professor of English at Florida Atlantic University. He is author of *Caribbean Literature and the Public Sphere: From the Plantation to the Postcolonial* (University of Virginia Press, 2011), a comparative literary history of the region. He is also coauthor of *The Latino/a Canon and the Emergence of Post-Sixties Literature* (Palgrave Macmillan, 2007), a study of the relationship of politics and the market to contemporary literature from the Hispanic Caribbean diaspora. His articles have appeared in journals such as *Interventions, Postcolonial Text, Research in African Literatures*, and *Small Axe*.

J. Michael Dash, born in Trinidad, has worked extensively on Haitian literature and French Caribbean writers, especially Édouard Glissant, whose works *The Ripening* (1985), *Caribbean Discourse* (1989), and *Monsieur Toussaint* (2005) he has translated into English. He is professor of French at New York University, and his publications include *Literature and Ideology in Haiti* (1981), *Haiti and the United States* (1988), *Edouard Glissant* (1995), and *The Other America: Caribbean Literature in a New World Context* (1998). His most recent books are *Libeté: A Haiti Anthology* (1999) with Charles Arthur and *Culture and Customs of Haiti* (2001).

Luis Duno-Gottberg is an associate professor at Rice University. He specializes in nineteenth- and twentieth-century Caribbean culture, with emphasis on race and ethnicity, politics, and violence. His work in progress, *Dangerous People: Hegemony, Representation, and Culture in Contemporary Venezuela*, explores the relationship between popular mobilization, radical politics, and culture. His translated and annotated edition of *Estela* (1853), the first Haitian novel, is forthcoming with Biblioteca Ayacucho. He is also the author of *Solventar las diferencias: La ideología del mestizaje en Cuba* (2003) and *Albert Camus: Naturaleza,*

patria y exilio (1994). He is the editor of *Miradas al margen: Cine y sub-
alternidad en América Latina* (2008), *Imagen y subalternidad: El cine de
Víctor Gaviria* (2003), and *Cultura e identidad racial en América Latina:
Revista de estudios culturales e investigaciones literarias* (2002).

Sibylle Fischer is the author of the award-winning *Modernity Disavowed:
Haiti and the Cultures of Slavery in the Age of Revolution*, as well as numerous essays on Caribbean culture and thought. She teaches in the Department of Spanish and Portuguese and the Center for Latin American and
Caribbean Studies at New York University. She is currently working on a
book on Simón Bolívar and the Spanish American racial imaginary.

Christopher Garland is a Ph.D. candidate in the Department of English
at the University of Florida. Born in New Zealand, he has also studied at
the University of Auckland and the University of Virginia. His most recent
essay is "'It is a very rough game, almost as rough as politics': Rugby as
Visual Metaphor and the Future of the New South Africa in *Invictus*," in
Hollywood's Africa after 1994 (Ohio University Press). His writing has also
appeared in the *New Zealand Herald* and *Nylon*. His dissertation is titled
"Haiti: Crisis, Western Imaginings, and Visual Rhetoric."

Professor **Clevis Headley** is an associate professor of philosophy at Florida Atlantic University. He was a founding member of the Caribbean Philosophical Association, serving as vice president and treasurer. Professor
Headley's research focuses on Afro-Caribbean philosophy, Africana philosophy, critical race theory, deconstruction, and ontology.

Jeff Karem is a professor of English at Cleveland State University. His
research focuses on twentieth-century American literature, with an
emphasis on regional and ethnic literatures throughout the American
hemisphere. His scholarship examines the changing canon of American
literature with the goal of expanding critical approaches to American literature beyond the national borders that have traditionally defined the
field. Karem has published articles on African American literature, Native
American literature, and literatures of the Caribbean and Latin American.
He is the author of two books, *The Romance of Authenticity: The Cultural
Politics of Ethnic and Regional Literatures* (University of Virginia Press,
2004) and *The Purloined Islands: Caribbean-U.S. Cross-Currents in Literature and Culture* (University of Virginia Press, 2011).

David P. Kilroy is an associate professor of history and Major Chair of International Studies at Nova Southeastern University in Fort Lauderdale. He teaches courses in U.S., world, and African history. He is the author of two books, *For Race and Country: The Life and Career of Colonel Charles Young* (Praeger, 2003), and *Days of Decision: Turning Points in U.S. Foreign Policy* (Potomac, 2011), and has published articles and reviews in the fields of U.S. foreign relations and military history.

Nadève Ménard is professor of literature at the École Normale Supérieure of Université d'État d'Haïti. Her research centers on the representation of political conflicts in literature. She has contributed to several journals and collective book projects, including *Conjonction, International Journal of Francophone Studies, Edwidge Danticat: A Reader's Guide, Haiti Rising: Haitian History, Culture, and the Earthquake of 2010,* and *Dictionnaire littéraire d'écrivains francophones classiques.* Her first edited book, *Écrits d'Haïti: Perspectives sur la littérature haïtienne contemporaine (1986–2006),* was published by Karthala in 2011. With Régine Michelle Jean-Charles, she recently launched *Tande,* a trilingual blog on Haitian culture and literature.

Dr. **Lindsay Twa** is assistant professor of art and director of the Eide/Dalrymple Gallery at Augustana College in Sioux Falls, South Dakota, where she teaches courses in art history and curates eight exhibitions each year. Her research focuses on the black diaspora and cross-cultural exchanges between African American artists and the Caribbean, particularly Haiti. Her publications include *Visualizing Haiti in U.S. Culture, 1910–1950* (forthcoming from Ashgate Press). She received her bachelor's degree in studio art and music from Concordia College and her M.A. and Ph.D. in art history from the University of North Carolina at Chapel Hill.

Index

Page numbers in *italics* indicate illustrations.

abolition, 6, 7, 9, 36, 40, 60
Adams, John (President), 9
Africa, 84, 87, 125, 137, 146, 179; and African Americans, 104, 157n6; British colonialism in, 77, 86, 91; Garvey on, 79; and Pan-Africanism, 79, 90–91; roots of Vodou in, 104
African Americans: and American national identity, 81–82, 92–93, 140; and civil rights, 114, 138; in drama, 139; and Haitian history, 5, 10, 11, 15, 18n19, 103, 115, 148; literature of, 112, 129n3; and lynching, 92–93, 111, 114; and Pan-Africanism, 15, 77–78, 84–85, 87, 115; and Pan-Americanism, 55; social position in the U.S., 82, 92–93, 114. *See also* Brown, William Wells; Chesnutt, Charles; Delany, Martin; Douglas, Aaron; Douglass, Frederick; Du Bois, W. E. B.; Gabriel's Rebellion; Harlem Renaissance; hip-hop; Hughes, Langston; Hurston, Zora Neale; Locke, Alain; Séjour, Victor; Vesey, Denmark; Washington, Booker T.; Young, Charles
African diaspora, 65
African Diaspora Studies, 3, 17
Afro-Cubans, 55, 57, 63, 65
Agnant, Marie-Celie, 227
Alexis, Pierre Nord, 100, 105
Alexis, Stéphen, 161, 169
anticolonialism, 8, 12. *See also* anti-imperialism

anti-Haitianism, 54, 55, 56, 68, 163
anti-imperialism, 56, 60–61, 66–67, 68–69. *See also* anticolonialism
Apaid, André "Andy," 193
Aristide, Jean-Bertrand, 191, 201; and Apaid, 193; opposition to, 181, 186, 190, 192, 194, 195n3; removal from office, 179, 185, 192, 196n4; supporters of, 180, 189, 185; and violence, 181, 185, 190, 192
art: landscapes, 152–55, 158n14, 167, 182; of the Harlem Renaissance, *140*; photography, *135*, 136. *See also* Basquiat, Jean-Michel; Douglas, Aaron; King, Alexander

Basquiat, Jean-Michel, 13
Battle of Savannah, 9, 17n7
Baucom, Ian, 115, 116
Benjamin, Walter, 179
Betances, Ramón, 14, 61
black Atlantic, 77, 85, 88, 90
Blum, William, 199, 201
Blyden, Edward, 84
Bolívar, Simón, 4, 14, 33; and Latin America, 31, 41–42, 48–49, 50; life of, 30, 51n1; military expeditions of, 8, 26, 29, 34, 51–52n3, 51n10; and people of color, 51n4, 29–30; relationship with Pétion, 25, 37–41, 44–48, 52n14; and Republicanism, 27, 29–32, 43
Bolivia, 32, 42, 49
Bonaparte, Napoleon, 43; constitutions of 1799 and 1802, 31, 46, 52n13; coronation of, 30; and the Haitian Revolution, 10, 103; regime of, 49; slavery and, 6, 9

About the Editors

Carla Calargé is assistant professor of French and Francophone studies at Florida Atlantic University. Her work has appeared in *French Forum, French Review,* and *Présence Francophone,* among others. **Raphael Dalleo** is associate professor of English at Florida Atlantic University. He is author of *Caribbean Literature and the Public Sphere: From the Plantation to the Postcolonial* and coauthor of *The Latino/a Canon and the Emergence of Post-Sixties Literature.* **Luis Duno-Gottberg** is associate professor of Caribbean studies and film at Rice University. He is the author of *Solventar las diferencias: La ideología del mestizaje en Cuba* and *Albert Camus. Naturaleza: Patria y Exilio.* **Clevis Headley** is associate professor of philosophy at Florida Atlantic University. He is the coeditor of *Shifting the Geography of Reason: Gender, Science and Religion.*